CLASSICAL GEOPOLITICS

CLASSICAL GEOPOLITICS

A New Analytical Model

PHIL KELLY

STANFORD UNIVERSITY PRESS

Stanford, California

Stanford University Press
Stanford, California

Library of Congress Cataloging-in-Publication Data

Kelly, Philip, author.
    Classical geopolitics : a new analytical model / Phil Kelly.
        pages   cm.
    Includes bibliographical references and index.
    ISBN 978-0-8047-9664-4 (cloth : alk. paper) —
    ISBN 978-0-8047-9820-4 (pbk. : alk. paper)
    1. Geopolitics.   2. International relations—Soviet Union.   I. Title.
JC319.K424 2016
320.1'2—dc23

                                                            2015021622

    ISBN 978-0-8047-9950-8 (electronic)

Printed in the United States of America on acid-free, archival-quality
paper. Typeset at Stanford University Press in 10/14 Minion.

Contents

Preface

Despite its usage in the press and occasionally in academic writings, the term "geopolitics" has stayed blurred in definition and misused in application, in part, because of its past associations with disreputable and discredited theories and ideologies. Only recently has the term experienced more visibility, although this has come largely in the media, where the label connects to international disruptions harmful to international tranquility and to stock market profits. It has not been available in a positive sense for extending the insights one might see in its potential yet hidden contribution. Accordingly, the goal of this book is to convince the reader that geopolitics should deserve a higher respectability and utility within the realm of international-relations theory and policy.

As a contemporary label, one can trace two paths of origin,[1] both arising around the beginning of the twentieth century. The first, the *organic*, reflected a Germanic concern with "scientific laws" that contributed to states' survival in an increasingly unstable world, its two spokespersons, Friedrich Ratzel and Rudolf Kjellén. The second, the *geostrategic* of British and North American interest, depicted geographic placement of states and regions as conditioning foreign affairs actions, with Admiral Alfred Thayer Mahan, Halford Mackinder, and Nicholas Spykman its standard bearers. Both versions enjoyed respect and consideration by foreign policy makers and scholars.

But following World War II, these classical sectors suffered, almost to their demise, from their alleged ties to General Karl Haushofer and his Munich school of geopolitics and to the aggressions of Adolf Hitler, both sources seen as linked in their promotion of war and racism. The tradition largely disappeared from the extant IR literature for the following decades, only later to be raised to a limited visibility in the statements and writings of Henry Kissinger.[2] Gradually, the term found increased notice from a variety of new places, certain of these being: the postmodernist "critical geopolitics" movement beginning during the 1980s; the numerous South American authors writing about their local territorial disputes and national developments during the period; the realist approach for North American academia that merged geopolitics within its focus of national power; and new generations of scholars and policy makers who have taken on its aura. A further instance of the new respect may be seen in the recent publication by the noted realist author Harvey Starr,[3] showing a title indicating also some academic resurrection of our concept.

Geopolitics has experienced of late at least two confusing and faulty meanings that have seriously diminished its legitimacy: (1) a "power politics" and *realpolitik* description of manipulation alleged to the larger nations, probably derived from the misperception that geopolitics resides within the *realist* international-relations model that emphasizes "power." Rather, the focus of geopolitics, away from realism, should rest upon states' geographic *positions* reflective of the term's spatial heritage; and (2) once more, an image of catastrophe and crisis—wars and threats of wars and other economic and political news depressing world financial markets—often heard in reference to Wall Street reporting. Neither of these versions receives any sort of definition; both are negative and reference a world at fault. Until these negative images are corrected and deflected from classical geopolitics, our study of *spatial impacts upon policy*—that is, geopolitics—will not see a full contribution. To repeat, that correction represents the goal of this book, the restoring of acceptance to classical geopolitics.

The traditional term offers an objective and neutral tool for students and statespersons to enlist as an insightful guide toward description and analysis within the milieu of foreign affairs, the assumption being that *geographic placement of countries can impact upon their actions*. This spatial linkage derives from pure common sense! Such a reliance upon a geographic location conditioning international events has been in evidence for millennia, perhaps being the earliest of military and foreign affairs models. This continued widespread practice of geopolitics as a policy and action guide in itself should lend some credibility as a usable IR model.

The author will structure this book according to these three objectives:

1. *Purpose:* to construct a classical geopolitical model.

2. *Aim:* with such a construction, to demonstrate the utility and the legitimacy of classical geopolitics as an important IR model.

3. *Approach:* three ways (below) that will show the benefit of classical geopolitics:

A first way will mark out a standard definition of the traditional version, a not-too-difficult task since it appears that most classical depictions tend closely to parallel, their emphases resting upon the geographic placement of states affecting their foreign affairs behaviors.

A second way will be to locate relevant theories that will enter the geopolitical model, a *model* being merely a container for theories that will fit the definition of "geopolitics." This author has located more than sixty generalizations that relate to the positional-geographic dimensions of geopolitics; all will be described and some applied later on in this book. This second way of locating relevant theories likewise will help to legitimize the traditional model.

Thirdly, and with more difficulty than the first two ways, any series of theories that attach themselves to a particular model should each be useful to shedding good insights into foreign affairs policies, actions, and events. In a later chapter, four methods for such theory-application will be suggested, followed by an assortment of contemporary and historical case studies as testing places for the gathered theories in the hope that these instances will further the author's goal of demonstrating the utility of geopolitics as an acceptable and useful international-relations model.

Classical geopolitics is the study of the impact or influence of certain geographic features—these being positions and locations of regions, states, and resources plus topography, climate, distance, immigration, states' sizes and shapes, demography, and the like—upon states' foreign policies and actions as an aid to statecraft. Accordingly, this study lends itself to a description and analysis both of theory and of policy.

The classical label is raised here to separate traditional geopolitics from postmodern "critical geopolitics," the latter differing quite extensively from the former.[4] The traditional emphasizes the gathering and applying of objective and interpretive theory; the critical focuses upon deconstructing alleged exploitation, blaming geopolitics itself for assisting in the exploitation, with theory largely ignored. This book is about the classical.

A *model* denotes a listing place for theories that correspond to the definition of a particular international-relations approach—in the current case, to geopolitics. One approach of this book lies with the collection of relevant theories, *heartlands, shatterbelts, checkerboards, sea-land power, buffer states, distance and location*, among many that are assembled within that model. Appropriate theories can be taken from the model when these might shed some light on a particular international incident.

The approach in this text, enlisting *theories* attached to *models*, differs from other international-relations models. Yet the author believes that his stance may contribute to the literature and particularly to a revitalized classical geopolitical perspective. The following example shows the confusion frequently seen in the contrasting of "models" with "theories," for the two labels differ.

The realist theorist Michael Mastanduno wrote the following description about his focus:

> It is critical to stress at the outset that there is no single "theory of realism" and that realism per se cannot be tested, confirmed, or refuted. Realism is a research program that contains a core set of assumptions from which a variety of theories and explanations can be developed.[5]

One may see both some confusion and some relevance in his description. Why mention a *single theory of realism*? This reference puzzles because realism contains a large array of theories that would pertain to that model's definition. Why would such a point need to be singled out? To attempt to clarify, an improved stance might be to insist that only one realist model and only one geopolitical model exist, but fitting into those structures or models will come respectively a variety of related theories that will fit each model's definition. Hence, in our case, one may visualize one geopolitical model but many theories that will assemble within that model. And to distinguish between the two, we might tend not to refer to a "geopolitical theory" but instead to a "heartland theory," this theory being a part of a "geopolitical model." A "geopolitical theory" does not exist.

Again to differ with Mastanduno, why cannot these theories be *tested, confirmed, or refuted*? If they cannot, why utilize their essence? Theories need to be applied to interpreting situations, or indeed, why have theories? Again, this book's approach differs in that the author wants to apply certain relevant theories, these corresponding to a set definition of a model, as a better way to understand international affairs. Nonetheless, the author agrees with Mastanduno's argument that realism, and geopolitics, represent research programs and that their study relies upon a core set of assumptions from which a variety of theories and explanations can be developed.

To summarize and to emphasize, "theory" and "model" differ, the first, theory, being a part of the second, model. One should, accordingly, insert "model" in place of "theory" in Mastanduno's description above, for a single *model* of realism contains a "variety of theories and explanations" that will correspond to the model's definition. In the second place, no problem would then arise in attempting to test, confirm, or refute a collection of theories, be they realist or geopolitical or other, the process being objective and appropriate to application.

In addition, Mastanduno and this book's approach would agree that, in both realism and geopolitics as "research programs," each will rely upon "a variety of theories and explanations." Yet one would add "applications" as well as "explanations" for this book's technique. For geopolitics, this author has located sixty theories that now reside within our geopolitical model, and these may be utilized for interpreting actions and policies within the realm of international relations and foreign policies.

Saul Cohen, a well-recognized classical geopolitics scholar, has authored articles and books in which, in constructing his model, he combined an assortment of elements that should impress the reader, at least at first.[6] He enlisted both systems and developmental models to show some dynamism within his geopolitics in addition to adding a variety of theories that provide a medium for comparing his "geostrategic realms," "geopolitical regions," and other transitional lands of interest. As within this book, his geopolitical model possesses an extensive display of spatial theories and connections that correspond to his classical definition. Nonetheless, unless one has misinterpreted, he completely failed to apply the theories of his model toward explaining their impact upon international relations. His text thus fails to fulfill the full requirement of testing his model by neglecting totally the final theory-application phase as promoted within the present treatise.

Nonetheless, another author, Jakub Grygiel,[7] makes just this application of theories, and admirably so. Grygiel defined his geopolitics as having three pertinent variables: (1) location of important natural and economic resources; (2) lines-of-communication linking these resources to nations' power; and (3) stability of associated frontiers. When these three factors became favorable to a governing system (he chose to study the rise and falls of Venice, the Ottoman Empire, and Ming China as Great Powers), the well-positioned empires rose to regional preponderance. Once the effects of the variables diminished, so also the empires declined.

This book's approach resembles that of Grygiel, the variance being that the present author will assemble sixty variables or theories compared with his three, and he will attempt applying that assembly of theories to a wider variety of contemporary and historical case-study examples.

In sum, Chapters 1 and 2 will describe geopolitical traditions and *models* and *theories* as this book will portray them. Chapter 3 contrasts the classical perspective with several depictions of distortions within the geopolitics of the past. Certain geopolitical assumptions are suggested in Chapter 4, as it is believed assumptions should form a part of a geopolitical model. Chapters 5 and 6 hold the most importance to the international-relations field, for in these sections the many classical theories that fit the geopolitical definition are introduced and then tested via application for their interpretive value to selected historical scenarios. In the final chapter, a call comes for a broadening of this book's initial stance, pointing out suggestions for continuing the contributions that should be the potential of classical geopolitics.

Perhaps this book's approach may appear to the reader to be rather simplistic—refining a definition, then placing appropriate theories into a container called a model, and later attempting to apply theories to interpreting international-relations happenings. No arrows linking inputs, outputs, and feedback and no complex mathematical parameters. Simplistic though this approach will be—but one quite practical and open to application—this author truly cannot imagine a better path to follow in the descriptions about classical geopolitics that lie ahead.

Finally, the author asserts adherence to an *objective* methodology. This objective approach will follow a *modernist* or *positivist* path, one devoid as much as possible of the author's personal bias and experience. Here, facts will rule over opinion, rationality over doctrine, and any claims to insight must welcome replication by others. Foreign affairs "realities" should be as easily observable by the reader as by the author before they render into generalizations and into applications. And such theories can be formulated by objective methods of research (observations of maps and history, statistics, experts' and scholars' experiences, and common sense and rationality). Indeed, objectivity spells the core of this text: (1) designing a standard classical geopolitical definition; (2) locating and clarifying appropriate theories; and (3) applying such generalizations with ease and understanding toward a more profound interpretation of international-relations events and policies. Objective methodology structures the primary aim of this book—to raise the visibility and utility of the classical geopolitical approach.

CLASSICAL GEOPOLITICS

1   Introduction

Several motivations prompt the writing of this book about formulating a geo-politics model. First, it is felt by the author that a strong potential for con-tribution exists in geopolitics as an international-relations practice and the-ory, despite its occasional capture by various factions intent on attaching to it their own ideological designs that have at times tarnished its reputation. The concept does not deserve a tarnished reputation, and correcting this image is desired so that geopolitics may be seen in a positive way as a separate and legit-imate international-relations model.

Second and related to the first, the term "geopolitics" itself has not been well defined, or not defined at all, in common as well as in scholars' usage. The true nature of the model should not be equated with the often pejorative expressions of Darwinian "science," fascism, power politics, hegemonic dom-ination, economic instability, or some of its other negative depictions. Rather, the best and most accurate description of "geopolitics" should be based upon its geographic heritage, that being, states' and regions' unique spatial positions and locations as impacting upon their foreign relations. Geopolitics must be kept objective and neutral to any ideology or partisan viewpoint, being instead a reliable tool for states persons and academics in their attempts to design some order to the usual complexity of foreign affairs. As long as the term suffers from the abuse of distorted images, its contribution can never be utilized fully.

Possibly, part of this fault of lacking clear definition may stem from the of-ten, but erroneous, connection made between the model of geopolitics and the model of realism. Many students of international affairs commonly place geopolitics as a theory within realism, but to this author, this is not a correct placement. Realism tends to focus upon power as a protector of nations in an anarchic or lawless world. The problem of containing chaos and violence in-duced from radical threats may be resolved within a stable balance of power configuration and within a consensus for moderation among the larger countries. None of these traits can be affixed to geopolitics.

Geopolitics rests upon the relative spatial positions of countries, regions, and resources as these may affect their foreign policies and actions. Such terms as states' and regions' locations, topography, distance, shape, and size will accompany these geographic features. And within these spatial structures, we may see certain patterns as depicted in shatterbelts, buffers, heartlands, sea power and land power, and checkerboards, among the numerous concepts-theories attached to the study of geopolitics. None of these features append to realism, nor do realistic theories enter the geopolitical model. The two descriptions inherently differ. Power defines realism; spatial position defines geopolitics.

Mackubin Thomas Owens offers a good example of the confusing of realism with geopolitics by his attempt to fuse the two.[1] He visualizes geopolitics as studying the relevance of geography to power, the "spatial aspects of power politics." But this leans toward a realist consideration, again, the intended focus upon power tied to security. Yet he neglects further development of this realist perspective, instead spending the rest of his article on classical geopolitical descriptions—pivotal binaries of position (core and periphery, sea and land power), the organic state and geostrategic theses, pan-regions, shatterbelts, and so forth. These latter topics are positional in space and not closely connected to power. The two models, indeed, can be utilized jointly as will be shown ahead, but the point here rests on the need to recognize two distinct approaches, the realist and the geopolitical, and not to confuse by melding them together.

In sum, in realism one should see the connection between power and geography, where countries' natural resources, placement, and size may sum to power and thus to national protection. But alternatively, geopolitics holds less interest in power and in security and more in the impact of nations' spatial positions and resources upon their international actions and policies.

Two further examples of these differences might help clarify. Both of these models, realism and geopolitics, describe balancing patterns among countries, although such equilibrium configurations differ according to the descriptions above. For realism, balance of power formations are measured in symmetries or asymmetries of strength—a power balance or imbalance among nations and alliances that might augment or deplete their protection and influence. The patterns within such configurations will show, for example, the number of "poles" or states and the competitiveness among these members, where the more rigid alliances may portend toward international conflict. A preference among contemporary realist scholars seems to favor as more peaceful a flexible multipolar structure over the present unipolar configuration led by the United States as global hegemon.

In contrast, balance patterns in geopolitics are visualized according to their regional or continental placements, such as a checkerboard configuration of allies being separated by opponents in leapfrog locations, these having little direct connection to power. This author has written about these geopolitical structures in the ancient Greece Peloponnesian war and in contemporary South American diplomacy,[2] and they will be included as examples below in Chapter 6. There, the intention has been to reveal the arrangements of states that might be affecting regional events and policies and again, not with the intention of showing their relative strengths but instead, their relative locations.

Geopolitical balances might even come in "falling-dominoes" or contagion patterns among a set of neighboring countries, one sort of action, riots or democracy, for instance, flowing across national frontiers. The configuration of encircling balances located at the east and west extremes of the Eurasian continent, with the United States as the offshore balancer at either margin, likewise, could be labeled as realism when power is emphasized, or geopolitics when position is considered. Nothing is askew when such models might overlap, for that happens. But the overlapping must be understood as per distinct definitional preferences. Again, it should be emphasized: geopolitics must be removed from realism and seen as a unique model itself.

A good number of references toward geopolitics go without any attempt at definition. Wall Street commentators commonly attribute erratic fluctuations in stock prices to global "geopolitical disruptions" but without further distinction. Certain academic sources sometimes use the geopolitical label to depict Great Power international relations in general. Two examples of books, among many that contain geopolitics in their titles, are Richard Falk (2004), *The Declining World Order: American's Imperial Geopolitics* (Routledge), and Charles Kupchan (2002), *The End of the American Era: US Foreign Policy and the Geopolitics of the Twenty-First Century* (Knopf), in which both authors opposed the neoconservative policies of the George W. Bush administration and agreed that such policies could spell a decline in US global influence. Both included geopolitics within their book's title, although neither pronounced a definition nor included any reference to the term in their concluding indexes. A more recent example would be Harvey Starr's (2013) *On Geopolitics* (Paradigm), it also lacking any definition of the term. Thus, one is left to guess in these texts the specific meaning of "geopolitics," although their labels of geopolitics apparently were rather positive ones, perhaps translating the term simply to relations among the contemporary Great Powers. Nonetheless, if true, their approaches on geopolitics differ substantially from the spatial designs of this book or of its traditional origins, those latter descriptions as described in the pages that follow, again, where the essential geographic and positional dimensions of the concept will be emphasized.

Another instance of an author neglecting to define, or even to give further mention of, the term "geopolitics," yet placing it within his title, is Robert Art's "Geopolitics Updated: The Strategy of Selective Engagement."[3] The article contains at least three references to basic traditional geopolitical themes, without labeling them as such: (1) his "forward-defense strategy" that favors US alliances with NATO, Japan-Korea, and the oil-rich Persian Gulf states, all reflective of Nicholas Spykman's rimland-base priorities;[4] (2) favorable Eurasian and rimland pivotal balances as vital US interests, again suggested both by Halford Mackinder and Spykman; and (3) "selective engagement" itself that resides within the domain of Spykman but with a different label and in the recent literature as offshore balancing. This neglect of definition should be corrected by an agreed-upon standard description that will stem the term's misuse.

A popular expression such as geopolitics, left without clear definition, confuses the meaning and application of the term, and it encourages a negative slant because of that confusion. This said, it seems evident that a clear definition of geopolitics can be devised and then applied effectively and consistently. That will be part of the mission of this text, and a complete definition will be offered below as it was listed in the Preface.

Third, the author is convinced that a systematic model of classical geopolitics can be constructed that will improve the utility of geopolitics. This will make it less susceptible to capture and abuse by ideologically bent factions and less associated to a dilution of identify by an incorrect merger into the power-politics image of realism.

For inclusion into this model, a deep but scattered foundation of concepts and theories already exists in a wide assortment of treatises and historical practices. To enhance this inheritance, this author has gathered and refined many of these variables for this book, added a description of the relevant geopolitical assumptions that underlay these theories, given contemporary and historical examples of applications enlisting the utility of the model's parts, and thus made the overall contributions of classical geopolitics broader, clearer, and more usable. What should still be needed currently is to expand upon and refine the extant areas of traditional geopolitics and to tie the essential elements into a solider framework that will fit a consistent definition. Accordingly, the motivation here—to first define a clear classical definition, then to collect and clarify the several dimensions of geopolitics (specifically, assumptions and concepts-theories), and finally to make the model more focused and tied together as a discipline so that logical applications to international events may be attempted. This academic mission will absorb the attention in the pages ahead.

In addition, a desire is present for bringing some clarification to the important functions of theories and of models in general, including but still moving beyond the domain of geopolitics, as the two labels, theories and models, have been made to be confusing and we have laid upon them too much expectation. Theories are none other than simple statements of predictability, and nothing else. As such, they offer us rather loose and not always predictable roadmaps for description and explanation, although of course, we are condemned to follow them, nonetheless. If "A" happens, there exists some probability that "B" will also happen as a result of "A." How much "probability" we might need must be left open as not readily possible to calculate with a minute precision. And likewise, one must note the difficulty of applying relevant theory to particular situations as being prone to error and as being a factor the student should take care in following the later reasoning of this treatise. Apply we must, with as much precision as will be possible.

As will be described in Chapter Two, theories are not models, and we need to note this important distinction. Whereas theories are simple sentences, models resemble more extensive gathering places or theoretical containers for all the assumptions, concepts, and theories that will fit the definition of whichever approach finds one's interest, including geopolitics. Once gathered, certain relevant parts of the model can be applied, but with care, to appropriate policies and actions for a deeper foreign-affairs understanding and prescription. Models are the passive containers; theories form the interpretive parts within those containers. More on these variations ahead in Chapter Two.

The geopolitical model of this book's description lacks a dynamic quality; it possesses no moving parts, no connecting areas and lines, no inputs, outputs, and feedback loops. It instead provides a typology or a container for gathering theories that fit the traditional geopolitical definition. Differing from models, theories offer a valuable explanatory medium for describing and analyzing the shifting policies and actions within global and regional environments. Theories do not change; instead, the environments and policies themselves change. As will be shown in later chapters, theories are timeless, enabling us to reach back into history or to stay in the contemporary, but they will still offer us interpretive tools of understanding. Geopolitics can counter critics' allegations of being "outdated" and "timeless" because its generalizations indeed are timeless and thus aptly qualify for flexibility and adaptability in facing a changing world.

Finally, and on a more personal bent, this author desires leaving some sort of legacy to others in the international-theory field for the rewards that his study of geopolitics has given him. If at all possible, he wants to contribute some part toward raising the clarification, legitimacy, and utility of the geopolitical model. This has been a long-time ambition, extending back to 1976 with a first article about spatial distance affecting the United Nations voting on intervention issues by the Latin American members.[5] This study utilized a statistical regression procedure, an early attempt to substantiate certain theories quantitatively that he has tried to enlist further whenever appropriate. In 1985, the author published another article in a London journal on the geopolitical writings of General Carlos de Meira Mattos of Brazil, the leading scholar of geopolitics in South America at the time.[6] There followed also an article dealing with refining the concept of shatterbelts, a further venture into statistically testing theories under the geopolitical label, on this occasion with a cluster-analysis routine.[7]

Most of the subsequent research on geopolitics has come from the inspiration of South America, and that focus has culminated in books coedited[8] and separately authored[9] about South American geopolitics in 1988 and 1997, and in a number of articles and chapters, all about analyzing theories and starting the journey toward constructing a more complete geopolitical model. South America has proven to be a fertile ground for the study of geopolitics, both in its unique topography, in its strategic isolation, and in its own scholars' and practitioners' interest and their application of classical geopolitical traditions to their republics' foreign affairs. Too, the author has appreciated the support and inspiration given him by its numerous authors, in particular that of General Meira Mattos of Brazil and of Bernardo Quagliotti de Bellis of Uruguay.

Of late and in part resembling an outline of this book, the author has had published a chapter in a political-geography text[10] and two articles[11] that show attempts at refining and describing shortened versions of thoughts about the geopolitical model. As an exercise in application, he enlisted with some ease and success certain theories (shatterbelts, distance, checkerboards, encirclement topography, contagion, sea power vs. land power) toward comparing the ancient Greek Peloponnesian war with the contemporary diplomacy of South America. The present book is to further that effort toward assembling all of these parts of prior study and to take them forward to as many steps beyond as one might be able to do.

Recently too, a necessary detour was taken into critiquing the "critical geopolitics" or postmodern variety of geopolitics,[12] a new and insightful school of deconstructivism largely within North American and British academic political geography, a rich experience for rethinking approaches toward the classical geopolitics. Nonetheless, in an interest in being a theorist, the author felt a strong need to separate himself from the critical school, one that largely dismisses theory in favor of pressing a radical deconstructivist agenda against the alleged hegemonic domination of the Great Nations, the classical geopolitics being depicted as a rather shameful tool used for such exploitation. Although respectful of the tenets of critical geopolitics, the author has kept himself away from the postmodernists in his traditional research after having authored that article. The two approaches just do not mix well. But the process is now set to write this present book about the classical version of geopolitics with the hope that the above-stated purposes will be rewarding to readers.

The primary intention of this book is *not* to formulate a defense of geopolitics. That torch of critiquing must pass on to others.[13] Instead, it is assumed that what geopolitics needs most from the present book is a clarifying of its definition and a gathering and applying of its extant assumptions, concepts, and theories within a common package that will be labeled as a geopolitical model. Indeed, a clarification and an expansion in themselves will offer a sufficient defense, for in tune with the remarks above, it is believed that the problems associated with the classical version of geopolitics appear to lie in its lack of precision and definition that has contributed to its sometimes tawdry reputation.

Accordingly, the present version on the subject of geopolitics is a positive and constructive one, that classical geopolitics represents one of the several available and useful interpretations and applications of international-relations models, albeit, a neglected and abused one. The mission again will be to assembly a typology of its parts that will facilitate toward developing a more complete general framework of geopolitics. And once this model-typology is assembled, the aim will be to utilize it to bringing an interpretation to a variety of contemporary and historical examples later on in Chapter 6.

These motivations now revealed, several additional comments appear to be in order before this first chapter ends. This book is written within the realm of a political scientist and not of a political geographer, and the author wants to avoid becoming entangled within the academic machinations toward measuring the intricacies that divide geopolitics from political geography.

Simply put, classical geopolitics focuses upon the structural, international, or strategic levels, and within this broader aspect it involves the study of the impacts of certain geographic features, such as states' and regions' positions and locations, resources, distance, topography, shapes and sizes, and the like, upon states' foreign policies and behaviors as an aid to statecraft and as a source for theory. In contrast, political geography is local and domestic in scope, stressing the impact of similar geographic features but upon policies and behaviors mostly within states' local political boundaries. Certain issues within these contrasting directions do overlap, such as immigration, pollution, violence, business, and transportation, but this overlapping should not negate the general distinctions. The concern is with geopolitics and not political geography, the international and not the domestic.

Political geography involves the immediate environmental impact upon the human, some sectors of this being the social, cultural, economic, and behavioral as reflected by the political and the governmental milieu. For instance: local policies affecting voting, income, crime, class, disease, and so forth within the spatial context as well as institutional solutions for green problems within the locale or the impact of space and resource limitations within the human condition. In contrast, the focus of geopolitics resides with states' interactions upon the regional and strategic stages. The realms of war and peace, alliance formations and balances of power, national security, regional and world government all would fit this more expansive level.

Clokie describes this contrast well in arguing:

> The geographers who have attempted to create a new super-science [of geopolitics] have failed because they do not understand what the political issues are. Geopolitics is, and will apparently remain, a fiction. At best it can be no more than statecraft, with emphasis on the craft. Geographers can, of course, contribute to the study of international affairs, but they cannot take it over bodily without ceasing to be geographers and becoming political scientists. Is there a master-science? This reviewer is not sure; but if there is, its name—as the reader would have guessed—is political science.[14]

As a political scientist, the author prefers geopolitics as both a craft of states' leaders and as a process for theory application. But he will disagree with Clokie when that author confines political geographers just to the academic and not also to the same policy interests that political scientists like to study. Nonetheless, geopolitics should rest more strongly with the foreign-policy specialty and the political geographers more strongly with the local-policy areas, and that focus on the domestic level could extend, likewise, to the decision-making realm of the postmodernist or critical geographers as well.

The design of this book is not concerned with the decision-making process in foreign affairs, that process instead being the reserve of the critical geographers. This author wants to escape study of leaders' biases as motivations for their actions and instead to point out rather the behaviors of states alone as relevant actors within the contrasting environments of the international scene.

Despite their differences, both political geography and geopolitics have suffered similar past disgraces, respectively, the problem of geographic determinism for geographers and the problem of fascism for adherents of geopolitics. Both problems, unfortunately, were associated in these respects with racism, and neither of the social sciences branches has escaped completely from its questionable heritage, a disgrace weakening to both. Fascism and racism speak of aggression, territorial and otherwise, against peaceful human existence. The dread of spatial expansion accompanies such exploitation. Neither must link with the neutral and nonideological parameters of geopolitics and political geography. Not to forget the previous harms, nonetheless one would think these past reputations need not continue to stigmatize our two approaches onto the present time.

And to complete this discussion of geopolitics and political geography, both hold similarities and differences that simply lack importance to the discussion made in this book. Indeed, the two fields overlap, and such cross-breeding strengthens both areas. Although the author prefers calling himself a political scientist interested in geopolitics, the label of political geographer is not offensive.

To continue on to a related theme, our discussion will turn to the facet of determinism/possibilism that will be a topic ahead in Chapters 4 and 5. But for this introduction, some further comment may be helpful, as these aspects touch upon geopolitics and political geography. Determinism, the quality of a rather absolute tie between one's environment and one's behavior, an earth dependency from which we humans cannot escape, is much too rigid for a classical adherence, and one should want to distance from its extremism. Obviously, we cannot escape from many of the constraints of our surroundings, as Nature places upon us certain conditions that do impact upon humans, consciously or unconsciously. Nonetheless, being both free and slave to our environments and without some balance between the two opposing aspects, neither branch of study, geopolitics nor political geography, can advance further to its potential. We need to retain both the "babies" of Nature's impacts and of persons' freedoms despite their occasional dirty "bathwaters."

Specifically, the possibility of spatial impact upon persons and nations alike is now favored by specialists in political geography and geopolitics. But the connection is implicit and not absolute. Placement may influence or condition actions occasionally and partly, but other stimulants, sometimes known but often unknown, will operate as well and normally with as much or greater frequency. Without this assumption that one's environment may impact one's actions (and this connection can only be an assumption and not a completely proven fact), neither study would be productive nor the constructing of a geopolitical model made even possible.

Still, we need to penetrate more deeply into this topic, once raised. Classical geopolitics, in its ontological foundations, assumes that some sort of a common reality does exist and that reality is clear enough so that many of us, author and reader alike, together can visualize and study it, and thus we can design theories of probability about particular likely outcomes. We will contrast this viewpoint with that of the postmodernists or of critical geopolitics later on in this first chapter.

In its epistemological foundations, the traditional version of geopolitics supports an eclectic methodology for locating these spatial realities, those exerting impacts from an environment that may influence behavior, in our cases, the positions of states and regions toward conditioning states-persons' foreign policies. These will briefly be described below relative to the various sources from which one may glean and evaluate the traditional theories, all toward a deeper understanding of geopolitics and its relevance to the international-affairs field:

Historical examples: Past events may offer our best source for finding theories, the events of history as these may correlate placement to action. This approach will be utilized in Chapter 6 by showing a variety of cases from which to study for geopolitical insights. The following quotation offers a good reason for locating theory in history:

> The substance of theory is history, composed of unique events and occurrences. An episode in history and politics is in one sense never repeated . . . . In this sense, history is beyond the reach of theory. Underlying all theory, however, is the assumption that these same unique events are also concrete instances of more general propositions.[15]

The realist theorist Christopher Layne, likewise, agreed with the reliance upon history for testing theory: "I use historical evidence to test my hypotheses about great power emergence."[16]

As much as with other approaches, history provides the empirical material necessary for gathering generalizations that we might accept for our geopolitical model. One would have had little difficulty in utilizing shatterbelts and checkerboards for a geopolitical interpretation of the Peloponnesian war of ancient Greece.[17] William Hay[18] drew insights from "specific events and historical periods" that have led to two recurring themes in European geopolitics: "first, the political fragmentation of Europe, and second, the historical division between East and West."

Scholars: An assortment of individuals have contributed insights into the relevance of geographic placement upon states' foreign involvements. The study of geopolitics has been very much influenced by Halford Mackinder, Nicholas Spykman, Zbigniew Brzezinski, Carlos de Meira Mattos, Saul Cohen, and a host of others in our understanding of classical geopolitics. Mackinder led the early way with his 1904 address concerning the Eurasian pivot, and both he and Spykman helped articulate the later parameters of strategic US defense policies in terms of their heartland and rimlands images.[19] The author recognized the dynamic of Paraguay as a lintel state,[20] one positioned between Brazil and Argentina and so protected that neither larger neighbor could thus absorb the smaller republic.

Common sense and logic: It would just make good sense to suppose that central and peripheral locations affect contrasting states' actions. Buffer states, it appears, restrict potentially hostile contacts among neighboring rival Great Powers. In South America, this cushioning effect of the buffers within the crush zone or corridor of conflict, one could believe, has helped stabilize the current regional diplomacy of peace,[21] again within a geopolitical format. Chapter 5 provides a number of concepts-theories based upon such notions.

Maps and important geographic locations: Maps reveal certain placement options for foreign-policy experts, as classical geopolitical treatises are replete with such visual illustrations. From these, we associate the locations of choke points, checkerboard patterns, encirclements, river estuaries, organic borders, distances and isolation, and other such spatial areas to happenings within the classical study.

Statistical or quantitative method: As has been attempted with certain spatial dimensions, distance weakening, shatterbelts, and borders-causing-wars, some generalizations associate with statistical approaches. But these instances appear limited because the majority of topics do not lend to quantification.

States persons: Elites or foreign-policy "experts" possess good instincts for spatial matters that guide successful policies. Robert Burr showed that nineteenth-century South American statesmen visualized balancing and positioning alignments of states for security and they established policies and actions accordingly.[22]

Rational-choice assumptions: Here, one should tread carefully in assuming that individuals, meaning policy-makers, will choose the best actions possible for achieving the goals they have set for their countries. This assumption has suffered contemporary scrutiny because of its alleged rigidity. Yet in this ideal, leaders will try to maximize benefits and rewards and minimize costs and risks. Said succinctly, people will instinctively choose the option with the greatest reward at the lowest cost, and within this capacity they will set priorities on the several options best considered, the better to the less attractive. The interest here is in the output of their rationalities, not in the bureaucratic processes that may speak of bias or err, because the aim is toward locating theories and not toward determining the motivation prompting states persons' actions.

For example, it is contended that statesmen follow Mackinder's heartland thesis because it lends itself to such rationality—a central position within the largest continent exerting pivotal impact outward. This said, the thesis tends to lack objective evidence of such spatial leverage. Nonetheless, because strategists believe its rationality, it remains important to national-security projects and represents a tradition within the geostrategic school of classical geopolitics. This rationality assumption fits nicely within the geopolitical compass, as leaders will be able to find the most profitable path to successful policies after considering these spatial tendencies based upon the geographic factors of importance to them.

Of course, dangers accompany this rationality, for governors do err or follow selfish and dysfunctional personal instincts and viewpoints or otherwise depart from cost-benefit formulas. Likewise, empirical testing of such assumptions could well be misleading or simply not possible. Reflecting these points, the "rational choice" advocates, no longer so dominant in contemporary political science, are facing increasing criticism.[23] The best solution to the rationality quandary is to be aware of such detours and to balance carefully the appropriateness of each of the seven theory sources now considered including our last option. And once more, one might avoid these difficulties by placing a focus upon the results of application, the worth of theories themselves when located and not upon leaders' decision-making motivations or the underlying contextual or ideological processes leading to the theories.

Several additional approaches are taken in this book that should receive further comments. First, our level-of-analysis fixes at the strategic or international or structural (these terms will be used interchangeably) with states the primary actors within the geopolitical scene. Differing from the postmodernists, whose concern plays upon leaders' subjectivities, for the most part our view will be to reduce foreign-policy-makers to playing rather passive roles, and the interest instead will pertain to the actions and strategies taken by countries themselves as the major performers of the regional and global theaters.

In an earlier article of the author's about a critique of critical geopolitics,[24] he compared these two levels-of-analyses preferences, the strategic or international of his own focus contrasted to the decision-making or individual-elitist perspective of the postmodernists. He sought to explain the major differences reflected in these two levels that separated the postmodernist critical geopolitics approach from the modernist classical geopolitical approach, the latter that is subscribed to in this book. One of the reviewers for the article, Klaus Dodds, suggested a method for joining together the two levels, a suggestion that was attempted but proved to be without good result. Truly, this author remains quite skeptical of a practical melding of the several levels, for this "levels-of-analysis-problem" realistically cannot be overcome.

Much of the focus of classical geopolitics concerns policy advice to country leaders. Halford Mackinder warned his government of impending strategic threats coming from Eurasian land powers. Admiral Alfred Mahan and Isaiah Bowman suggested sea-power alternatives to several US presidents. Hence, the level of interest of the classical shows this preference for the interplay of states. Nonetheless, a global perspective has risen of late,[25] wherein classical geopolitics may also address remedies of worldwide concern, global warming, energy and water scarcities, overpopulation, terrorism and nuclear proliferation, pandemics, and the like.

The book will not be concerned with historicizing or contextualizing the motivations of scholars and states persons as they formulate their foreign-affairs plans, for to us it is not important whether such persons were "imperialists," "conservatives," or hegemonic. Indeed, the historic context of authors, decision-makers, and the theories derived by them, finds little note because again, the interest rests upon the theories themselves within the model and not upon the motivations behind their creations. A model and its theories tend to be, of necessity, objective, ubiquitous, and timeless, although one must be aware of the dynamics of technology, human biases and cultures, and other such qualities that might alter the relationships among nations and regions within the transformations of history and of the shifting international environments.

For instance, we need not blame the motivations and social environments for any supposed human frailties of Halford Mackinder during the composition of his heartland thesis.[26] Rather, the importance lies in his theory alone, detached from judgment of the author's intention. A perfect example of this comes from Gearóid Ó Tuathail, a leader in the critical-geopolitics movement who wrote an insightful and well-researched article about the historical Mackinder with a focus upon his purported conservatism, elitism, and even racism, faults that might have contributed to the British colonial and hegemonic regime.[27] Ó Tuathail saw Mackinder's concept of geopolitics only as a tool for exploitation, and he ignored Mackinder as a modern founder and contributor of geopolitics itself, the originator of the heartland thesis that has continued to be one of the most influential theories within the classical model. Again, this book's focus rests upon the theories of our model and not upon backgrounds of the authors who created them.

The present volume will treat geopolitics as a neutral approach to making international affairs more understandable by enlisting classical theory, conforming instead to this much-repeated statement by Nicholas Spykman: "Ministers come and go, even dictators die, but mountain ranges stand unperturbed . . . . The nature of the territorial base has influenced [foreign-policy-makers] in the past and will continue to do so in the future."[28] The examples of Spykman and Ó Tuathail bespeak the contrasts between the two geopolitical approaches and their levels of interest, one of the traditionalists, the alternative of the postmodernists. Again, in this book we will follow the norm of Spykman and of the traditionalists.

The "scientific approach" tends to confuse many within traditional geopolitics because its misuse has caused difficulties to the study's reputation. The originators, Kjellín, Ratzel, Haushofer, and others, sought a "scientific" foundation to legitimize their spatial studies, and they enlisted the organic, evolutionary, and similar theories of their time for substantiating their ideas about geopolitics. Unfortunately for our later classical version, such concepts became outdated or blended within extremist ideologies, National Socialism in particular, that distorted their focus. Their "scientific" attachments find abrupt rejection within the notions of this book.

Interestingly, South American writers of geopolitics today commonly speak of their "scientific" approaches to geopolitics. These traditions tend to derive from the German heritage of the region's geopolitics when embassy military attachés taught in the Southern Cone's military academies the classical versions of organic, *raum,* and associated spatial definitions. We continue to see such influences in South American military education formats and in Southern Cone bookstores today. For instance, such can be gleaned in a textbook for officers in *Introducción a la Geopolítica,*[29] a treatise reflecting National Socialist themes of racism and territorial expansion but also expounding relevant generalizations of states' placement and access to natural resources.

Certain results of such past involvements carry some legitimacy (organic borders, for example); yet, these should not take a "scientific" label. As Cohen has done with attaching systems and developmental approaches within his geopolitics,[30] nothing can damage by attempting such additional linkages, if done carefully and, again, if they could be seen as valuable. But these attachments should not carry a "scientific" designation.

Nonetheless, in the contemporary sense, modern geopolitics can make use of natural-sciences methodologies and of statistical hypothesis-testing, these legitimately appended to classical geopolitics as "scientific." But quantification is limited in our case of geopolitics because numbers do not equate well with its usual approximate nature. How can one quantify heartlands, buffer states, influence spheres, and checkerboards? Unfortunately, with great difficulty and normally, not at all. So, where statistics can apply to certain concrete characteristics—say, frontiers, state size, distance, and demography—the results might satisfy such a rigid methodology.[31] Still, most of the spatial theories gathered in this book are not scientifically derived in this way but instead must rely upon other objective selection formulations. Specifically, geopolitics appears more an "art" than a "science," and our mission rests on making its methods as objective as possible in its normal process of theory gathering and in its application of relevant generalizations.

This book's epistemological and ontological assumptions are distinctly modernist. In the first instance, a common reality is possible, resting on the premise that one can visualize our environments void of excessive bias. And in the second, we possess sufficient practical and objective means for researching this vision of "reality" such that the probability requirement of theory is possible. One's self and one's vision are separated enough so that some amount of generalization and measurement can be ascertained from what we may visualize "out there." This common reality among individuals can derive through historical example, logic, common sense, visualization, statistical analysis, and rational choice, the measures outlined above. In either case, the "actual" or the "outside" stages exist and can be seen by significant groupings of persons in sufficiently clear probabilities that will make it possible to utilize objective approaches. Without such modernist assumptions, the formulation, testing, and use of classical geopolitical theory would not be possible.

We will not read in this book much about the history of geopolitics,[32] although brief sketches, mainly in Chapter 3, are given where some background would be appropriate. Whereas the term originated with Rudolf Kjellén and Friedrich Ratzel more than one hundred years ago, clearly the practice of geopolitics came much earlier with the first diplomatic contacts among the beginnings of ancient societies. It has continued to be utilized as a normal procedure in the composition of national political and military strategies, those being to take into consideration for policy-making and action the positions of various lands within continents and regions, these aligned astride mountains, rivers and oceans, and natural and energy resources. Other such geographic factors as distance, climate, topography, and size and shape of countries and continents that might affect a country's foreign affairs were assumed to be important also.

These reflections all lead to a summation by Francis Sempa, who portrays these traditions in the following:

> Lord Palmerston famously remarked that nations have no permanent friends and no permanent enemies, only permanent interests. Geopolitics helps statesmen determine their country's interests, and helps them distinguish between enduring and transient interests.[33]

The United States, for instance, has a rather permanent security strategy of maintaining a favorable balance of power within the rimlands of the Eurasian continent, enabled by its marine strength and by bases in certain pivotal areas (Western Europe, Persian Gulf, and Korea/Japan). Its allies and opponents might vary from time to time; yet, North America will continue unrelentingly toward this secure rimlands position framed within its advantages of great distances and isolation from likely foes,[34] no matter what other global and regional transformations may appear. This US focus on neutralizing strategic dangers to its security from Eurasian threats has remained relatively permanent since independence, although such a concern may be more evident during periods of stress and not in others of calm.

In contrast to North America, South America, in a different world location, remains isolated and not much affected by Eurasian balances. The republics there will direct their interests and involvements toward threatened frontiers, regional development and integration, and continental power balances among the larger powers and the buffer states, and consequently the region maintains currently a rather stable regional "zone of peace."[35] Their geopolitics do not reflect a strategic or global concern; rather the attention draws inward as an independent and isolated world region.

One further point requires mention. A single overall model of international relations simply lacks possible design and implementation. Rather, each of the other IR models described in Chapter 2 holds insight and utility, for it takes different models including geopolitics fully to understand the various foreign-affairs scenes. As with the others, geopolitics should merit inclusion within this grouping.

Now, with these basics of the nature of classical geopolitics examined, we move on to other aspects of theoretical modeling.

2   Model and Theory

Some initial thoughts concerning theory should begin this discussion of theories and models, the themes for this second chapter. To summarize from the last chapter, theories are merely simple sentences of probability, composed as "if-then" statements. If a state occupies a central position, this location may then lend to that state certain advantages and certain disadvantages. A nation residing distantly from an event of concern will likely see its immediate impact upon that event diminished, a distance-weakens proposition. Shatterbelts in the Caribbean will violate the Monroe Doctrine because these pose strategic intrusions into Middle America by Eurasian opponents against North America.

It is not the intention in this book to delve into a survey of others' depictions of IR theory. Yet some comments should assist relative to what appear to be the more common directions of theory-definition within the field of international relations. Here, the descriptions vary widely; yet that shown above parallels others for the most part. For instance, please note this reference from the classic Dougherty and Pfaltzgraff text: "A theory sets forth a systematic view of phenomena by presenting a series of propositions or hypotheses which specify relations among variables in order to present explanations and make predictions about the phenomena."[1] Or Stephen van Evera: "[Theories represent] general statements that describe and explain the causes or effects of classes of phenomena."[2] Again, it seems these and others alike may approximate what this book is attempting to define relative to classical geopolitics.

Interestingly, some authors simply ignore propounding any definition of theory. Knud Erik Jorgensen takes a more expansive approach, describing certain "categories" and "traditions" of generalization, somewhat attuned to this author's use of "model" instead.[3] Despite the concept placed within his book's title, he fails even to list the term "theory" within his glossary of terms. Somewhat similarly, Martin Griffiths notes this confusion happening despite his failure to correct by alleging theory as a "diverse collection of worldviews" that ignores any helpful specificity.[4] Finally, Kenneth Waltz travels a very different path, arguing that theories are "speculative processes introduced to explain [laws] . . . . Laws remain, theories come and go."[5] Were one to follow his guide this book could not have been written, because geopolitics simply lacks any totally predictable "laws" and instead can claim to a wide assortment of theories based upon predictability! To assemble all of these diverse notions into one defining guide extends much beyond the present author's intelligence and patience! Better to "keep it simple" by staying with what has already been given the reader: theories are simple sentences of probability.

The function of theories is to provide objective filters for obtaining a better assessment of which reality might be "out there." They attempt to simplify, explain, scrutinize, even predict, the policies and actions of our interest. Theories reveal the obvious, although they can also find what is sometimes hidden.[6] In the words of Jack Snyder:

> Each theory offers a filter for looking at a complicated picture. As such they help explain the assumptions behind political rhetoric about foreign policy. Even more important, the theories act as a powerful check on each other. Deployed effectively, they reveal the weaknesses in arguments that can lead to misguided policies.[7]

The "misguided policies," indeed, reveal the difficulties of theories because theories, wrongly selected and applied, can easily lead to serious mistakes. But they can as well provide some better chance for insight and predictions. Our real challenge is to seek some balance between the guidance of reliable theory and the chance of being misled.

We come to accept these generalizations based upon their likelihoods of showing a consistent and predictable relationship between variables. This connection sometimes happens, but not always. Yet some degree of consistency and probability in these predictions should be sufficient for us toward accepting these associations as theories. Were the "if-then" results always to occur, an unlikely case, the relationship instead would not be a theory but would figure as Waltz's "law," and we do not have any of these absolutes in geopolitics, unfortunately.

At what point do repeated actions become predictable theories? How do we "test" phenomena for a probability that might rise to the level of solid generalizations? This author's admittedly sketchy but, it is hoped, objective approach toward locating reliable theories simply is: (1) to recognize their existence—

that is, to utilize carefully the seven criteria for selection as outlined in the previous chapter, these being historical examples, scholars' judgments, common sense and logic, maps and important geographic locations, statistical or quantitative methods, states persons' actions, and rational-choice assumptions; and (2) to evaluate as closely as possible the selected theory applications to unique situations where they might offer us some understanding. This book can submit no better methodology other than the limited occasions when statistical hypothesis-testing can be utilized, and the quite scarce instances of the statistical approach can mislead as well.

Accordingly, if a statement bears a reasonable chance of explanation and prediction, it probably will enter our classical geopolitical model. Or when an outstanding scholar or states person utters a conclusion that seems logical or consistent within the flow of historical experience, it too will see acceptance. Common sense, rationality, repeated observations, and the like will fit closely enough to the objective and empirical format of this book to approximate a likely appearance of theory, these similarly passing the test of probability and theory recognition.

Most authors of the social sciences would much prefer their topics and models to render to statistical testing where the methodology of the "hard sciences" might be more dependable in hypothesis testing. Unfortunately, geopolitics is not one of those fortunate areas, because the majority of theory candidates in geopolitics are not amenable to numbers. But neither would any of the other sectors of "model building" within the foreign-affairs domain either hold these hard-science advantages.

Once more, the statistics path is available but in very limited fashion for calculating the spatial linkages that we would call theories as set within the geopolitical definition. In later chapters will be described a statistically tested contagion or spread of political and other conditions across borders.[8] Or the quantitatively relevant thesis which posits that "the number of state borders correlate significantly with the number of wars suffered by states—the more borders, the more war involvements."[9] A cluster-analysis routine was enlisted to formulate shatterbelts.[10] Distance statistically associated with UN voting by the Latin American states on the issue of collective intervention.[11] All of these instances contained variables that were readily susceptible to enlisting numbers, and hence to the more exacting quantifiable comparisons. Frankly, beyond these and other meager examples, one can seldom see anything else in statistical testing for proving the reliability of our spatial theories. Other quantifiable mixtures within geopolitics may be located as well, but these will prove to be quite limited in number.

As outlined in Chapter 1, most geopolitical theories arise from events of history and also from national security policies, common sense, logical and rational thought, as well as from the empirical suggestions of maps and writers. But again, no other set rules are offered in this treatise for recognizing when a generalization comes to be accepted as a theory for our model. Consequently, each author decides intuitively the presence of generalizations, and that, too, will be the author's approach. If a respected individual calls a statement a "theory," that will normally settle the matter of acceptance for the geopolitics of this book.

Nonetheless, a positive might be suggested for having such an open gathering format for the more important theories for our classical typology. It is believed that spatial generalizations do actually exist, naturally, in practice, in thought, and also in relative abundance. In a broader sense, we simply could not exist as humans without reliance on theories, of whatever coloration. The same with geopolitics. The impact of states' spatial positions upon their policies and actions is rather obvious and visible to states persons' and to our own understanding of international relations.[12] These theories serve as filters for our attempts at interpreting the international scenery. Because they exist, they can be located and utilized!

For instance, in describing four historic geopolitical features of Peru's border disputes with neighboring countries, Gorman admits to their permanency by stating:

> The geopolitical interests of nations, it may be argued, tend to remain relatively fixed over extended periods of time and reflect certain real or perceived environmental influences, opportunities, and/or constraints of a geographical nature.[13]

He outlines ambitions of "consolidating [Peru's] control over what might be called peripheral areas on its frontiers" that have waxed and waned since independence but still have stayed consistent within the horizons of the republic's leaders.

Hence, our task with theories is to select a reasonable statement that might apply to explaining a consistently happening situation, then make practical interpretation as carefully as we can. This slippery work lies ahead in the selection of the primary classical theories, but nonetheless, the author felt sufficiently confidence in his selection procedures to locate more than sixty theories as acceptable to our geopolitical model. His various choices must await further examination and application later on in Chapters 5 and 6.

Now, we shall proceed on to models. Models differ from theories in their much wider scope of description. Models encompass all of the relevant assumptions, concepts, and theories that will extend over our entire geopolitical realm, their boundaries or entry points distinguished by the particular definition we hold for classical geopolitics. Thus, models are simple containers or typologies or structures for all the relevant parts of geopolitics including theories.

Models are passive; they do not interpret or explain anything. They possess no moving parts, although they may enhance the bundling of related theories that may be relevant to certain events. But they play no further function except to hold what we place astride them! To repeat from the first chapter, the interpretive quality of geopolitics rests, not with its model, but with its theories that will assist with describing and analyzing the often-changing events and environments of the international system. The model will stay passive and unchanged.

Second, other authorities have retained this designation of model. For example, Joseph Berger and colleagues' depiction of a "theoretical research program" closely follows the above depiction of model, theirs being a "family of interrelated theories" or "an interrelated set of theories together with theoretical research relevant to them and applied research grounded in them."[14] Accordingly, these assortments of common theories join within "families" or "sets" that adhere to a familiar definition, these generalizations enjoying clarification and testing within that definition when necessary. Individual theories or bundles of theories are then available as taken from this "program" to attempt interpretations of events of interest.

Frankly, none of the other international-relations models have been so fully packaged as is being attempted here with geopolitics. This contrasting process groups within one configuraton all relevant parts for study and for guidance to statecraft. Perhaps this technique may prove useful to some growth in these directions for the other international-relations models as well?

Importantly, one begins to assemble a model by first composing a definition of that model that will assist the scholar and statesman toward selecting the appropriate assumptions, concepts, and theories that would fit within the framework described by that definition. Indeed, a model cannot exist without such a definition. Hence, a model's definition functions as a gatekeeper or funnel or entry point for pertinent assumptions, concepts, and theories passing into that container we will call a model. Specifically, it serves as a device for recognizing what should enter the bounds of the structure and as a barrier for restricting other elements that do not fit the exclusive definition of the model.

A geopolitical definition denotes the first starting part of the geopolitical model, and perhaps this phase represents its most important part because all else that we will be calling geopolitics will have to conform to that commonly accepted definition before it can become part of the model. And the refinement of a model's definition is one of the most neglected factors in model building, for most if not all international-relations models appear to be lacking this distinguishing and necessary defining quality.

Particularly in the case of geopolitics, the absence of a clear definition, as pointed out in the first chapter, has been one of the chief weaknesses of geopolitics in the past. This lack has led both to attacks for its promoting a diabolical power politics and to its capture by certain ideologies that have distorted its reputation. In some of his past publications,[15] this author has called for some consensus on formulating a common definition of geopolitics that could be helpful to a broader acceptance of the model. He makes such a call for a standard designation among concerned scholars ahead in the final chapter of this book.

Definitions of geopolitics will vary widely and certain ones are cumbersome, negative, contradictory, and confusing. But that said, the majority stay within the rough parameters of geography or country position as conditioning states' foreign affairs. Accordingly, we have many instances of relatively standard depictions to rely upon from scholars who reside within the field of geopolitics.

The author's suggestion for a consensus definition of geopolitics follows this path: "Geopolitics is the study of the impact or influence of certain geographic features, positions and locations of regions, states, and resources, plus topography, climate, distance, states' size and shape, demography, and the like, upon states' foreign policies and actions as an aid to statecraft. Accordingly, this study lends itself both to theory and to policy."

This description emphasizes the original geographic thrust of position, location, and the other features where all of the parts will pertain to the structural or international spatial domains of states, regions, and resources. These all function to assist in the creation and application of both policy and generalization.

Additionally, the following definition extracts from Jorge Atencio's influential book among South American scholars published in Argentina, *¿Qué es la Geopolítica?*:

> Geopolitics is the science that studies the influence of geographic factors in the life and evolution of states, with an objective of extracting conclusions of a political character . . . . [Geopolitics] guides statesmen in the conduct of the state's domestic and foreign policy, and it orients the armed forces to prepare for national defense and the conduct of strategy; it facilitates planning for future contingencies based on consideration of relatively permanent geographic features that permit calculations to be made between such physical realities and certain proposed national objectives, and consequently, the means for conducting suitable political or strategic responses.[16]

Later on in another chapter will be discussed specific variations between the North and South American approaches to geopolitics, but Atencio's definition of geopolitics closely parallels the tack taken above. His description departs in two ways: (1) he favors the earlier German designation in taking Friedrich Ratzel's lead for a "scientific" and organic feature toward the "life and evolution of states"; (2) along with his reference to the importance of geopolitics to the national armed forces that is neglected in our first submission.

Another more recent definition of geopolitics corresponds to both the first definition and to Atencio's, that authored by Saul Cohen:

> A . . . modern geopolitics is . . . a scholarly analysis of the geographical factors underlying international relations and guiding political interactions . . . the analysis of the interaction between, on the one hand, geographical settings and perspectives and, on the other, political processes. The settings are composed of geographical features and patterns and the multilayered regions that they form. The political processes include forces that operate at the international level and those on the domestic scene that influence international behavior. Both geographic settings and political processes are dynamic, and each influences and is influenced by the other.[17]

Cohen then proceeds to outline five stages of modern geopolitics to reveal how this definition has emerged, showing also a dialectic feature that pushes these stages onward to a fuller development. His definition includes his "multilayered regions" characteristic of this overall structure to geopolitics. But otherwise, he too connects the impact of geographic features to foreign policies and actions. More on his geopolitical model later on in this chapter.

In sum, with the three definitions of classical geopolitics taken together, their common elements include certain geographic factors that may affect a country's foreign policies and actions. For ease and clarity, this book's definition will stick with the first description of classical geopolitics.

In all of these ways, geopolitics shows a neutral, objective, and ideologically free tool for use by foreign-policy experts. It is state-centric in that the focus of study sets mainly upon the relationships among countries within the international system. It holds a predictable quality where its theories stay consistent over time. Further, it tends to ignore the motivations and machinations of decision-makers and rather its emphasis is upon locating and applying theories that may assist toward understanding international phenomena. Finally, the "geo" prefix emphasizes the "geographic" and less the "power" aspect of international relations. Accordingly, the definition, and therefore the theories of the model themselves, emit a structural design in that the bounds of their activity would be intercontinental, cross-continental, or at least regional parts of continents, and the various strategic actions and reactions of concern that happen within a systemic configuration.

One final description of definition: geopolitics associates with both peace and with war. All international-relations models must deal with conflict, obviously, because conflict resides throughout the global realm as well as within human activity. But IR models, likewise, will consider resolution of such rivalries and will assist in other ways to bring more stability to problems of global disharmony, geopolitics among these contributors. As for geopolitics, we can contrast the heartland and shatterbelt theses most probably to conflict, whereas checkerboards and buffer states may reflect either conflict or resolution of strife, and finally integration, distance, and gateway and lintel states will resemble more pacific outcomes. Consequently, geopolitics rests upon the positioning of states, regions, and resources as impacting upon their policies and actions, with some of its consequences associated with international violence and others with structures of accommodation.

This method of defining a model does deserve some positive notice for several good reasons. It gathers together all of the extant assumptions, concepts, and theories within a standardized definition so that we can recognize and utilize the whole expanse of the elements within the model. Settled within the fabric of the definition, the individual assumptions and concepts-theories can be studied more closely and clarified if needed. Others can be added. We also now have a device that distinguishes the specific elements of the geopolitics model that will depart from those of the other models, so we avoid the confusions and captures of the overlapping frameworks.

And we are also able to form theoretical linkages or bundles of generalizations that may contribute more broadly to an interpretation of issues of regional or continental interest. For instance, in a later chapter will be the attempt to enlist the concepts of checkerboards and shatterbelts to analyze the similarities and differences between the Peloponnesian war of ancient Greece and the contemporary diplomacy of South America.[18] Interestingly, checkerboard structures featured both areas, but shatterbelts, common to the Greek conflict, have not appeared of late in republican South America. The point raised here is that groupings of variables may extend understandings, these assembled within a set definition and a clustering enabled by a functioning model.

Once again, a model's definition sets the parameters for the selection of theories. Lenin's imperialism thesis would fit a socialist/communist model, and Hitler's master-race a fascist framework. Of course, neither imperialism nor race superiority would be applicable to the spatially oriented and nonideological geopolitical definition, and they consequently could not enter into its basket or model. The occasional competition between maritime and continental states, because of the positional and geographic natures of these dichotomies, would pertain to and become part of the geopolitical model, fitting its definition and thus passing into the model. Similarly too, the impacts of distance, energy resources, central locations, and river watersheds, as these will impact upon foreign affairs and other such questions of a political nature, would likewise fit nicely within the geopolitical model.

Often neglected in most model constructions, assumptions are simple but normally impossible-to-verify statements that describe the underlying features of a model. They show a nearly universal agreement among their students about the basic natures of IR approaches, geopolitics in our case. Indeed, they must be accepted or we cannot proceed further into the model. We assume a state's location and position relative to other states and regions do exert some impact upon foreign policies. As such, states persons are somewhat conscience about these influences, and they do act upon the spatial stimulants whether they are aware of these or not. These spatial influences are permanent, like theories, although theories are more testable and they do not demand the trust that we must place upon the assumptions.

Assumptions differ from theories in these ways: (1) assumptions are not validated by their probability; they stand alone as being widely accepted and as exhibiting patterns of consistency; (2) they are imagined to be true, for there is no further test for their justification; (3) they are more abstract and tend to be broader than theories; (4) they are not directly applied for interpreting international events; and (5) they form the basis for an entire model, its basic foundations. Sometimes assumptions and theories can overlap, but normally one should ignore this problem by accepting both parts when such a duet happens.

The obvious initial premise of geopolitics is that geography can affect a state's actions. We do not set out to test this ideal, for indeed such a premise cannot be proven. We merely must accept that connection to be true. Otherwise, geopolitics itself lacks a solid spatial foundation and it would be very difficult to proceed further. Moreover, we must imagine that foreign-policy-makers and actors will perform within this geopolitical assumption of environment-affecting-action, whether we can be assured of such connections or not. We must take these "leaps of faith" rather blindly because we simply have no other choice! Chapter 4 will describe various of the assumptions undergirding geopolitics.

Concepts appear as locations, symbols, or abstractions of patterns or features within the political and physical landscape that would fit within the spatial/geographic definition and assumptions of the geopolitical model. In a sense, they are the vocabulary and the descriptive materials of geopolitics that can be expanded into the forming of assumptions and theories. One can occasionally have difficulty separating concepts from theories because the two can run together, as we experienced with assumptions. But such need not be a problem because, for convenience of explanation, the two phenomena, concepts and theories, will combine into one in Chapter 5 within the designation of concepts-theories. But for ease of discussion, normally just "theory" will be utilized.

Examples of concepts include heartlands, checkerboards, shatterbelts, buffer states, pan-regions, and organic frontiers. These factors are passive and not abstract; they provide descriptions and examples for the creation of assumptions and theories. They do not articulate an assumption or argue a thesis. And again, all such designations should adhere to the spatial definition of geopolitics. It would be consistent within our model for an investigation to gather the whole expanse of concepts within one "tent" such that this multitude can be appreciated, utilized, and refined.

To repeat, all four parts, a set definition in addition to assumptions, concepts, and theories that fit that designation, together form a complete model that enables a listing and describing for these parts and a forum for clarifying, composing, testing, joining, and applying the various spatial dimensions to foreign policies. These two facilities, a topology of gathered elements and a forum for testing, represent the primary utilities of models. We simply can go no further in our constructing after applying all of these geopolitical factors to international relations!

This book's version of the classical geopolitical model will differ from that of David Easton's "political systems framework,"[19] one that is nicely patterned with arrows showing inputs, outputs, and feedback loops, and that features an internal mechanism for converting demands and supports into actions. One could visualize here a factory at work: raw materials entering, being processed into a completed product, and finally having reliable feedback loops for evaluating the effectiveness of the finished product. Were that all models might be so clearly proportioned! Alas, ours lacks arrows and all the rest!

Nonetheless, within international-relations theory the other models, too, lack these input-output flows. But are these really necessary in our case? And can they be successfully attached, anyway? At least for the structural or international level of analysis wherein lie the leading IR theories, the actors perform as states, not individuals. We study how states interact within strategic and regional spaces, not how the actions and policies themselves become formulated by elitist policy-makers. The levels-of-analysis differ here, with decision-making specific enough for erecting depictions of arrows and flow charts. But in our interest, we observe the broader actions of states within regions and continents where policies and actions represent our focus of theory application.

The Talcott Parsons and Edward Shils designation of four levels of theory (or models) might give some further indication of where our geopolitical model may locate.[20] Their "ad-hoc classification systems," the lowest level, simply assembles rather arbitrary categories for arranging collected data. A higher grade, "taxonomies," broadens that data by offering descriptive links among categories. "Conceptual frameworks," similar to Easton's above, will offer explanations and predications but be without axioms or assumptions and without strong facilities for inter-relating data systematically. The patterns of the present treatise for outlining the geopolitical model would resemble the highest order, that of a "theoretical system" that combines taxonomies and conceptual frameworks and thus would facilitate a more systematic interconnecting of descriptions, explanations, and predictions where the parts of the model can be linked together and expanded into broader packages for interpretation where possible.

The geopolitical theoretical system formulated within this text accomplishes what would be expected at this highest level of modeling. It gathers all of the parts within a common description or definition, clarifies and applies these according to empirical review, and provides the chance for linking common concepts-theories together for broader and new approaches for interpretation.

Now, we must proceed on to a further topic on this quest for depicting models and theories, that of attempting to place the other leading internation-al-relations models within the framework just given to geopolitics. Nonetheless, the descriptions that will follow will be brief for the most part because this author admits to being not sufficiently expert to have delved extensively into their main features. But he thinks these models, too, lack the full development they require, similar to geopolitics. His method of model construction might widen the general discussion of models as well as broaden our understanding of geopolitics. This chapter will then conclude with an evaluation of the two geopolitical models drawn by Saul Cohen and by Jakub Grygiel. Their attempts, to this author's knowledge, represent the only models roughly similar to that formulated in the present book.

Realism: We will start with realism, a favorite of the author because he finds it quite usable as a model and quite "realistic." His sole objection to this model: its "capture" of geopolitics, submerging our classical model into a foreign framework not appropriate to its separate contribution. We still require some brief repeating of the earlier descriptions of geopolitics' merger into realism because a complete decoupling merits importance to the legitimacy cause of our topic.

In a recent manuscript and typical display of realism,[21] the writer depicted geopolitics as nothing more than a fixture within realism. He stated: "[G]eo-politics has been seen as subordinated to the broader area of 'realist thinking,' where states are regarded as driven to maximize their power position in an anarchic system." This author is correct in his description of realism visualizing an "anarchic system" where power maximization could bring security. But expressed earlier, the "power" factor does not affix to classical geopolitics.

Nicholas Spykman wrote in both realist and geopolitical directions. In his earlier articles that define as geopolitical,[22] he examined the spatial factors impacting upon nations' behaviors and security: their size and location, the factors of topography, competition between land- and sea-power configurations, and the inevitable territorial expansion of states. All of these geographic features conditioned foreign policies, he predicted, thus revealing their spatial natures. Nonetheless, in his classic, *America's Strategy in World Politics*,[23] Spykman saw the world in mostly realist terms, enlisting such descriptors as an anarchic and dangerous world with a never-ending struggle for power among nations and with limited periods of peace only arising between inevitable and longer periods of warfare.

He stayed within geopolitics when he altered the importance of Mackinder's heartlands by suggesting the more vital pivotal positions of rimlands that lay between the central portions and the outer lands beyond, with sea power as important as land power.[24] In terms that would later influence George Kennan's containment thesis, he predicted North America's defense lay in a favorable balance of power within the Eurasian rimlands and not in a fortress America posture.

Nothing is harmed by enlisting two or more models jointly, a practice deepening foreign-affairs insights. But of necessity, realism must relinquish its supposed ownership of geopolitics and allow the free rein of our classical stance to make its full mark within the assembly of all IR models. This poses a substantial aim for this book and one that it is necessary to keep pointing out.

The realist visualizes the world anarchic and lawless, violent and dangerous, and devoid of international security institutions such as a protective United Nations and readily enforceable laws punishing violators for wars and radical revolutions. This security void unfortunately will continue so long as states only seek safety unto themselves. The answer to the security problem arrives in a collective endeavor, moderate nations joining in unison to satisfy the protections not delivered by their own efforts or by the existing international system.

A fixation upon power-for-security, where most realist scholars and states persons have placed their emphases until lately, is gradually seeing some revision. Simply put, the traditional thesis, now questioned, alleges that states gain security through their own "drive to maximize power." This author remembers in his undergraduate days studying whole chapters in college IR textbooks devoted to the realist assembling and measuring of national power. That textbook focus, thankfully, has waned because, frankly to realists, of a dawning awareness that unilateral quests for security by one country inevitably raise a daunting "dilemma"—does "maximizing one's power" really deliver protection when other countries of equal resources will likely respond similarly with their own increases in power, thus negating the whole enterprise of a single country seeking its own safety? When one monarch builds his castle walls higher, his immediate neighbors, alarmed in the next castles beyond, will do so also when they feel threatened by the adjacent higher castle walls. Arms races (or higher castle walls) will ensue, bringing more threats to the original security difficulty.

In asymmetric comparisons, United States versus Mexico or Canada, this security dilemma can be ignored. But if contemporary Russia flaunts its nuclear weaponry, one could expect China, Germany, and the United States to become alarmed and take appropriate security measures to counter the Russians. This dilemma has not been convincingly answered by realist authors. Perhaps, no good unilateral response exists to settle this difficulty.

Good security answers may come in two different tracks of collective configuration conceived since Hans Morgenthau's classical realist portrayal of the problem,[25] the first from Henry Kissinger's consensus submission,[26] and the second from Kenneth Waltz's[27] balance of power path.

To Kissinger, with President Richard Nixon in agreement, an international "framework for peace" or a dependable consensus or agreement among the larger states presents at least a temporary solution to the security attainment. This consensus translates to the greater powers subscribing to a solid trust and confidence among themselves where none will undermine the security of the others. A status quo of moderation and compromise would establish a common support for a collective security. That description could approximate our present global framework, at least until Putin's Russian adventures in Ukraine and despite the current era of North American global hegemony. One might see the major countries cooperating against terrorism and piracy, nuclear and chemical warfare, environmental threats of warming, pollution, and pandemics, and global financial stability. We probably will still encounter local and regional conflicts and rivalries within regions, but fortunately these may not escalate more widely into shatterbelts (the exception being contemporary Ukraine) because the major powers would surely move to prevent these spreads of violence—that is, China with North Korea, Russia with Iran and Syria.

Accordingly, a consensus among Great Power moderates will bring peace, a stability however tenuous that would assist a resolution of the security dilemma within the realist model. A vital pivotal role is imagined for the visionary statesman, a Metternich, Castlereagh, Bismarck, Churchill, or Kissinger, for example, who would guide nations to the consensus the realists would want for protection, including his following tasks and characteristics:

1. A statesman recognizing and then isolating or destroying revolutionary leaders who might rise in the larger states, a Napoleon or a Hitler. Radicals disrupt desired consensuses and bring conflict and war, a return to harmful

anarchy. Moderate leaders cannot negotiate profitably with revolutionaries, for radicals by definition will work to break any existing consensus. They must be absent for moderates to enhance and continue that stability.

2. A statesman implanting moderate actions and policies within his country as a nonthreatening example to other nations and as a trust re-enforcing to the consensus. Realists criticize excessive US "crusades" in Iraq and Vietnam because these immoderate adventures destabilize and weaken a framework of trust that underpins peace and thus security.

3. A statesman working to construct and/or maintain the consensus among the leading state actors by his skilled diplomacy, his establishment of alliances and power balances, his success in fostering international trust and dependable communications, and in like accomplishments to encourage stability through compromise and moderation.

4. A statesman coordinating efforts among Great Power allies to prevent catalytic or escalatory wars by reining in rogue and pariah states that might harm the strategic consensus. This may translate to recognizing others' spheres of interest and in pulling back armed forces from positions that may threaten the concerns of neighboring states and in erecting "fire-breaks" to halt shatter-belt escalations.

In sum, security equates to Great Power consensus drawn on moderation and collective assurances of conflict management, void of radical disturbances that might disrupt the stability.

A second variant for resolving the security dilemma pertains to the collective management of power for this security against an anarchic world: either a power balancing among states or a collective security should be applied. In the first description, the international system seeks a harmony or equilibrium among the great states. Conflict unsettles the balance but nations will strive to restore the former stability by counterbalancing against whatever is creating the disharmony. Weighting strength against strength dampens strife, it is alleged, and the ensuing stalemate translates to peace.

In the second description, a collective security makes each alliance partner protector of the others by resisting peace-violators with a collective response to wrongdoing. More feasible on paper than in practice, this approach awaits success in stopping aggression, its future dependent on enhanced international unity. Yet, it figures as a possible solution to the power dilemma inherent to realism.

The collective-power-management theme suffers some confusion because the assumptions tend to differ. For instance, which sort of balance spells security, an asymmetric or imbalance or a symmetric or equilibrium? Garnham found the former case more frequently awarding protection,[28] and perhaps his conclusion represents the norm. Similarly, the number of state players or "poles" and their interactions, whether "flexible" or "rigid," figure into this security nexus as well. Here, the classic nineteenth-century balance of a flexible relationship among five primary states of Europe was alleged to have delivered a near-century of strategic peace. Once that structure became rigid, warfare ensued into the next century.

The Cold War ending, the global structure has turned from a fairly stable bipolarity of the Soviet Union and the United States into a never-before-seen in modern times unipolarity of North American paramountcy, a coming era whose longevity and stability have caused much debate among realist scholars. How long will the United States persist as sole global hegemon, momentarily or for a lengthier time? Will the stability of this "unipolar moment" stay or gradually revert to strategic rivalry, the Great Power consensus evaporating and an instable world arising?

A number of realist commentators predict the eventual rise of challengers poised to defeat US leadership, their opposition gaining traction by a hegemon's coming bankruptcy and by the equalizing of technology and wealth among the leading rival states.[29] Such a reversal of leadership will arrive naturally within this system, perhaps stalled for the moment because of American power and to its being a more benign and less threatening leader-state. Others contest this argument, asserting instead that an American and non-European hegemon differs from the past structures by being able to balance regional contenders for a longer interval in Europe and Asia to its favor from a safe and distant American platform and to offshore balancing on the Eurasian flanks with its two-ocean navy for a similar advantage. Time will tell the outcome for this realist debate.

The systems model stresses actions that will prompt reactions, these seeking an eventual equilibrium that will alter the environments of both actors and reactors. Always evolving into something different, the structure of study connects its parts into a fluid blend of outcomes where some states may benefit, others may suffer. The world is composed of a multitude of systems, mostly interconnected and residing at different levels of involvement. Thus, their boundaries often are not clear and actions and reactions will spill beyond their immediate confines. In these same ways, all of our structural international-relations models tend to be systemic including geopolitics. But this model focuses exclusively upon such parameters and the interactions within.

Examples abound. During the Cold War rivalry between North America and Russia, Nicaragua took on more importance than it would normally deserve, caught within the bounds of the Monroe Doctrine and of the Reagan administration's opposition to the Soviet-supported Sandinista Revolution within the country. This systemic linkage of rivalry and strife among the three countries quickly evaporated once the Soviets experienced their Cold War collapse. Daniel Ortega's re-election in 2010 in Nicaragua drew little attention in Washington, whereas his rule in the 1980's suffered US covert intervention. One system's actors and interactions replaced a very different description of actors and interactions after a short interval of years.

While many works depict the parts of this model, that of Robert Marks merits display.[30] His assumptions tend toward: a contingency phenomenon, or the contention that major world events normally are not isolated but instead will stay tied to other happenings that inter-relate upon a wider plain of events; historical accidents, for instance, in climate changes as these may affect a variety of random patterns that will advance or prohibit the prosperity, stability, and other conditions of countries and regions; and conjunction, where several of the factors noted above might come together to form a unique historic moment that would impact upon regional or international events.

For instance, what caused the Europeans to expand across the oceans, soon to found colonies around the globe? Marks's answer: partly, blocked land routes to Asia caused by Muslim and Mongol invasions across Central Asia. Why did industrialization begin in England and not elsewhere? Mark's answer: in part, the location of ample coal deposits lying near London, this eventually prompting steam power linked to locomotives, textile looms, and military battleships. Why did China and India, once strong manufacturing competitors to England and Europe, decline as commercial centers so quickly after England industrialized? Mark's response: the European powers, taking advantage of steam-powered industrialization, deprived a divided India of its textile industry and its independence. Eventually, a united China, too, was overcome by the Europeans by defeat in the two Opium Wars because of iron-clad steam-driven warships. More favorable climates in North America and Europe during the past several centuries assisted the West as well. In all of these situations, such historical actions/reactions within regional and global systems advantaged the Europeans against the Asians.

Might China and India both rise once again to equal Europe's prosperity and power in the near future, when systemic conditions could reverse? Possibly: new energy sources beyond the coal and petroleum eras will place the Asians on a par with or even an advantage over the Europeans and Americans. Marks visualized a new Pacific Era lying ahead, with China and India resuming their earlier positions of influence.

We conclude this systems model by stipulating (1) a definition with (2) assumptions that would underlie and spawn (3) concepts/theories that can be applied to an understanding of contemporary and historical transformations.

A dependency model shows a structure of contrasting levels of wealth and technology, a core of abundance encircled by a periphery of poverty and a lack of technology. This design resembles powerful northern regions placed against weakened and dependent southern regions. Statistical data substantiate this description,[31] and the wealth gap between the two sectors appears destined to widen further. The dysfunction of these patterns rests in the increasing destitution of the outer layer that likely will foment disease, crime, terrorism, and broken states that threaten capitalist riches and security of central ecumenes and thus upset global stability.

Two primary causes for wealth imbalances seem the most plausible: (1) the natural resources already abundantly present in the prosperous core regions but absent from the poorer lands; plus (2) the advantages in technology and power of the rich in taking profits from the poor, either in normal capitalist competition or in exploitation. Accordingly, blame and solutions derive in several different explanations, the more moderate to the more radical.

One moderate stance points to the inherent monopolies of capitalism, particularly the global variety without strong institutions and regulations for protecting the unprotected. Simply put, the rich just get richer through successful competition and to the plight of the less successful and competitive. But a voluntary reversal of wealth by the core nations to the periphery, called the "New International Economic Order," has been proposed as an attempt to adjust the imbalances between the two sectors by taking various measures including some sort of global progressive taxing system that would give aid to the periphery. Little progress toward this redirection of riches, nonetheless, has yet taken place.

Another solution offered to dependency, also within a moderate assumption, is globalization, or the expansion of technology and outsourcing of employment from core to periphery worldwide, its motivation being to gain core entry into the emerging markets and their cheaper labor and natural and energy resources. This pattern includes involvement of investment capital and currencies and a tighter linkage among national economies, core, peripheral, and emerging. With such a concentration upon the economic factor, this structure seems more distant to geopolitics, but it is reflective of dependency.

Leninist imperialism figures within this dependency structure, too, a radical alternative of not only claiming capitalist exploitation but also of military plotting of the Great Powers to dominate poorer regions and peoples and to keep them stuck within their feudal stages of development. The profits derived from imperialist subjugation go to capitalist coffers, slowing the dialectic progression from capitalism onto socialism. The solution arrives in revolutionary violence in the southern regions, the cutting of the alleged profits extracted by capitalism, this causing depression in the industrial worlds and a resumed dialectic course on to their own socialist revolutions, thus ending the dependency of imperialism itself.

An extension of the radical approaches, the semiperipheral zones inserted between core and periphery, has seen description also within this system—for example, the focus of the central Great Powers upon Iran, Iraq, Pakistan, and North Korea, rogue countries that might hold the capacity for gaining nuclear weapons technologies that challenge the military dominance of the core. In the contemporary era, such a scenario could explain the US occupation of Iraq and its policies to isolate or to terminate the dangers of these rebel intermediate states.

Parts of dependency theory could be placed within the geopolitical model. For instance, our earth has not distributed its resources evenly throughout its lands and oceans, and it is clear that certain areas have benefited the most in natural wealth, North America, Western Europe, and China perhaps the most. Here have risen, or will rise, the strategic powers and the most prosperous states of the present and future. Africa, the Middle East, South Asia, and most parts of Latin America probably will never grow a global superpower because the natural resources infrastructures simply do not exist in those places.

One could, likewise, include aspects of Robert Mark's systems model within the dependency theses, the rise and fall of the Asian states in the face of European industrialization, this transformation caused in Europe by its abundance of coal in England and elsewhere nearby, its ability to develop steam power from this resource, and its military and political utility in exploiting the peripheral regions. Yet, the age of petroleum may have evened this "playing field," and China and India could be emerging to stake their claim on the world's resources and trade. This elevation in status and wealth may bring more instability and threat than balance.[32]

Once more, the dependency model shows a definition of its common characteristics, along with pertinent assumptions and theories. Too, the model overlaps with parts both of the geopolitics and of the systems models, a feature not infrequent to most patterns of international-relations study.

A number of cyclic models carry theories that approximate the geopolitical description, one being the hegemonic stability thesis of George Modelski.[33] His depiction features a rise and fall of hegemons or leader-states resting on the premise that certain favored states have each dominated during one-hundred-year periods, these appearing during the last five-hundred-year span of history. The hegemon gains global leadership during the midcentury decades after having won the previous world wars and having constructed institutions that stabilized the peace. Yet that state's eventual decline would gain momentum in the later century decades, and the world system ultimately would collapse into defeat from warfare during the years at the turn of a century, the decline in part caused by the leading states' overextension and thus their exhaustion of wealth. Modelski's hegemons came as sea powers (Portugal, Holland, England, and the United States) because the maritime sector offered better access to resources and wealth based upon the new technologies of navigation and transport.

Finally, a functional or liberal model should be added to our IR listing, now recognized in academic study in nearly as high of esteem as has been given realism. Its definition would fit traditional progressive thought including an optimistic view toward world peace and toward a decline of national sovereignty and an expansion of international institutions and law. The assumptions here rest upon a lessening of the anarchy so feared by realists. Resolving that anarchy, it was felt, would come in the increasing numbers and successes of regional and international organizations that would encourage trade, prosperity, peace, and democracy. To liberals, the globe will become more integrated, travel and communications more facilitated, and the potential for a federal world government more assured. The democratic-peace thesis claims that such nations are more peaceful, this holding some statistical proof, and despite some rough periods of growth, the European Union, and on a lesser order the Southern Cone Common Market, represent integrationist goals within the functional model.

In sum, all of these structural IR models overlap in some common areas, although these are relatively few, and each model's definition and characteristics should be distinct and separated from the others. None of the models including geopolitics are particularly well developed as per definition, assumptions, concepts, and theories. To strengthen that focus once more is the goal of this book toward refining more extensively the geopolitical model.

Practitioners of foreign affairs sometimes err in wrongly applying a certain model or theory to an event or policy where it does not fit, frequently leading to failure. Or some models briefly glimmer in scholarly attractiveness, to be later replaced by others that might gain center stage. Accordingly, we have to be careful in utilizing our several models and constantly to test the appropriateness of that model over others in its "best fit." And occasionally theories just will not pertain to any interpretation and should be ignored, and practicalities and common sense, instead, should rule.

One might take both directions in this dilemma of deciding which model might best apply with several recent examples. It appears that Nixon and Kissinger, fortunately, did get the correct model in place for the transitions then happening in the late 1960s into the 1970s by applying realism and discarding the containment thesis of Cold War geopolitics of earlier presidents. Their successes in reducing ideological and military tensions would pay rewards later during the instabilities of the Soviet Union's fall, leading to what would be the realist consensus among the Great Powers that we enjoy to the present time.

Wrongly applied models can be seen as well, with the US intervention in Vietnam representing a good example. Several frameworks played out in those conflicts, as is the case in most situations, but the ideologically framed Cold War falling dominos thesis that prompted the United States toward the Vietnam conflict misled our policy-makers toward a costly failure. That thesis assumed, without much evidence, that China, under the control of Russia, held ambitions to expand its domain eventually through Vietnam and beyond.[34] Were the United States to ignore this aggressiveness, it was alleged, the expansion would only happen more quickly, endangering the security of the entire Free World.

Instead, an ideologically neutral checkerboards pattern would have brought a clearer picture to the conflict, that being an international configuration less partisan but yet geopolitical. In this pattern, a united Vietnam had traditionally opposed the Chinese. Consequently, had socialist China even sought to advance southward across Vietnam and beyond (an unproved assumption) as the dominoes thesis had predicted, what better block would have existed but a strong and united Vietnam? And the checkerboards would have shown, in addition, that the Chinese were not subservient to the Russians. Might North America to the contrary have either sided with North Vietnam or refused to intervene in the first place? Subsequent events appear to have substantiated these assertions.

This second chapter will conclude with a description and evaluation, first of Saul Cohen's geopolitical model and second of Jakub Grygiel's geopolitical approach.

Cohen's model is drawn from a variety of his publications, and particularly, from Chapter 3 of his *Geopolitics: The Geography of International Relations.*[35] Cohen's writings span more than half a century; yet his basic approaches have stayed quite consistent within the definition of classical geopolitics, with some minor additions over time that have expanded certain areas of his approach. His and the author's may represent the only two extant models of geopolitics that have carried over some decades a set definition and the entry of refined and applied theories.

He gave us three separate but inter-related approaches in forming his model: a systemic design, a developmental approach within a dialectic progression, and a geopolitical labeling of several types of regions and concepts. For clarity, his first two aspects are separated here, the systemic and the developmental, although he may have intended to have joined them in this refrain: "For over a decade, influenced by some environmental perception research . . . , I applied the developmental approach in general systems theory more fully to geopolitical analysis."[36]

His systemic endeavor shows Cohen's placing a dynamic quality within classical geopolitics, an alleged weakness of the model as raised by some postmodernists and others. A system at equilibrium will bring international peace and progress, "a condition of equal balance between arrays of opposing forces operating at different geographical scales—is the desired state [for countries and regions] . . . . Equilibrium is dynamic . . . [its natural condition] at rest or homeostasis."[37] Cohen explained this further in this passage:

> Any system that is in dynamic equilibrium will be characterized by short-term disturbances or perturbations. As long as the system is open to change as a result of such pressures, and as long as it progresses toward higher states of integration [development], it can maintain its equilibrium.[38]

Thus many of the world's current perturbations are energizing events that operate within open systems, or serve to open relatively closed systems, and strengthen these systems.

Much of Cohen's description paralleled normal systems theory, but his emphasis did bring him confidence that global politics steadily were moving toward equilibrium and consequently toward global peace, thanks to the various systems being receptive to an ultimate and inevitable return to stability after the "perturbations" or disturbances to the balance. Indeed, such perturbations figured as bringing further development to the system.

The second feature also extended Cohen's prediction of a likely transformation of countries and regions into a more stable and peaceful global politics, that being a "developmental sequence" or thesis that would move countries from "atomization and undifferentiation to differentiation, specialization, and specialization—hierarchical integration" within their systemic routines.[39] In an "action-reaction process—a form of [Hegelian] dialectic,"[40] conflict and other factors will cause a "disequilibrium" within any system, but "equilibrium will be restored when the system achieves a higher form of [developmental] specialization."[41] And Cohen argued that movement toward more complexity would be inevitable: "As with any set of life organisms, the world system can be expected to evolve from its most simple form to its most complex" through the various levels of development, the progression, again, creating more stability and peace.

Several factors move states and regions forward within this developmental progression: (1) his "perturbations" or "short-term disturbances" that will lead to an eventual "dynamic equilibrium" based upon the natural homeostasis or need for balance within states;[42] (2) an "entropy," or "the availability of energy to do work,"[43] comes more frequently from the smaller and the "gateway" states that will encourage more specialization and integration within the system; (3) "convergence zones,"[44] being areas of outside Great Power competition, will evolve either into "shatterbelts" or "gateway" regions, but if the latter, this would represent "the strongest guarantee of a stable, global geopolitical system"; (4) "asymmetrical states,"[45] being such second-order states that will "provide a challenge to the regional leaders to rethink long-held positions and, in effect, to open their systems more widely . . . . While these regionally destabilizing states may well exhaust their own energies, the perturbations caused by them play a useful role in forging more cohesive regional structures"; and (5) "gateway states" or "mini-trading states with qualified sovereignty" that will "represent no military threat to their larger neighbors" but will serve the purpose of stimulating global economic, social and political interaction, thus creating "boundaries of accommodation."[46]

Cohen's third factor revealed a geopolitical ordering of maritime and continental states composed of "geostrategic realms," "geopolitical regions," and "states and subnational unit areas."[47] These levels do not reflect developmental stages, but instead they will appear according to "spatial orders" or geographic sizes. At present, three "realms," the United States, Maritime Europe, and China in a Continental-Maritime combination, dominate their respective areas. Cohen designated nine "geopolitical regions," for the most part as "sub-divisions" of realms, although certain ones are independent without such an attachment. Cohen's designations of these various labels changed over time, so for example, China has recently separated from Russia in occupying its own "realm," with Russia relegated to a geopolitical "region." The chapter content of Cohen's 2009 textbook followed the nine geopolitical regions in some historical detail.

Other types of states and regional conditions placed additional complexity on to this geopolitical structure. "Compression zones" lie between regions, these zones being "torn apart by the combination of civil wars and the interventionist actions of neighboring countries."[48] Similarly but less violent, he described "convergence zones" that have "drawn the interest and possible serious competition of outside Great Powers," and these areas could evolve into "gateway" or "shatterbelt" regions. "Gateway" states or regions reflected smaller countries engaged in commercial involvement, and they tended to encourage stability and development because of the wealth they are able to attract.[49] "Shatterbelts," in contrast, came as regions suffering outside intervention as mixed with regional conflict. Cohen saw sub-Saharan Africa in such a state, where China competed against the Western powers for its resources. Already described above would include "asymmetrical" or rebel states that, by their contrariness, stimulate development and stability, the larger states learning from the changing parameters. All of these concepts are clearly drawn, and all correspond to a classical geopolitical definition.

His model attempted to combine these three approaches: (1) a systems structure that focuses upon stability, and in this he optimistically predicts a more peaceful future based upon an inevitable movement within the members of the system toward equilibrium; (2) a developmental sequence of growing complexity that eventually will end in a balanced stability according to a dialectic progression of stages; and (3) geopolitical zones drawn worldwide that show an evolution of maritime and continental realms, regions, and lesser spaces that will progress into higher levels of modernity and thus into global peace.

Cohen's works exhibit precise classical geopolitical definitions, and this book's author has found useful his maps and descriptions of the dialectic evolution of global realms, regions, and national states. One likewise could applaud his attempt at bringing the stability and development modes into his geopolitical model.

But three main problems have arisen particularly in his 2009 text despite his contributions, and one may come away generally disappointed with his effort. (1) His descriptions were scattered throughout his several publications; one has to read and combine all sectors before getting a complete vision of his contribution. They lack a summation that might locate all the separate aspects together in one source. (2) He did not integrate convincingly his three separate approaches: systems, developmental, and geopolitical. The reader may remain confused as to how they join together because no apparent attempt is made toward linking the members. Instead, what he presented are scattered descriptions with no guide for integrating the several sectors. (3) And above all, he made no effort to apply his model, probably because the model itself is so disconnected, and thus it becomes not usable. For instance, the nine chapters of the 2009 text that pertain to each of the "geopolitical regions" lack any connection to his systemic and development attachment outlined in his Chapter 3, denoted "Geopolitical Structure and Theory." Instead, they describe only the various spatial features of each region: countries' histories, geographic landmarks, capital cities, ecumenes, boundaries, and several other such labels, these all more political geography than geopolitics. We seldom see even a portrayal of any description of the wider geopolitical concepts attached to these sections.

Accordingly, our geopolitical model as drawn earlier in this second chapter does not synchronize with that drawn by Cohen. The author has taken several of Cohen's concepts (gateway states and regions, asymmetrical states, convergence zones) and sequestered them within his typology, as will be outlined ahead in Chapter 5. His use of systems terminology does not lend much assistance, as most structural international-relations models also would accord this feature within them. And his development sequence is interesting but it does not connect well with the classical geopolitics because of its vagueness.

In contrast to Cohen's structures, Grygiel's approach fits a more precise description and one that reflects more of what one should be attempting to do in model-construction.[50] His path limited the geopolitical definition to just three variables: the location of important natural and economic resources, the lines of communication linking these resources to countries, and the stability of a state's frontiers, whether hostile or friendly. "Geography" was a combination of rather fixed geological features, and "geostrategy" described how a state will direct its military and diplomatic efforts toward controlling the three geopolitical features. Within this system of factors:

> [W]hen there is a disconnect between the geostrategy of a state and the underlying geopolitics, that state begins its decline. The state loses control over centers of resources and lines of communications and consequently relinquishes much of its influence over other states. . . . A foreign policy that does not reflect the underlying geopolitics cannot increase or maintain the power of a state.[51]

Geostrategy was the most changeable of the three factors and the most difficult to adjust to geopolitical realities because it served as the security policy of the state. Thus, it must reflect shifts in international geopolitics and blend these with the other parts of decision-making—ideologies, domestic politics, leaders' idiosyncrasies, and so forth that often may depart from such geopolitical realities.

Grygiel submitted this analysis to three historical examples:

Venice (years 1000 to 1600): The republic extended its sea power to controlling east-west communications of trade in the Eastern Mediterranean, greatly increasing its wealth and power. When trade routes changed to ocean routes beyond Venice's control, and when the state sought territories within Italy, destabilizing its frontiers, the republic waned in power.

Ottoman Empire (years 1300 to 1699): It correctly aimed its power toward Vienna, where it could control European trade communications. Unable to gain the city, combined with hostile frontiers elsewhere that reduced its thrust northward, the empire declined.

Ming China (years 1364 to 1644): Not able to protect itself from frontier threats from Mongol and Manchu tribes, the dynasty failed. In addition, the Ming rulers were prevented from developing sea-power communications over the China Sea, Indian Ocean, and beyond that would have brought trade wealth and have blocked the later European entry into and dominance of Asia.

Furthermore, Grygiel offered advice to contemporary US policies resting upon geopolitics, urging control of Asian sea lanes of communication, balancing Chinese naval power by maintaining a strong presence in Central Asia, and keeping its own borders with Mexico stable.

The geopolitical model outlined in the present book, nonetheless, contrasts to Grygiel's in its definition of geopolitics, the author's being more extensive. Yet, Grygiel precisely defined his three geopolitical variables within the three systemic patterns (geography, geopolitics, and geostrategy), and later, he adroitly applied the concepts/theories to four historical scenarios. His model closely resembles the present book's construction, except that this author offers more variables and more applications. One should applaud Grygiel's effort for being successful.

So, in concluding this second chapter, the main points emphasize: (1) how theories and models differ, the former being parts of the latter; (2) the importance of having a precise definition for a model, this providing an entry point for related assumptions, concepts, and theories; (3) a recommended geopolitical definition plus a container analogy of the model; (4) benefits and drawbacks of models and theories; and (5) comparisons between geopolitics and the other major international-relations models.

This chapter now completed, we will turn to an examination of several geopolitical approaches of the past and the present as a further way to an understanding of the classical geopolitical model.

3 Several Geopolitical Approaches of the Recent Past

In this third chapter, four distinct geopolitical schools or approaches will see review: (1) the German or Munich *Geopolitik* of the 1920s and 1930s as led by General Karl Haushofer and his associates; (2) the Cold War containment or "power politics" at mid-twentieth century; (3) the postmodernist critical geopolitics, first appearing in the 1970s and 1980s that is today headed by scholars within academic political-geography that challenges this author's traditional geopolitics; and finally, (4) the classical geopolitics of which the present author is constructing its model. The latter two approaches, the critical and the classical, will be summaries of his previous essay on critical geopolitics.[1]

The intent will be to contrast the first three versions against the classical. Specifically, the three all possess rather strong ideological taints that set them apart from the objective paths of traditional geopolitics. In reviewing the differences, the hope will be to rescue the original classic from the stigmas so damaging to it from the past.

Before starting on the several approaches, a good introduction might be to explore the question of why geopolitics has been "captured" by partisans of "left" and "right" who have distorted its original theme and purpose. The author proceeds with this query because he does not see these abuses happening to the other IR models.

One does not have to look far to find criticisms of the classical. This quotation is typical from an article entitled "Dreams of the Eurasian Heartland: The Reemergence of Geopolitics," authored by Charles Clover, the Kiev bureau chief for the *Financial Times* and published in the influential journal *Foreign Affairs*.[2] He begins with this polemic: "Few modern ideologies are as whimsically all-encompassing, as romantically obscure, as intellectually sloppy, and as likely to start a third world war as the theory of geopolitics." An "eccentric" Halford Mackinder of the heartland thesis has inspired, Clover alleges, Russian nationalists to advocate an aggressive geopolitical doctrine of "Eurasianism" that will confront the Western states and drive Russia back to the belligerency of the previous Soviet era:

> Many Russian intellectuals, who once thought their homeland's victory over the world would be the inevitable result of history, now pin their hope for Russia's return to greatness on a [geopolitical] theory that is, in a way, the opposite of dialectical materialism. Victory is now to be found in geography, rather than history; in space, rather than time.

All of this aggressiveness is blamed on "geopolitics," making Clover's diatribe disturbing and also irresponsible.

Clover neglects defining geopolitics or considering a balanced evaluation of the concept, wrongly staying with past ties to foreign ideologies. He submits a simplistic depiction of geopolitics as a destructive practice that somehow has helped to create a renewed Russian expansionism. The present author could not locate further explanations by Clover, his brief descriptions and negative allegations apparently approved by the journal without rigorous review to substantiate his claims.

Another misuse of the term, often associated with gloomy stock-market predictions, comes from its supposed causing of international disruptions, terrorist attacks, political instabilities, environmental disasters, and military confrontations that will dampen business prosperity, often with higher prices for oil. Again, we see a similar vague and sinister label, never with definition or review for fairness and accuracy. From among a multitude of instances, this description offers insight:

> Stocks got rocked for a second straight day Thursday. Mounting *geopolitical* concerns in the Middle East, which lifted oil prices to record highs, exacerbated pressing concerns about earnings prospects in the face of a slowing economy.[3]

These accusatory ways distance the classic from its geographic source. Here again, somehow raw and arbitrary power of the influential countries and of terrorists-wrought instabilities associate with a threatening geopolitics.

Accounts similar to Clover's and the stock markets are common elsewhere as well, particularly within critical geopolitics that show geopolitics a powerful instrument controlled by Great Power rulers bent upon global exploitation with the advancement of raw capitalism. A good example is the following by Gearóid Ó Tuathail, a leading exponent of critical theory:

In the conventional conceptions that dominated the twentieth century, [classical] geopolitics was a panoptic form of power/knowledge that sought to analyze the condition of world power in order to aid the practice of statecraft by great powers. Embedded within the imperialist projects of various states throughout the century, geopolitics generated comprehensive visions of world politics while also proposing particular strategies for states to pursue against their rivals.[4]

Geopolitics rates as a facility utilized by imperialist powers for advancing the shameful interests of the wealthy states. The spatial or geographic connection is removed; no reference to theory is uttered. We see in this radical stance a power-thirsty aggression against the weak.

Once again, why this pejorative focus against geopolitics and not against the other international-relations models, of geopolitics a ruination of global violence within the aura of aggressions and greed? Being not completely certain, this author can submit but these suggestions for the easy blame of geopolitics for its being something inherently bad.

In its possessing a rather romantic and "catchy" name, the term "geopolitics" exhibits two suspect traits within one title, geography and politics. "Geography" and "politics" may attach to certain sinister expressions within American culture, "secret alliances and treaties," "multinational regulations and organizations," "balances-of-power," "depleting our national sovereignty," "foreign entanglements," "joint-international actions," and like suspicious activities abroad. These foreign configurations entrap our republic into dangerous adventures against our control and interests. As the geopolitics concept has been more harshly treated in the United States than elsewhere, anything related to foreign affairs coupled to *realpolitik* and power politics would tend to alert American resistance. Since one does not see such negativity toward the term in Europe and in South America, this North American distrust of international spatial-power engagements seems to hold some validity. One more point: the image of realism hints of a positive bearing, for we Americans tend to appreciate something "real," forceful, and masculine, and these depictions would advantage that particular label.

Second, geopolitics represents the oldest academic theory of international relations, having arisen before World War I within German and English universities. It became connected to the conservative "balance of power" and "secret agreements" machinations so criticized by liberal statesman including President Woodrow Wilson. The Great Game image of Russian-British intrigue in

Central Asia of the late nineteenth century may also have prompted this conspiracy theme. Geopolitics' longevity in the foreign limelight may have translated into a negative inheritance by default, the other models more sequestered within the classroom.

Further, the organic state factor connected to the earlier thinking about geopolitics, the premise that states themselves held human characteristics including growth and inherent values. Some countries possessed greater spatial consciousness, and consequently they drew ambitions for territorial expansion in seeking greater power and wealth. Other nations, as the theory states, tended not to be so aware of this law of inevitable growth or decline, and they shrank and disappeared accordingly. The notorious ideal of lebensraum, being connected to later German fascism, legitimized the value of taking "living space" from weaker nations. Always wary of aggression, these earlier spatial "laws" may have attracted some popular dread.

As such, a whole generation of North Americans became exposed to decades of accusations tying fascism and other negatives to geopolitical-caused disruptions. Popular articles wrongly associated General Haushofer to his dominance over Hitler in directing the war in Europe. This faulting toward traditional geopolitics found its way into the major American universities and into the media, and its residence in these areas continues.

US expansion over North America and beyond was not framed within such a widespread hostility. Our Manifest Destiny held nationalist pride and even religious underpinnings but was not observed as aggression. Our sphere of influence over Middle America came as our inherent security, as well as the Monroe Doctrine, intended to keep the Caribbean isolated from Eurasian influence and subservient to our needs. All three of these terms could be defined as geopolitical; nonetheless, they find acceptance to our publics. Ironically, such doctrines were applauded by Haushofer himself,[5] but such a connection has been ignored.

Later in the postwar period of containment and beyond, geopolitics continued being victim to an entanglement within this darker ideological and organic inheritance, becoming attached to a broader explanation of Russian and Chinese expansionist threats, an attachment it has suffered to the present times despite the demise of the Soviet realm. A new opponent tied to geopolitics apparently is now the rise of Islam terrorism and the instabilities it might create for Western security and prosperity.

This half-century of hostility maintains in the teaching of many North

American social scientists, further prompted by European exiles from fascism who entered universities and wrote negatively about geopolitics. Cold War strategists enlisted Mackinder and Nicholas Spykman as inspirations for containment policies, and in these applications the link between "power politics" to geopolitics became more legitimized, yet still unpleasant. Such entanglements are central to the criticisms raised by theorists of critical geopolitics, who themselves have lent their ideology against the traditional within the postmodern focus of deconstruction, normative theory, and radical emancipation.

Finally, geopolitics, like other social sciences theories, has lacked precise and universal definition and theoretical refinement despite possessing an assortment of theories, some of which were rather farfetched but never modified or discarded by testing and application. Lebensraum would count among these. When a framework such as geopolitics lacks status and clarity, it tends to open itself to absorption by outside ideologies, this being more the case with geopolitics than with realism, liberal/functionalism, dependency, and systems analysis.

Our attention now turns to summarizing the leading historic approaches as contrasts to classical geopolitics. The intention is to present their characteristics to broaden out for the reader the author's construction of the classical model.

1. German Geopolitik

The origins of academic geopolitics first surfaced in the works of Friedrich Ratzel and Rudolf Kjellén, the former a German, the second a Swede, professors of geography and political science, respectively. Kjellén and others saw during the final decades of the nineteenth century a global scarcity of lands and colonies still available to the expansionist European states. They feared this closure could spawn rivalries and warfare.[6] The fear led to a naturalistic form of thinking, that "scientific" principles could be applied to predicting the growth or contraction of countries' size. Here, Kjellén found a theoretical grounding in the organic/spatial theories of Ratzel that posited a rationale for territorial expansion.

Fitting the intellectual dynamics of the times, Ratzel visualized the state as a biological or organic entity, existing and growing on the resources and environment within its territorial space. He visualized a state's survival resting upon the interplay of the two concepts of *raum,* or territory, and of *lage,* or location, these factors of natural wealth and position either enhancing or depleting the abilities of states to grow and prosper. States as organic beings were subject to natural laws, its lebensraum or "living space" the most prominent and notorious because successful states should grow spatially, thus enhancing their power and wealth in order to survive in a brutal international system that was competing for increasingly scarce territories. Those state leaders most conscious of this spatial reality and necessity, the requirement for territorial expansion for survival, would be the most successful in this rivalry.

Fundamental to Ratzel's thought was the adoption of environmental determinism,[7] the "physical environment as a molding influence on the character and development of human society." Specific individuals or governments might in rare moments influence important events, but they could do so only within the "scientific" application of appropriate natural laws such as Darwin's evolutionary "survival of the fittest" thesis. In these applications of law to policy, Kjellén, Ratzel, and others rejected racist theories, Ratzel even applauding the mixing of diverse races as beneficial to societies, his views at odds with later fascist arguments. It might be added that "scientific" in that day reflected more a consistent application of these "natural laws" to state actions rather than to the statistical or quantitative procedures that we would apply today.

Kjellén termed the study of this new science *Geopolitik*—the objective search for universal laws of a spatial nature that would apply to the promotion of states' foreign policies and security. The emphasis was grounded in geography—the location and position or states, regions, and resources, the benefits and detractions of these spatial elements, the search for "laws" or theories that would clarify these factors, and eventually the application of them to states' foreign relationships. These qualities are similar to those expounded within this book but with less emphasis upon the organic features of territorial expansion and colonization and more upon the positions and locations of states, regions, frontiers, and resources.

Karl Haushofer, the organizer of the Munich school of German *Geopolitik*, followed the earlier traditions of Ratzel and Kjellén, particularly their organic, territorial, deterministic, and objective tenets. A geographer, nationalist, and retired army general, Haushofer and his colleagues also saw geopolitics as a solution to many of Germany's postwar difficulties. The journal he edited after 1924, *Zeitschrift fur Geopolitik,* sought to publicize this new "science" of political geography by finding objective spatial laws that might apply to the advantages of Germany's pivotal location in central Europe and to its ambitions of extending its sovereignty further.

His contributions can be roughly summarized thus: first, he placed emphasis upon the value of space, stating that "space governs mankind's history" and that a nation must grow into new lands or it would perish.[8] Smaller states would be submerged into the gigantic nations he predicted for the future. Here, he admitted his respect for North America's Monroe Doctrine, asserting that this could be an example for Germany's necessary expansion. Autarky or national economic self-sufficiency was advised in the form of pan-regions, a global structure of northern-world command of southern-world resources and labor.

Second, Haushofer admitted that Germany's spatial orientation was that of a land power and that landward expansion eastward would be desirable. Nonetheless, a sea power facility would prompt overseas expansion for colonies and riches, he noted, and Germany should not err in being only a land power, for it required naval authority as well. Third, he warned against Germany's fighting wars on two fronts, although France and England were declining powers to the west and could be easily controlled. His country should not take the initiative in beginning a war. He said little about the United States beyond pointing to its strategic rivalry with Japan, but he once referred to it as "the only geopolitically mature country." In a move toward grand strategy, he advocated alliance between Germany, Russia, China, and Japan, although he recognized that Germany might eventually be forced to war against some of these if the occasion warranted.

But for our immediate notice, it is not only Haushofer's geopolitics that should interest us, but likewise his alleged tie to Hitler and fascism that has so damaged the reputation of classical geopolitics. Evidence shows that Haushofer did bend to pressure from the National Socialists when he accepted a limited racist viewpoint within his institute's geopolitics.[9] This and other such links lent to the later unsavory connection to the German Nazi *Geopolitik*.

The connection between fascism or *Geopolitik* and Haushofer originated with Rudolf Hess, the general's aide-de-camp during World War I and his later university student. Via Hess, Haushofer met Hitler in 1923 while the future Fuhrer was incarcerated. Nonetheless, according to Fifield and Pearcy, the Haushofer-Hitler association:

> was very limited . . . . [N]o intimate friendship ever developed. Yet, Chapter Fourteen of *Mein Kampf* reflects the influence of Haushofer on Hitler, especially regarding the importance of space . . . . [T]he fate of Haushofer is not necessarily bound to that of Hitler.[10]

Bassin outlines the Haushofer-Hitler dissimilarities also:

> Geopolitics as conceived and developed by Haushofer and others in the 1920s did not play the role of a state science under the Nazis, and could not have done so. Geopolitics, deriving essentially from the scientific materialism of the 19th century, was conceptualized as a law-seeking discipline . . . . The human element was seen as subject to this external influence. The ideological orientation of National Socialism . . . differed in fundamental ways from geopolitics [for it favored] a Romantic recourse to the emotions and sentiments [and was infused] with racial qualities . . . . After the Nazis came to power in 1933, these divergences in perspective became increasingly problematic, and resulted in official attacks upon geopolitics.[11]

The charge of Haushfer's Nazi taint tends toward exaggeration, but whether exaggerated or not, his past reputation continues to be harming to the legitimacy of contemporary geopolitics.

In summary, the intent once again in making this description of German *Geopolitik* comes twofold: to remove the fascist connection that has tainted the classical geopolitics, and to show the similarities of Ratzel and Haushofer to certain of the justified theories of traditional geopolitics.

2. Cold War or Containment Geopolitics

This second geopolitical alternative is included in our discussion for several reasons. First, the Cold War approach utilizes many of the traditional concepts of classical geopolitics: heartlands, rimlands, containment, spheres of influence, contagion, land and sea power, and so forth. Second, it fixes these precepts within the realist thesis, and in particular it adds the power politics thrust and an anticommunist ideological flavor, these both foreign to our objective emphasis of classical geopolitics. This combining of geopolitical images to realist approaches within an ideological and anti-Soviet demeanor provides the opportunity of not only revealing how the several trends have become connected but also of showing the wrongful attachment of the ideological labels to traditional geopolitics.

Cohen describes these aspects nicely with the following depiction:

> American Cold Warriors embraced geopolitics as a basis for a national policy aimed at confronting the Soviet Union and international communism. Building on early geographically derived geopolitical theories, and holding static interpretations of global and regional spatial patterns, they introduced such political-strategic concepts as containment, domino theory, balance-of-power linkages, and linchpin states into the lexicon of Cold War geopolitics. In this context Halford Mackinder's heartland theory played an instrumental role.[12]

George Kennan's warnings,[13] in addition to Winston Churchill's Fulton, Missouri, "Iron Curtain" speech and the Truman Doctrine, formed the ideological foundations for containment.

US containment following World War II framed three basic assumptions: (1) a supposed ideological and/or Russian territorial expansion sought by the Soviet leadership that would launch the USSR onto the rimlands of Eurasia and beyond. Accordingly, (2) the necessity for stopping this expansion depended on the resolve of the United States and its democratic allies to construct "rimland dykes" along the Russian periphery that (3) either would force a Soviet mellowing and submission or an internal implosion within the empire that would break it apart and possibly raise tensions to the level of strategic warfare, all of these outcomes caused by Soviet failure to expand in territory and influence.

Several Cold War theories accompanied this containment thesis.[14] A possible domino contagion was thought to extend communism outward from the Soviet-controlled heartland and into Third World regions. The Western belief in this expansion prompted engagements in Vietnam and later in Nicaragua and elsewhere. Such a contagion created strategic rivalries between the Russian and American allies, forming a variety of shatterbelts that would spread beyond Eurasia and into sub-Saharan Africa and Middle America. Western linchpin states and key-country allies (for instance, Germany, Iran, South Korea) could be counted upon to assist in containing communism. Finally, a claim of linkage, blaming the Soviet Union for instabilities within the world's periphery, offered a further rationale for fighting against Russian and Chinese expansionism.

The strategic policies of the United States since the last world war rested consistently upon an emphasis of balancing off the states of Eurasia as the best way for gaining American security against a Eurasian intrusion into the Americas. The Monroe Doctrine, of preventing rival Eurasian bases in Middle America and of negating a shatterbelt in the Caribbean, fits into this framework, as do extending the republic's Manifest Destiny beyond the continent and its sphere of influence over Middle America, protecting the "soft underbelly of North America" and projecting American power onto pivotal rimland areas of Asia and Europe. A fortress America of defensive bases on the outward perimeters of the hemisphere was never contemplated because, like the English balancing traditions, a divided Eurasia was seen as the best defense for America. Again, the essence of these theories arose within classical geopolitics but without the realist, nationalistic, and ideological parameters of the Cold War strategies.

In part, these approaches originated in the insights of George Kennan, the acclaimed architect of containment. Nonetheless, the basic ideas first came from Halford Mackinder and his heartland and from Nicholas Spykman and his rimlands. In the quotation that follows, observe the attachments that Kennan holds to the original heartland structure:

> It is essential to us, as it was to Britain, that no single continental land power should come to dominate the entire Eurasian landmass. Our interest has lain rather in the maintenance of some sort of stable balance among the powers of the interior, in order that none of them should effect the subjugation of the others, conquer the seafaring fringes of the landmass, become a great sea power as well as land power, shatter the position of England, and enter, as in these circumstances it certainly would, on an overseas expansion hostile to ourselves and supported by the immense resources of the interior of Europe and Asia.[15]

Mackinder's framework focused upon a likely struggle for world domination between the land-based heartland countries in opposition to the sea-oriented offshore states, with the inner and outer "crescents" passive to this struggle and acted upon or ignored by the two strategic competitors.[16] Spykman's rimlands were more strategically pivotal to this struggle, but the Americans were to meld together these diverse visions.

The North American Cold War strategy would be that of aggressively intervening in Eurasia with bases, troops, and alliances within the rimlands, specifically in Western Europe, the Persian Gulf, and Korea-Japan, and wherever else a rimland threat might appear. The aim again: to stop an expansion outward from the heartland core and to bring about a favorable Eurasian balance that would secure American safety against becoming encircled by threatening forces of Asia and Europe. This feat included deflecting Middle American countries from alliances with Eurasian enemies, framed within the Monroe Doctrine as a way to preventing shatterbelts to the immediate south of the United States.

Problems lay in determining the true intentions of Russia and its Chinese allies. Indeed, did their leaders hold ambitions of outward expansion and eventual world conquest, or were they merely less dangerous emerging Great Powers? The former contention was assumed under the containment doctrines but never substantiated. Moreover, if one visualized a Soviet nationalist or ideological goal of Eurasian expansion, would containment translate into intervening against all such threats throughout the extensive rimlands? Indeed, were the trouble spots of Vietnam, Nicaragua, and Afghanistan immediate threats prompted by an aggressive Russia and thus in need of strategic containment?

Did not, in contrast, this "rimland dyke" encourage a Western "over-reach" of indiscriminate global intervention that eventually could weaken and even bankrupt the proponents of containment? But a strategy of "selective engagement" proved difficult,[17] politically in addition to militarily. The concept of effective containment itself was flawed, both in its suspect assumptions of Soviet expansionism and in its enforcement requirements.

The Nixon-Kissinger foreign policy was noted for its geopolitical parameters, Kissinger's terminology raising the visibility of the classical. Nonetheless, Kissinger never defined the concept in traditional terms, instead speaking in "equilibrium" and in power terms that reflected more his realism than a clear depiction of geopolitics. Within this perspective, one can see regional balances enlisting key nations that would resist Russian influence within strategic rimland spots,[18] and retrenchment of American power where such threats did not appear. These approaches reflected the power and ideological perspectives that set the Cold War apart from the classical depiction of geopolitics.

In sum, this Cold War containment strategy offers a second alternative to classical geopolitics, one that, like the German *realpolitik*, diminishes the traditional fixtures within geopolitics. Containment shied from the classical label by attaching the power aspects of the realist vintage and by bringing both an ideological character and aggressiveness that distanced it from the original definition. Nonetheless, some of its parts stayed within the original fold of Mackinder and the other classical authors, as these are based upon placement, central position, and other such spatial features that would correspond to the traditional geopolitical perspective.

3. Critical Geopolitics

The postmodern critique of classical geopolitics, with its depiction of geopolitics as a corrupt tool of global capitalism, merits our close examination. This approach presents the most active of depictions of the study and application of geopolitics today, and consequently the following review should shed further light upon the classical description.

Why so much academic enthusiasm for this radical political-geography contrast to the traditional? Several possibilities could be raised. First, the postmodernist thesis has gained popularity in Europe, rising originally among an assortment of outstanding philosophers. In the words of Richard Jones,[19] these thinkers sought a "process of emancipator social transformation" with an emphasis on the "emancipator potential inherent in communications." Its normative and deconstructive parts appeared appropriate to a critique of past and present-day problems.

A later generation of postmodernist professors arose within North American, British, and Canadian political geography offering a protected and stable basis for the new ideas. The critical academics have been advantaged by numerous publication outlets in related books and journals (for instance, the Routledge publishers and the *Geopolitics* journal, both of London) that show an assortment of treatises on their brands of geopolitics. And lastly, we can visualize in contemporary global affairs likely examples as targets for the postmodernists' blames—in the expansion of unregulated capitalism internationally and in the various Western-led interventions in Vietnam, Africa, Iraq, and Afghanistan/Pakistan.

Several themes below describe the critical,[20] and later the same themes in turn will draft similar comparisons for the classical.

The postmodern look especially toward decision-making in foreign policy, where the stress rests upon elitists' motivations in their conduct of foreign affairs by deconstructing their "scripts" or written or spoken statements. This emphasis upon leaders' corruptions conditioning the actions they take ignores any reference toward spatial or geographic placement of states, regions, and resources and any attempt at theorizing these effects among countries. The involvements of the larger countries score highly in their attention.

According to Gearóid Ó Tuathail:

> The focus of critical geopolitics is on exposing the plays of power involved in grand geopolitical schemes . . . . Fundamental to this process is the power of certain national security elites to represent the nature and defining of the dilemmas of international politics in particular ways . . . . These representational practices of national security intellectuals generate particular "scripts" in international politics concerning places, peoples and issues. Such "scripts" then become part of the means by which [Great Power] hegemony is exercised in the international system.[21]

Once more, the placement rests upon expecting and exposing hegemonic wrong-doing as committed by the elites of the leading states, these "experts" or "intellectuals" holding capitalist backgrounds and intentions more prone to gaining power and business profits than to exhibiting the traditional images of rational states persons. This decision-making postmodern dimension, of individual and small-groups, marks a clear departure from the more expansive structural or internationalist level of the classical posture.

Critics assert that an objective truth, one most of us can readily see and agree to, is not possible. Instead, we humans inherently can visualize only subjectively what is before us—that is, we see our own individual realities and viewpoints separate and exclusive from most others. Consequently, a single reality is not reachable. Since this happens, too, for the elites of societies, our foreign policies are as subjective as are we humans and thus open to exclusiveness and to corruption and manipulation. Again, this focus upon the biases of decision-makers holds for the critics' deconstructing concerns.

Applying theory to policy is voided because attempting generalization relies upon a common view of reality, followed by some measure of predictability in associations within that vision after replication and testing. Such processes are completely lacking to the postmodernists because they find such unity of vision not existing and the varied interests of rulers extending toward greed and subjugation.

Policy-makers, the critics assert, apply their "imperialist projects" or schemes of domination to their ambitions of amassing power for controlling peoples and nations:

> All power requires knowledge and all knowledge relies on and reinforces existing power relations. Thus there is no such thing as "truth," existing outside of power .... Postmodern international theorists have used this insight to examine the "truths" of international relations to see how the concepts and knowledge-claims that dominate the discipline in fact are highly contingent on specific power relations.[22]

The critical version sees geopolitics, itself, as an elitist tool tainted by this thirst for power.

In the realm of the traditional, Simon Dalby charges, "Critical geopolitics can be broadly understood as the critical and poststructuralist intellectual practices of unraveling and deconstructing geographical and related disguises, dissimulations, and rationalizations of power."[23] As a "problem," blame extends in these charges toward classical geopolitics as a facilitator of the masters' dominance. Once again, the critics postulate the exploitation by elites of the leading states around the globe, and they find themselves emancipators to exposing evils by deconstruction and contextualization of leaders' goals and by offering solutions for restructuring international affairs, although little of this promise for remedy appears in the extant literature.

Because objective reality nowhere exists, all actions and policies reflect this all-encompassing subjectivity and its accompanying biases that have contributed to elitist subjugation. As offered by Leslie Hepple:

> The texts of [classical] geopolitical discourse are not free-floating, innocent contributions to an "objective" knowledge, but are rooted in . . . "power/knowledge," serving the interests of particular groups in society and helping to sustain and legitimate certain perspectives and interpretations.[24]

Elitist ambition directs toward accumulating more power, personal and national, an accumulation readily possible because corrupt leaders have created artificial "constructs" and other control techniques over their subjects. Again, the task of the critics is to expose this hegemonic domination in these ways:

> The superficial and self-interested ways in which orthodox geopolitics "reads the world political map" [do so] by projecting its own cultural and political assumptions upon it while concealing the very assumptions . . . to expose this power politics to scrutiny and public debate in the name of deepening democratic politics.[25]

To the postmodernists, revealing Halford Mackinder's imperialist and racist background is more important than studying his theories because that background conforms the leaders' goals of subjugation.

Where does "reality" reside in the case of classical geopolitics? Writes Ó Tuathail:

> As an unreflexively eurocentric and narrowly rational cultural practice of "experts" in powerful Western institutions (from universities to military bureaucracies to strategic "think-tanks") [classical] geopolitics is not about power politics: it is power politics.[26]

The classical presents nothing more than a "condensation of Western epistemological and ontological hubris, an imagining of the world from an imperial point of view."[27] Being a tool of suppression, classical geopolitics should be discarded as tainted beyond all usefulness. The "geo" fixture of the term dims; the "political" part stands out, albeit, in a very negative stance.

Traditional geopolitics, claim the critics, fit into a "state philosophy" of exploitation that serves the more powerful classes against the poor. It provides a tool for corrupting that system, particularly at the domination of the larger countries. Alleges Ó Tuathail:

> The study of geopolitics is the study of the spatialisation of international politics by core powers and hegemonic states . . . . [The term is] convenient fiction, an imperfect name for a set of practices within the civil societies of the Great Powers that sought to explain the meaning of the new global conditions of space, power, and technology.[28]

Geopolitics associates as a helpmate to such pejorative depictions as war, repression, and imperialism, locked into advancing the elite castes within global capitalist networks.

An exposure of these practices establishes the prime deconstructive interests of the critics, as described by Klaus Dodds:

> Critical geopolitical writers have argued that geopolitics is a discourse concerned with the relationship between power-knowledge and social and political relations . . . . [They] propose that understanding world politics has to be understood on a fundamentally interpretative basis rather than on [accepting without review] a series of divine "truths" such as the fundamental division of global politics between [the classics'] land and sea powers. For the critical geopolitician, therefore, the really important task is interpreting [the contexture within] theories of world politics rather than repeating often ill-defined assumptions and understandings of politics and geography.[29]

Deconstructing scripts, discourse, and intentions of elites and intellectuals involves a rigorous review of their literature and speeches, revealing the brutal nature of international politics, with traditional geopolitics being the willing servant in assisting in the exploitation.

The "divine truths" alleged to the classical by Dodds—the heartland, land power/sea power, and other generalizations—are misleading, biased, and simply lead to nowhere, since human and state actions reflect the subjectivities gained through script propagandas that prescribe Great Power dominance. Theories become meaningless in such subjectivity.

Claim the radicals, the classical is "decidedly old fashioned and out of place. Indeed, a number of strategists and politicians have proclaimed the end of geopolitics altogether . . . . In many analyses, [such a] geopolitics has been left for dead."[30] The traditional assumptions and theories do not pertain, since the permanent features of the geographic landscape have been replaced by the ideological stratagems of elitist foreign-policy-makers and actors. The "power" factor of geopolitics now replaces the "geo" or spatial feature within this conspiracy.

The final product arrives with a "new" geopolitics, or even of an "anti-geopolitics" according to Paul Routledge, that would repair the damage committed by the traditional actions:

> Anti-geopolitics represents an assertion of permanent independence from the state *whoever is in power,* and articulates two interrelated forms of counter-hegemonic

struggle. First, it challenges the *material* (economic and military) geopolitical power of states and global institutions; and second, it challenges the *representations* imposed by political and economic elites upon the world and its different peoples, that are deployed to serve their geopolitical interests."[31]

Shifting away from the tradition of exploitation, critical geopolitics, being an "anti-geopolitics," would radicalize toward an emancipation of those suffering in the present hegemony, taking an activist character that would remove the former exploitations and replace these with an improved order.

Relief from the exploitation, an "emancipation," follows the success of "deconstruction" in postmodernist movement toward an improvement where the individual must first understand his enslavement before seeking his freedom. Forceful removal of entrenched leaders will be necessary before that ideal might be achieved. The traditional concepts and theories offer no assistance toward this emancipation. Radical action, after substantial reconstruction, offers the only remedy for relieving the slavery of capitalism. Seeing no other path, the entrenched leaders must be removed violently, they refusing any limited reform and compromise.

To evaluate the tenets above of critical geopolitics, the following suggestions are raised.

First, the criticisms seem excessively harsh against the traditional, such diatribe as "fantasies," "fiction," "divine," and "timeless truths" not being productive. Might a more balanced slant better serve our purpose:

> Such harsh indictments overstate an attack against the classical and leave comparison of the two versions as an either/or selection when I would again suggest a more constructive acceptance and expansion of *both* yet contrasting approaches as most productive toward growing the field of geopolitics. The critics have not been clear as to their stance toward traditional geopolitics, whether, that is, to destroy it or to resurrect it.[32]

To discard all of the classical contributions without making closer examination of its common-sense merits may over-reach.

Despite "disguises, dissimulations, and rationalizations of power," theory earns its place in scholarship and policy application and should be recognized as legitimate where it can be reasonably tested and applied. Why study foreign affairs and geopolitics for their consistencies without an interest in locating, refining, and applying replicated generalizations, when such theories have been utilized by states for so long and with some insight and success? The listing of sixty such theories in Chapter 5 below and the applying of appropriate theories to historic events in Chapter 6 should offer some profits to foreign affairs.

In addition, it seems the critics do a disservice when they ignore the clear fact that placement of states, regions, and resources may impact foreign policies. If we agree, we lose some credible insight and value, observed by many commentators, historic and contemporary, of a rather blunt common sense: again, that position conditions behavior.

Ideological accusations attacking the classical weaken its utility, infecting its methodology and blunting its connecting of theory to event. Bias cancels the value of objectivity, an important contribution of the traditional but the critics' prime weapon. Themselves excessively ideological, the critics' attachment of bias to the classical just does not fit well.

These unsubstantiated charges against the traditional, the focus of "problem," distracts for writer and reader the main purpose of the present text, our earlier stated threefold way toward raising the visibility of the original: designing a common definition of the classical, constructing a model for containing theories that correspond to that definition, and studying whether certain theories will provide satisfactory insight into foreign events of interest. Very much to the contrary, a hunt for bias, conspiracy, and exploitation simply lacks interest to the student of classical geopolitics. Nicholas Spykman states this best:

> The factors that condition the policy of states are many; they are permanent and temporary, obvious and hidden; they include, apart from the geographic factor, population density, the economic structure of the country, the ethnic composition of the people, the form of government, and the complexes and pet prejudices of foreign ministers; and it is their simultaneous action and inter-action that create the complex phenomenon known as 'foreign policy.'[33]

Merely to focus upon supposed ills of elites ignores the real complexity and contribution of theories adjusted to policy, A simple deconstructing of leaders' statements could mislead toward locating their intents, a methodology tedious to say the least without much gain and needlessly generalizing the specific, when common sense, logic, and experience might provide better conclusions.

The fixating only on larger countries and their ambitions reduces the reach of study of the international. Evidence of Great Power dominance may be available, but the aggressive states may suffer failure, disunity, and disarray as well. They may also seek peace and accommodation rather than conflict and supremacy and perform altruistically at times.

We pass over the geopolitics of the smaller states that possess similar geopolitical characteristics in their foreign policies. Why only the Great Nations within the critics' parameters? Geopolitics of the classical is ubiquitous, an interpretation of how geography impacts upon policy and action regardless of the location and strength of individual states and regions, great and small.

This author set about examining the geopolitics of Paraguay, clearly not a significant power even within the Southern Cone. It facilitated an understanding with assembling the various traditional theories to depict Paraguay's regional relationships, of elastic frontiers, buffer states, continental "hinge" or pivotal states, hydroelectric power along the Paraná River, heartland pivoting, and so forth that fit the geopolitical model.[34] Geopolitics as a foreign-policy technique holds a worldwide utility with the geopolitics of the smaller countries taking on similar spatial insights the critics reserve for the greater powers. Paraguay will receive study as an application example in Chapter 6.

Finally, in their rather rigid bent on subjectivity and ideology, one has difficulty locating what indeed is "real," when a conclusion could assert that an objective reality does not exist at all. Hence, we possess none of the consistencies upon which theories depend because all is biased, subjective, and exploitative. Consequently, one can only conclude, where might we go because nothing else of value can exist beyond deconstructing this bitter truth of failure? How can we build upon such a harsh reality? Unfortunately, it appears we are left "hanging" and without hope for betterment, other than violent revolution, and this reference stays ignored. Any further help given the reader seems to be lacking.

4. Classical Geopolitics

Repeating the rather obvious, the traditional variation differs substantially from the critical. To continue our comparing with again intending to bring understanding to the classical, we proceed onward within the topical framework taken above for the critical.

We see different strata of study in the decision-making of individual statesmen and small groups for the critical and in the structural, strategic, or international levels of the classical, the latter bypassing the decision-making process entirely. The broader classical comes with the interplay among states and regions within a designated system, showing the effects of geography where location, position, resources, frontiers, and other spatial features may be pertinent. The following is an example of the global emphasis with awareness to structure and theory:

> The reality that confronts President Reagan's administration is that the super-pow-
> er-dominated global order has disintegrated . . . . The new global order that eventu-
> ally emerges will be strongly affected by the behavior of [new] regional forces. There
> is need for a geopolitical theory that will take into account the structural relations
> between these first- and second-order powers, and the relationships of states in the
> international hierarchy to states of lower orders.[35]

No concern with leaders' decision-making or about their subjectivity. The contrast derives from the systemic interactions among the countries and regions
of interest and from certain generalizations pertinent to these states' actions
within established international realms. Individuals do not count within this
nexus, with only states relevant to study. These divergent levels-of-analyses
simply cannot be integrated; the traditionalist can only go with the higher levels found in the regional and the international.

The "rational" stipulation surfaces again, the traditional perspective that
states persons will perform predictably toward the interests of their nations.
Such an assertion must be on trust, for in discovering and implementing theory, one should not be distracted by the idiosyncrasies, errors, and ambitions
of individual leaders. Little can be done about these aberrations except to ad-
mitting to these and proceeding onward without hesitation. Once more, theory
derives from the consistent actions among states and not from the involvement
of individuals in foreign affairs.

The emphasis leans on a confidence that an objective methodology can extend to locating and testing generalizations that might be gleaned from sources
within the social sciences. A value-free environment may enlist statistical approaches, as shown in earlier chapters. One gains theory from historical example, logic and common sense, and the experiences of scholars and diplomats.
Rationality can contribute to this collecting and applying of theories, an assumption of expected utility from the regular play of states' leaders.

The task of exposing prejudices and misuse within foreign affairs lacks concern within the classical argument, as stated by this depiction:

> [T]hose of the classical see themselves as neutral, doing a rather fixed, problem-solv-
> ing, even common sense and natural application of environmental opportunities
> and constraints upon foreign and military policies and actions.[36]

The appropriateness of a neutral and practical tool in geopolitics for statesmen
is assumed, the locating and testing of theory and later to applying its possible

applications to instances of policy and action. The "problem" rests more in the clarification of generalizations and in the connection of theory to situations or policies, making these methods as certain as possible to coupling the correct theory to the correct situation.

Frederick Teggart asserts the movement of forces extending from the heartland on to marginal areas is "not a theory, but a conspicuous fact," and that:

> We are led to see a succession of empires [Greece, Rome, medieval Europe] based upon sea power, each of which has been overthrown finally by a land attack. The success of land power, in each case, has come from a broadening of the field of operations and the seizure of the seaman's base of supplies.[37]

This land power/sea power dichotomy relates well to the ancient Peloponnesian war, where the final Spartan victory came in its construction of a sea power capability that eventually brought defeat to Athens.

This quotation needs inclusion, too, from Ó Tuathail and Dalby, attesting to the neutrality of the traditional version:

> Classical geopolitics is a form of geopolitical discourse that seeks to repress its own politics and geography, imagining itself as beyond politics and above situated geographies in a transcendent Olympian realm of surveillance and judgment. The response of critical geopolitics is to insist on the situated, contextual and embodied nature of all forms of geopolitical reasoning.[38]

To the modernists, reliance upon the "gaze of statesmen" possesses sufficient confidence for proceeding into formulating theory based upon such "gazes." Motivations of persons formulating policies are ignored despite possibilities that some leaders could well be as biased, mistaken, and exploitative as the critics allege. But such flaws do not factor into impartial theories; in truth, they cannot be considered if we are to travel in unison within the traditional.

For the classical, a spatial reality exists "out there" where most can visualize a common view within available environments, despite this the process being better done by "experts" who are experienced in their professionally honed instincts. Our human perspectives perform to unify and to make simpler these observations, not complicated by accusations of hegemonic conspiracy, human greed, and other such elitist motivations. Most of us can agree that a nation's geographic placement conditions policy, and this facet can be observed, replicated, and formulated into theory for conducting diplomacy satisfactorily.

Reflecting the example of Halford Mackinder, Zbigniew Brzezinski posits this viewpoint relative to the objective professional:

Ever since the continents started interacting politically, some five hundred years ago, Eurasia has been the center of world power .... American foreign policy must employ its influence in Eurasia in a manner that creates a stable continental equilibrium, with the United States as the political arbiter. ... [I]t is imperative that no Eurasian challenger emerges, capable of dominating Eurasia and thus also challenging America.[39]

Here, no suggestion of tainted contexture by Brzezinski arises, and we honor his practiced visions of the spatial generalities of traditional American strategic policies.

We must assume that associations among geographic factors and policy alternatives are apparent to a good number of observers, as the viewer and the object are joined for neutral and objective empirical study. Being a problem-solving exercise, geopolitics "takes the existing power structures for granted and works within these to provide conceptualization and advice for foreign policy decision-makers."[40] Said differently, the classical approach contributes an objective tool for persons who would study their country's position as related to possible outcomes within the foreign-affairs regime.

As stated above, although the larger countries dominate global affairs, the practice of geopolitics extends to all countries alike within international topics. Geopolitics contributes a technique for understanding how countries act and react to influences stemming from the placement of nations, regions, resources, and other spatial features. This includes all nations, large and small. The point of "great power bias inherent in most realist theory and geopolitics" is raised by Hans Mouritzen.[41]

Again, this author and a colleague[42] saw Paraguay buffering the expansionistic tendencies of its two more powerful neighbors, Brazil and Argentina. Its security and prosperity rested upon either a bandwagoning strategy of favoring Brazil over Argentina, as happened in the construction of the Itaipú hydroelectric dam on the Paraná River, or during other eras a balancing strategy by playing off one rival state against the other. The late General Carlos Meira Mattos once confided that Brazil shared the Itaipú construction with Paraguay as a way to stabilize and dominate its junior partner. One could visualize, in a similar stance, Paraguay as a lintel state, positioned between its two neighbors as a stabilizer for the Southern Cone region.

The Paraguayan strategist Julia Velilla posited that Paraguay's pivotal location at the center of the Southern Cone had impacted strategically across the continent:

[Asunción is an] area of welding, a crossroads of encounter and union. It linked Atlantic with Pacific, united the Banda Oriental [Uruguay] with the ports of Upper Peru [Bolivia]. It is the meeting of the Amazon with the Plata, and it was union and equilibrium among Portuguese and Spanish powers in the Plata, impeding the *bandeirantes*' [Portuguese] advance.[43]

She saw her country part of a triangle providing a "true balance of continental equilibrium," a "key to continental domination" that lent itself to regional integration. Whether the real impact of Paraguay rises to a continental level could be questioned, but her statement derives in her depiction of her country as a geopolitical actor and a facet toward stabilizing the continent's checkerboard structure despite its limited resources and isolation.

A good reason for improving the study and application of geopolitics relates to refining the assumptions, concepts, and theories that might connect geographic factors to nations' foreign policy. A related goal of this book comes in grouping these possibilities into a more complete typology or model that might be utilized both by students and statesmen. Hence, one studies diplomatic history where spatial relationships might show some predictable level of generalization. Does a spatial application impact upon policy considerations and actions—the positions and locations of countries, regions, and resources as well as topography, passageways, rivers and coasts, mountains and deserts, and the similar conditions of geography? One could assert that the evidence is ample and logical.

Examining maps assists in locating theory—for instance, the importance of strategic areas and resources as described by Halford Mackinder:

Europe, Asia, Africa, and the two Americas are thus included within the visible hemisphere; but the chief feature even of the land-half of the globe is the great arm of the Mediterranean ocean, Atlantic and Arctic, winding north-ward. No flat chart can give a correct impression of the form of the North Atlantic. Only a globe can suggest its vast bulging centre, and the relative insignificance of its Arctic, Mediterranean, and Caribbean recesses.[44]

Practitioners of geopolitics are especially interested in evaluating strategic significance, in particular land and maritime areas that may hold leverage beyond their points. Others have followed his lead. The northern middle latitudes give special impact for their landward positions of wealth and power.[45] As one distances, the outlying peripheries become less significant, this labeled the *camino del oro*. Henry Kissinger has referred to the diminishing importance of the southern world as well.[46]

Spykman also noted similar favorable locations: "History is made between 25 degrees and 60 degrees north latitude," with the "most favored state in the world from the point of view of location [being] the United States."[47] Likewise, the "northern Atlantic is today the most desirable body of water on which a state can be located." Indeed, Western civilization has risen around great bodies of water, and such civilizations have steadily gone further west and north, a portrayal sometimes voiced by geopolitical writers.

The traditional faces criticism for theories lacking dynamic qualities, an inability to keep up with technological changes within countries and regions. Nonetheless, this charge can be met in two ways: (1) theories remain permanent; they pertain to all times, locations, and situations; and (2) the dynamic quality resides in the foreign policies and spatial environments themselves, for in these would be felt shifts in development and modernization. Nicholas Spykman stated these points as well:

> Ministers come and go, even dictators die, but mountain ranges stand unperturbed . . . . The nature of the territorial base has influenced [policy-makers] in the past and will continue to do so in the future.[48]

This permanency within our geopolitical model simplifies the study and implementation of geopolitics and its relevant theories, for one may examine the full extent of history and place in comparing geopolitical situations. The point made here: the political environment shifts, not the theories.

One is able to utilize the checkerboard phenomena for two separated historical events: the ancient Peloponnesian war of ancient Greece contrasted to the geopolitics of contemporary South American diplomacy,[49] with the two regions exhibiting very different patterns of involvement within their checkerboards, the former an instable and harsh antagonism and the latter a stable and peaceful multipolarity. Similarly, the shatterbelt could be observed at the Ohio Valley frontiers in the decades following US independence, where French, English, and Spanish alliances with the several Native American nations sought to contain the westward expansion of the new republic.[50] The same with the shatterbelt of the Cuban crisis of 1962.

This author has experimented with his students in a sort of laboratory simulation, a study of imagined or fictitious maps of the moon but filled with oceans, rivers, and mountains, or seabed topographies on earth with the same intent. In these, we considered our various theories and plotted outcomes. River valleys tended to unify peoples; strategic mountain passes attracted states' competition. Locations of abundant natural resources attracted rivalry;

countries astride seacoasts spawned naval forces. In such artificial settings, spatial concepts could be applied with probable outcomes, war or peace, unity or disunity, sea or land power, for instance, and within a pedagogical intent.

A historical (but racially biased) map of pan-regions can be examined by students, this depiction designed by the *Geopolitik* school that attempted similar structures but found differing patterns within. Here, divisor lines of longitude exposed three or four large regions that joined northern and southern land and sea areas, the purpose being to create zones of autarky or self-sufficiency. One could conclude from study of the pan-regional design that the international outcomes of this structure tend toward the northern domination of the south and a checkerboard conflict among the hemispheres, as shown in George Orwell's novel 1984.

We see once more a feature more to the liking of the postmodernists, the deconstructing of messages to reveal Great Power aggressions. But this interest in overcoming elite conspiracies, however beneficial, passes by the modernists, whose emphasis draws upon utilizing geopolitics as a neutral, objective, timeless approach to theory and policy application, geopolitics seen as an "aid to statecraft" without any exposing of power abuses. The "levels-of-analysis" problem arises again: either a critique of leadership or an emphasis upon theory among states by themselves. We cannot have it both ways, and the classical method of country actions within the structural realm is the alternative that is promoted within the pages of this book.

Several limitations confront traditional geopolitics, some of these described in the initial chapters of this book. Certainly, a large part of the often-times negative description of geopolitics comes, as we have seen, from its lack of a common definition, one that associates a spatial setting conditioning foreign affairs, its original intention. Once supporters of the classical locate an agreed-upon definition, the "power-politics" label should transfer back to its original realist home.

The assumption of "rationality" poses difficulty for the classical, the focus upon countries as actors while ignoring the intentions of decision-makers. The idiosyncrasies of leaders, at times, have brought spontaneous outcomes to foreign actions. One could cite President Nixon's invasion of Cambodia as possibly stimulated by his viewing of the movie *Patton* before his decision to invade. Or Mackinder's conservative and imperial views tainting his strategic concepts. Or Brzezinski's Polish background in forming his anti-Russian biases. Unfortunately, this levels-of-analysis problem simply lacks a good solution, as the two levels, the decision-making and the state-centered, cannot be readily joined.

The postmodernists have good reason to accuse the traditionalists of not asserting the normative or critical, of not taking stands against corruption and domination. Neglecting the subjective has its just place in international relations for correcting abuses. Nonetheless, classical geopolitics must simply step aside from such normative prescription because its theories depend on objectivity and methodological preciseness if they are to be of any use to students and statespersons. We should leave any judgments to the critics and others who have promised themselves to reconstruction.

What represents the positive to classical geopolitics derives from the locating of extant assumptions, concepts, and theories within a clearly formulated definition and model, once more, the ambition of this book. We should find it useful to affix theories, once located, to examining foreign policies and actions as an "aid to the statesman" and to students alike. This traditional model, like other models of international politics, has yet to be thoroughly described and applied, but the potential for development and increased usefulness is certainly a possibility for geopolitics.

4   Classical Geopolitical Assumptions

Once a definition of classical geopolitics has been established—that being for this book, the study of the impacts of certain geographic features, such as states' and regions' positions and locations, resources, topography, distance, and the like, on states' foreign policies and actions as aids to statecraft and to theory—an assortment of assumptions about geopolitics can be examined, a first step toward a later depiction of theories in Chapter 5 and then certain theories applied to foreign events in Chapter 6. Assumptions are one of the more interesting phases of the model-building process, a feature that clarifies the basic nature of classical geopolitics and yet one that does not receive much attention in model construction.

Geopolitical assumptions are simple but quite abstract statements that help define what underlies the essence of geopolitics, its basic beliefs, parameters, and foundations. These must be taken for granted for being true with minimal possibility of proving them to be accurate. For assumptions, one must simply take a "leap of faith" that certain "truths" will form what is essential to the nature of classical geopolitics. We would falter in our understanding of geopolitics without having agreed to them.

Harold and Margaret Sprout had this to say about the relevance of spatial assumptions, equating such axioms to "percepts" regarding "the state of the environment" that would be of interest in applications to foreign affairs:

> All geopolitical discussion . . . is carried on with reference to some set of percepts or assumptions regarding the state of the environment. The theorizer starts with a set of ideas about the layout of things in space and their movements and changes through time. He makes assumptions, or reaches conclusions on the basis of evidence, as to which factors of the environment are most significant and which are undergoing or likely to undergo significant change during the time span under consideration.[1]

Accordingly, the fruitfulness of geopolitical descriptions must rest upon these initial foundations or axioms because, like a definition of the topic, they perform as "gatekeepers" to recognizing the theories that will enter into the full extent of the model. Again, one must accept these basic spatial "truisms" before proceeding onward toward examining the other contents of the model itself.

Those who engage in research, teaching, or policy-making often overlook or disregard the assumptions built into their models. This tends to foster uncritical acceptance of geopolitical propositions and to spawn later rejections of hypotheses that may fit the definitions required of a particular model. Tying together all parts of the model, assumptions, similar to definitions, help to maintain a consistency within the theoretical framework.

For instance, fascism would make little sense to its believers without first the adherents accepting the assumption that certain races are superior to other races. With this thesis once accepted on faith, the rest of racist doctrines will fit logically into place. The same with realism, socialism, conservatism, liberalism, and other such models including geopolitics—we must pass this "trust" hurtle before proceeding on.

On the surface, assumptions may closely equate with theories, for they both arrive as simple sentences of explanation. The dividing point is often difficult to discern, and we will experience that problem ahead. Indeed, examples shown in this chapter as assumptions may arise again in the next chapter as theories. Frankly, this difficulty of contrasting assumptions against theories seemed so unwieldy that the author considered just eliminating this chapter altogether as being too confusing to proceed. But he decided to keep intact this section's short descriptions because geopolitical assumptions appear too important to neglect.

Assumptions and theories each serve different purposes. We should keep in mind that theories explain, analyze, and predict, whereas assumptions are but simple abstract beliefs that underlie the general description of the model's concepts and theories. Assumptions reveal much more the esoteric; they are more simplistic and not based upon probability; and they do not lend at all to rigorous logic or statistical testing. Theories, being more concrete and more testable, challenge us to understand their consistency and to predict their outcomes. They are more functional because they have faced a rigorous scrutiny; they offer precise descriptions, explanations, predictions, and prescriptions; and they occupy the highest level of sophistication within the geopolitical model. Whereas the profit of theories comes in their application, assumptions do not go that far. Instead, they merely describe the basic understandings or groundings of the model.

Several examples continue this discussion of contrasting assumptions with theories:

A geopolitically defined assumption: A state's immediate environment conditions its international behavior.

A geopolitically defined theory: The position of a state, whether central or peripheral within a region, conditions its international behavior.

Here in two simple instances, the assumption of a conditioning environment is the more abstract and not readily available to proving, whereas the theory of a particular position within that environment tends to be more complex, concrete, and open to translation. A testing of theory still would be difficult, but comparisons of some concrete distinctions between core and marginal states could be attempted.

In a majority of cases, the divide between assumptions and theories exposes a blurred distinction. Worse yet, many show identical stances. Another example brings this difficult distinction to light:

Mackinder's heartland assumption: The state or coalition of states controlling central Eurasia possesses an advantage for world domination.

Mackinder's heartland theory: The state or coalition of states controlling central Eurasia possesses an advantage for world domination.

Assumption and theory, identical in this case, still separate according to function, the first contending a belief, the second an assertion. A precise divide must be set aside if we are to continue with constructing this model.

The fault lies in large part on methodology, a reliance upon the objective features of selection and application for theories, since the vast majority of these cannot adapt to quantitative or scientific proving. Assumptions do not require this rigor. Accordingly, we should tread carefully for the remainder of this chapter, choosing a short list of the most obvious assumptions that will fit the traditional geopolitical definition and thus become part of the geopolitical model.

We begin our discussion with a repeat of an observation made earlier: (1) The immediate environment affects a state's behavior. With this, we are subjected to accepting without testing this initial hypothesis as true, if we are, indeed, able to describe and utilize the entire basis of classical geopolitics. Many reasonable examples can be raised that demonstrate this common sense. In teaching students, the configuration of classroom seating may impact upon one's instruction and upon one's learning as well as upon the extent of discussion and interaction and the attentiveness of students. A round table may encourage more dinner conversation, at least offering each person seated an equal chance to talk. The position of a listener within an audience could enhance or limit that person's attention. These spatial features should be evident enough to most of us, although such conditionings with structure and placement cannot reveal objectively. Of course, the same lies with states within their particular environments, being likewise abstract and simple although difficult to showing clear relevance.

Again, Harold and Margaret Sprout delved into this environmental setting of policy-making. They assert a distinction between a perception of opportunities, in our present case being assumptions, and an actual accomplishment of these in the attainment of goals:

> Environmental factors, whether constant or variable, can affect human affairs in only two ways. Such factors can be perceived, interpreted, and taken into account by the human actors under consideration. In this way, and in this way only, can environmental factors "influence" attitudes and decisions. The relation of environmental factors to performance and accomplishment . . . is quite different. Such factors comprise a sort of matrix, figuratively speaking, which limits the execution of decisions. Limitations on performance and accomplishment are not necessarily dependent on the actor's perception. *Such limitations may be operative irrespective of whether or how the limiting factors are perceived in the process of reaching decisions* . . . . What matters in the explanation of decisions and policies is how the actor imagined his environment to be, not how it actually was, whereas what matters in the explanation of accomplishments is how the environment actually was, not how the actor imagined it to be.[2]

As the Sprout's contend in a later article on this topic:

> The statesman's *psychological* environment (that is, his image, or estimate, of the situation, setting, or milieu) may or may not correspond to the *operational* environment (in which his decisions are executed). But in policy-making, what matters is how the policy-maker images the milieu to be, not how it actually is.[3]

They followed these environmental contentions by drawing a spectrum of likely relationships between man and his milieu:[4] environmental determinism, where man possesses no choice but to be driven by "some set of environmental causes"; free-will environmentalism, where man is able to choose, and be influenced, beckoned, or pushed; environmental possibilism, where limits, that may be visualized, will restrict human and state action; cognitive behaviorism, in which "what matters in decision-making is not how the milieu is but how the decision-maker imagines it to be"; and environmental probabilism, where past images and associations become paramount on human reaction. All yield a picture of an abstract platform upon which geopolitical assumptions must rest.

(2) The immediate environment of a country conditions its decision-makers, imprinting on them conscientiously or unconscientiously a spatial bearing in their actions to further the interests and objectives of their nation. To repeat from our last chapter, one ignores the idiosyncrasies, mistakes, and ideologies of rulers in preference to our judging more broadly their state's settings and actions, with states, not individuals, the prime actors within the international realm. Here, geography "matters" in the cases of states-as-actors performing as one among others, although again such cannot be proven objectively. Leaders submerge passively within the rational goals of their states, although we assume their awareness of country setting parallels that of the state itself, as argued above by the Sprouts.

Additionally, (3) the relative location of a state within a region impacts upon its behavior and policy. This assumption differs from the first axiom above in its relativity—a setting conditioned by other states' locations nearby. The United States since its beginning has tended toward aloofness, isolationism, messianism, exceptionalism, interventionism, and unilateralism, all apparently based upon its rather remote and isolated island mentality and its separation as a result of its distance from a potentially threatening Eurasia. This helps explain the history of the country—the immigration and development patterns, the Manifest Destiny of continental expansion, the Monroe Doctrine that shields Middle American from becoming a shatterbelt, the overseas projection of forces onto rimland bases, and the enforcement of power balances on both the eastern and western extremes of Eurasia. But once more, these connections are assumed relevant; we certainly cannot offer much solid evidence for their exactness.

Centrally positioned nations tend to experience different perspectives than marginally positioned states, a basic premise of most writers of geopolitics including Halford Mackinder and Nicholas Spykman. Statistically, some evidence is shown that countries holding a greater number of international frontiers suffer the most involvements in warfare.[5] Interior countries may be less democratic, being less exposed to international trade. Coastal nations may reveal sea power tendencies and be more democratic and cosmopolitan. Such premises derive more on conjectures and common sense than on provable generalizations because objective methodology simply will be lacking.

We assume the sixty theories chosen for this book are valid, all (4) set within the spatial or positional definition of classical geopolitics—where states' and regions' relative positions may impact upon their foreign involvements. Since theories selected for this book's model are necessarily personal and approximate and without the rigor of the "hard" sciences, the author has given careful attention to noting the spatial elements within each generalization. But, do heartlands, checkerboards, shatterbelts, and the rest really hold sufficient relevance for us to proceed on? Our answer: we are assuming so. We must trust as reasonable and pertinent the theory selections later examined for inclusion into our geopolitical model.

In the acceptance of theory in classical geopolitics, the modernist stance is taken and the postmodernist claims rejected. (5) Accordingly, it must be assumed that the environment "out there" is separate from oneself, and enough others can join us in locating consistencies within that environment. And what is within these surroundings can be seen as recognizable, predictable, and continuous sufficient enough to visualize the predictability required of theory. Without this assumption of confidence in locating and utilizing theories, the contribution of classical geopolitics would be lost.

(6) Geopolitics fits all sizes of countries, large, median, and small, its application being appropriate to all levels of foreign affairs. Hans Mouritzen offers a good slant on this common state-centric assumption, that of his "present and past geopolitics" dichotomy.[6] All types of countries correspond to his descriptions. His "present geopolitics" feature would fit our traditional definition: state's position impacting upon policy. In contrast, his "lessons of the past" in a country's geopolitical memory that Mouritzen labels as "theoretical assumptions," instead, will influence domestic decision-making when security dangers are minimal. He states that past geopolitics "can be afforded only under favorable external circumstances. Its role will vary with the state's external action space, that is, its ability to remain unaffected by other [external] actors. Decreasing action space means less room for past geopolitics, while increasing action space means more." For instance, Poland's deep mistrust of both Russia and Germany, its "past geopolitics," characterized its post–Cold War diplomacy toward its gaining NATO and EU membership, in part, because it also enjoyed "a significant [safe] action space" at the present moment. In sum, the point raised is that he described all states in this study, not just the Great Powers.

A seventh assumption admits to the thesis (7) that certain world areas hold more relevance to regional world affairs than do other places as a result of their wealth, positions, and locations. This hydraulic factor of "important places" within geopolitics holds a strong historic tradition, one that yields to a variety of assumptions. Simply stated, the earth's surface is not even in its resources, and thus the distribution of riches, position, and other geographic rewards shows advantages to certain benefited regions and states.

"History is made between 25 degrees and 60 degrees north latitude, with the North Atlantic today the most desirable body of water on which a state can be located," so assumed Nicholas Spykman.[7] This fixation on the global northern temperate zones is a commonly voiced assertion in traditional geopolitics, such pivotal positions being places "that count." Saul Cohen adds a similar "hierarchy of levels" in which Eurasia and Africa together constitute 66 percent of the earth's total land area and 85 percent of global population.[8] Likewise, the Northern Hemisphere embraces 80 percent of land space and a similar 85 percent of its peoples, showing this favorable concentration of wealth and power.

General Julio Londoño Londoño of Colombia described this same scenario in his *el camino del sol* configuration, where the locations of those land occupiers closest to a northern latitudinal line extending from Beijing and Tokyo through Washington, DC, and on to the major capitals of northern Europe, translated into geopolitical importance.[9] Those most distant from this assumed line spelled impotence and irrelevance. Henry Kissinger's pentagonal design that advised an exclusive US focus upon China, Russia, Europe, and Japan resembled this preference for northern significance. These presumptions, if visualized important, diminishes the strategic importance of Africa, Australia, South Asia, and South America. Such positional aspects figured as axioms and theories together, it being difficult to distinguish between the two. Accordingly, they will repeat occasionally both in Chapters 4 and 5.

Mackinder's heartland thesis further substantiates this traditional interest— that whichever state or alliance comes to dominate the vast interior of Eurasia, containing two-thirds of global territories, populations, and wealth, will eventually come to dominate the earth. Such a contention, of course, eludes quantitative testing;[10] yet as an assumption (and a theory) it holds the most notable spot within the literature of classical geopolitics, and it has formed the foundation of contemporary and historical British, Russian, and US strategic security policies. Whether assumption or theory, it tends to be believed, and this belief substantially promotes its importance despite its being quite impossible to substantiate historically!

South America could be labeled an independent region within global geopolitics,[11] an area without a strategically important Great Power state or close ties to an alliance with the greater states of Eurasia and North America. Brazil, at times, has claimed a friendship to North America, but lacking the endorsement of its Spanish neighbors or of North America, its search for greater status has failed. Such historical resistance by its neighbors also helped block its continental ambitions toward reaching the Pacific coast, consequently decreasing its pivotal impact within South America and beyond. Hence, with little strategic linkage from the region to northern power balances or alliances, and no shatterbelts appearing since independence, South American geopolitics perform internally without any military or political ties to extracontinental allies. Its interests have lain mostly in border and territorial conflict and more recently in development and integration.

Furthermore and within this broader category of assumptions, certain seas and oceans receive notice by the authors of geopolitics as linked to enhanced political and economic impact. In a European-focused milieu, the Mediterranean Sea was the "cradle" to Western civilization and global advancement, and later the North Atlantic coupled nations together in Western security during the Cold War. For the United States, the Caribbean has long represented a security vulnerability to the Monroe Doctrine. And for the new millennium, the Age of the Pacific may also be dawning.

Among the larger countries, some observers contend that North America's position is the most favorably placed on earth in terms of geopolitical advantage, its location in the healthful northern temperate zone but distant from Eurasian power struggles, its isolation in America among smaller and nonthreatening nations, its seafaring island image favored with good harbors and internal navigable rivers and lakes, its wealth blessed with abundant natural and energy resources, its citizenry enhanced by talented immigrant populations, and its consolidation of an American empire spreading over the rich lands reaching from Atlantic to Pacific Oceans—all spelled national development and international greatness. Areas of Western Europe and East Asia compare similarly to North America in many of these attributes as well, although perhaps not in the abundances to compete effectively with the power and position of the United States.

North America, likewise, holds the best power position to balance off the larger countries at both Asian and European flanks of Eurasia, a pivotal advantage of offshore balancing. This enables North America not only to resist threats coming from the Grand Continent but also to erect and maintain favorable regional balances to further enhance its already secure place. One could contend that the present "unipolar moment" has been extended, at least for the coming decades, based upon these factors of American positional and resources advantage.

Various other land and maritime areas possess strategic importance, such zones pivotal to countries because of their control over more extensive territories and resources. Mountain passes, ocean straits, river estuaries, pivotal islands and canals, clean water and energy-resources, and central locations all contribute to these strengths. For the United States, the Mississippi River and New Orleans, the Great Lakes, Mexico, the Caribbean Basin, and Hawaii come to mind as important. For South America, the Amazon and La Plata watersheds and estuaries, the Malvinas Islands, the "Atlantic narrows" between Africa and the Brazilian bulge, the Charcas heartland,[12] and the hydroelectric power complex at Itaipú on the Paraná River. One could easily locate additional pivotal places that would exert impacts beyond.

Another geopolitical assumption (8) rests on the notion of unique and contrasting spatial patterns occurring within systems or structures. Here, one examines the interaction of events within a particular configuration, a "ripple effect" among the elements within the borders of a dynamic system where a thrust by element A will tend to impact upon elements B and C. We might see here an attempt among national actors to restore some sort of equilibrium once the system has been disturbed. Our assumption, consequently, is that the various patterns of activity within the several geopolitical structures will lend themselves to some sorts of interpretation and prediction of a spatial nature and design.

For instance, the ending of the Cold War caused the Middle American shatterbelt to end, where Soviet ties to Cuba, Nicaragua, and elsewhere quickly evaporated, and thus also US interventions into Central America. Daniel Ortega, president of Nicaragua in the 1980s, had posed an ideological-security threat to North American that drew Washington to support the rebel forces against his regime. But Ortega's re-election in 2008 drew little northern notice, although he was still disliked by North Americans. Indeed, all of the shatterbelts arising during the Cold War years abruptly faded because of the Soviet collapse; yet the potential for new shatterbelts could happen, these arising in Ukraine and along the central Eurasian belt.

Certain geopolitical structures approximate inclusion as assumptions: pan-regions, checkerboards, and lintel states. A pan-regional design divides the world longitudinally into three or four separate formations, Pan-America, Pan-Europa/Africa/Middle East, Pan-Russia/India, and Pan–East Asia and Oceania. One alleged purpose was to expose each sector to a north-south trade regime in which commodities and resources would feature northern domination of the south. East-West relations among the sectors could be strained and a checkerboard pattern might emerge, drawing a scenario similar to the world described in George Orwell's 1984, with almost constant warfare among the several partitions.

The structure of a checkerboard reveals contrasting patterns of actions and reactions and thus outcomes. Among the South American states, a leapfrog design of "my neighbor, my enemy, but my neighbor's neighbor my friend," has risen during several eras of South American diplomacy that encompassed Brazil, Chile, and Colombia aligned against Argentina, Peru, and Venezuela.[13] The best contemporary portrayal of this structure appeared during the 1982 Malvinas/Falkland Islands war between Argentina and Great Britain, in which Argentina's strongest ally was Peru, Chile assisting the British and Brazil remaining neutral.

Normally, one could assume such checkerboards might encourage strife. But unlike the pan-regional design, a contrary scenario might visualize checkerboards being also more peace-prone than war-prone at the moment,[14] showing a "structure of peace." Several reasons prompt this suggestion. In exhibiting their leapfrog patterns, countries within the checkerboard might wish to avoid facing costly two-front wars or at least significant frontier tensions, a feature encouraging conflict escalation and exhausting wars, although these historically have been infrequent among the major South American states. The vast expanses of sparsely populated hinterlands among the major countries and the cushioning effect of the four buffer states within the clash zone interior also would move this assumption in a more stable direction.

A final example of the structural assumption arrives in the lintel state configuration, Paraguay again being the example.[15] In this pivotal situation, the placement of Paraguay between its two larger neighbors, Brazil and Argentina, may have helped fix stability in Southern Cone diplomacy by preventing territorial absorption by either of the larger nations at the expense of Paraguay. Like a lintel stabilizing two adjoining columns betwixt a window or door in architectural terms, Paraguay, if it is able, holds fast to its autonomy by balancing or bandwagoning its two dominate regional powers. As will be discussed later in the next chapter, this buffering quality within the South American interior, too, has helped prevent an escalation of warfare among the major players within the checkerboard of the Southern Cone.

One could contend (9) that most geopolitically based themes will persist over some time regardless of contemporary issues that may prompt crises and change. Environments, technologies, and foreign policies may shift; yet our spatial qualities will remain largely intact. The United States will continue to look upon Middle America as its own sphere of influence and the area being within the vision of the Monroe Doctrine, as will Russia similarly envision Central Asia. Paraguay will balance off Brazil against Argentina, and the checkerboard of the La Plata Basin will persist, all over time. While these concepts will remain unchanged, the scenery will shift instead.

Colin Gray raises the theme of (10) conflict as inherent to geopolitics by arguing thus:

> The importance of geopolitics, and hence of Sir Halford's [heartland] theory, lies precisely in the fact that it addresses a major dimension to international conflict, the geographical, and that it seeks to identify and explain patterns in international conflict behavior. These are simply existential claims. International conflict has been endemic to the course of history, never more so than in the Twentieth-Century, and *geopolitical grand theory inevitably has reflected that reality.*[16]

Gray's assumption of conflict represents an important feature to the study of classical geopolitics, and we must elaborate on it.

Let us first take care to state that all IR models contain assumptions that highlight regional and global conflict. Indeed, such competition for valued resources comes centrally to all considerations of politics,[17] for without such rivalry in the face of scarcity, politics like government would "wither away" in Marxian terms. Most nations and peoples suffer some form of "scarcity," no matter their position or wealth.

In the case of geopolitics, the conflict assumption reflects both a conservative bias and a security tradition within geopolitics. It is conservative in that it agrees with the premise that struggle occurs naturally within all political relations—that being the case in human nature as well as in states' behavior. The world stage reflects an environment of danger; thus nations should focus upon national safety to survive. Statesmen will guide their countries in line with attaining their safest positions and with safeguarding the necessary resources available within their immediate environments. This latter aspect of national security rests as well on the successful competition for valued places that will render enhanced security. Thus, placement awards safety.

But again, we must be reminded that this conflict aspect has erred in merging traditional geopolitics within the "power politics" feature of the realist model in rather negative and pejorative directions, so harmful to our classical reputation, while the other international-relations models appear to have largely escaped this tawdry reputation. Strife attaches to all foreign-affairs considerations, but the geopolitical emphasis stays with states' placement and not with states' power.

For geopolitics, solutions for limiting dangers of conflict are found within a variety of geographic configurations, these being rather permanently set within the spatial realm. Smaller states may enlist bandwagoning or balancing strategies when facing larger states that neighbor them. Checkerboard patterns might diminish threats posed by shatterbelts. Buffer and lintel states could assist in reducing regional tensions, and economic integration and bridge-countries will promote globalization and peace. Checkerboard balancing may render some relief from hostile neighbors and establish allies for guaranteeing a joint security.[18] Having to face two fronts of hostility also could limit an encirclement and escalation by opponents.

Finally, it is assumed that (11) various topographic and other physical features of the geographic landscape may show certain national and regional traits of pivotal significance. Many of the world's major river watersheds exist within the larger countries, such as the Amazon of Brazil, the Mississippi of the United States, the Nile of Egypt, the Indus of India, the Yangtze of China, and so forth, providing a platform for unifying these nations as well as for strengthening commercial and transportation facilities within. Regions that form around such river basins seem to offer higher potentials for economic and political integration, two examples being the La Plata Basin for the Southern Cone Common Market and the European Union on the Danube, Rhine, and other rivers.

In contrast, disruptive mountain ranges, jungles, and deserts divide countries and regions. In this respect, consider the spatial challenge given the young United States to extending its sovereignty across central and western North America and onward to the Pacific coast, assisted by Ohio and Missouri river transport and not unduly impeded by the Rocky Mountains and the surrounding deserts. Yet Brazil could not parallel this Manifest Destiny success in the southern continent, being unable to conquer the brutal Andes mountain range nor the expansive interior jungles. The Pacific coastal lands of South America already were firmly settled by Spanish immigrants who were ready to oppose Brazilian expansionist intentions, a difficulty not faced by the northern republic in the more vacant California lands and the Northwest.

Interior and isolated spaces within continents could spawn conservatism and weaker political systems, whereas coastal environments could encourage financial progress and more democracy. A study by the author compared the variable, distance from Santa Cruz de la Sierra, Bolivia, one of the alleged South American heartland sites, with the ten South American capital cities, with a democracy variable based upon a composite of rankings from the Fitzgibbon democracy scale for Latin America.[19] From this "more isolation/less democracy" concept came a statistically significant association by enlisting a Spearman rho bivariate coefficient; our rho score of .567 was slightly higher than our hypothesis-acceptance score of .5494, showing a relevant association.

The shapes of these nations, their river systems and natural resources, the strategic natures of straits, the difficulties or advantages rendered in achieving national unity—all are just too basic to the geopolitics model to argue otherwise. Of course, we will investigate most of the geographic configurations associated with such positions later on as well. But again, these are assumptions of the classical mode, not easily rendered to theory but nonetheless relevant to the beliefs of geopolitics.

The above eleven examples of geopolitical assumptions could be extended, but now the model's explanation needs to shift to an exploring of an assortment of sixty theories that have fit the geopolitical definition.

5   Classical Geopolitical Theories

In this chapter we arrive at theory selection, a second way toward demonstrating a utility and legitimacy for classical geopolitics, the already-stated purpose for authoring this book. The reader is reminded of the first way, a drawing of a standardized definition of the classical in Chapter 2, and the third way, a coming application of selected theories to certain international happenings in Chapter 6. These three ways, again, represent the author's approaches toward raising the visibility of geopolitics as a viable and separate international-relations model.

Classical concepts and classical theories, that both fit the geopolitical definition, will be combined in this chapter and not kept apart. Several reasons prompted this choice. First, it appeared quite cumbersome to disconnect these two parts of the model. For instance, one chapter might introduce a description of a concept, but once studied, are we to abruptly await further analysis until the next chapter and start up again with outlining the same concept, although now a theory? To avoid this confusing disconnect, examination of both concepts and theories will come together jointly for clarity, convenience, and consistency. Second, attempting to define precisely the line separating a concept from a theory in most cases would be rather tedious because that separation is just not important or even possible. Once more, we face the failure of precision in our classical methodology, with the best solution being to just ignore the division and to forage on ahead, nonetheless.

And for a third reason not to face a distinction between the two, frankly concepts and theories interconnect so tightly, they truly should not be kept separate when applied to interpreting an international event. In studying an international happening, does not one start with recognizing the concept initially, but then proceed directly on with the theory of the same label? First the premise and then the conclusion? That is, if a shatterbelt [the concept] appears to be arising, then at that point, the potential for a conflict escalation might ensue [the theory] in the aftermath. The flow seems continuous and uninterrupted—the shatterbelt is identified and its likely impact described in nearly one sequence.

Or, if we see a contagion [the concept] of revolution occurring within one state among an array of states, the potential increases for that revolution sweeping within and then out from the one country, soon to be spread to nearby countries [the theory]. The transition between the two cannot be clearly located, and its precise boundary between the two features is not that vital to our understanding and utility anyway. In sum, we must begin with the vocabulary or definition before we set off on a description of the theory-to-application that forms from that flow of interpretation. But the joining of concepts and theories becomes a convenient necessity and this should not diminish our result.

As well, consideration of hypotheses as susceptible to becoming theories is avoided, since again the divide between these precepts and theories is also quite blurred. Hypotheses are "guesstimations" or untested yet possible associations that could eventually be called theories if a probability occurs. But determining when a sufficient probability exists so that we might see a transition from hypothesis to theory would be difficult to measure. Hence, we will push away this dilemma of sorting out this hypotheses-moving-to-theories question altogether.

We must still keep in mind that concepts and theories are separate qualities and they continue to serve distinctive functions within our model. Concepts appear first in line as passive descriptors of a possibly emerging situation, whereas theories will provide a later facility for showing the likelihood for interpreting and predicting an international action.

Concepts represent the vocabulary of a model, being passive and descriptive, and they are limited to providing the definitions and materials for explaining both assumptions and theories within the geopolitical model. Concepts portray certain spaces, events, and other geographically relevant phenomena that will relate to foreign policies and actions. Unlike assumptions, they are not so abstract. And differing from theories, they do not lend themselves to interactions among spatial factors or to being involved with testing, predicting, and prescribing likely associations. No probability characteristic exists here. Instead, concepts represent the concrete definitions of the landscape, the signposts and the describers. But concepts, too, often overlap in the descriptions associated with theories, as the line dividing the two phenomena, again, is not clear.

In contrast to concepts, theories are simple statements that show probable associations among variables. Normally just composed of short sentences, they often are quite limited in scope—if "A" happens, then there is a good chance that "B" will happen as a consequence of a stimulus induced on "B" from "A." The key word is "probability," as we place some reliance on predictability. Unlike concepts, theories require a certain amount of testing and replication for locating that predictability.

Once more as given in Chapter 2, it is hoped that this depiction of theory will be useful to the field of international-relations study. The tact is quite simple, a theory being none other than a mere sentence linking two elements into a prediction of probability. In contrast, "model" is used more broadly, a complete yet passive package of assumptions, concepts, and theories, all wrapped together within a common definition. This model-as-container includes all that is offered to us by classical geopolitics—hence, we speak of a total geopolitical model, but also of separate theories (with assumptions and concepts) that correspond to the geopolitical definition, all being a part of that greater basket collection.

Scholars' use of "theory" and "model" often confuses the reader. Their usual description of "theory" would resemble roughly this book's present depiction of "model." Likewise, their "model" may come as some sort of decision-making process where certain variables are tested for association to policy and action, in some cases with arrows and lines showing evolving actions moving toward a result. But on the structural or international levels, the human realm of decision-making cannot so easily be observed. Hence, our conclusion: theory appears as a mere sentence of probably and model as a passive container for associated assumptions and concepts-theories.

Stated once more as in Chapter 2, the theory-selection process of the present chapter will be made as objectively as possible. A majority of our sixty-odd generalizations below derive either from history or from scholars-practitioners, with the remainder from maps, logic, common sense, statistics, and rationality. If a candidate for theory arises that seems a reasonable choice based on these criteria—the link between proposition and probable conclusion—it will likely find membership within the present listing. The best "test" for usefulness and reliability will be their ease and accuracy for yielding good insights when attached to historical or contemporary foreign-affairs events. This process will happen in Chapter 6.

Mackinder's suggestion of a heartland, Spykman's of a rimland, Cohen's of a gateway region, Gray's of an imperial thesis, or Kelly's of a lintel state, all represent fairly clear choices. In North American history, such terms present as Manifest Destiny, the Monroe Doctrine, offshore balancing, containment, and spheres of influence. Common to international relations generally would be encirclement, balances of power, land and sea power, dependency, shatterbelts, and checkerboards, to name just a few. Accordingly, the author's efforts at collecting his sixty deserve some praise; yet, a large majority would be recognized quite readily by most international-relations students.

In a limited number of cases, some supposed generalizations failed even the rather open selection criteria above. One example could stand for General Londoño Londoño's triple-border points thesis,[1] where he imagined that a place crossed by three different nations' borders would be more prone to international conflict, a common-sense conclusion. Nonetheless, that thesis could not pass statistical inspection, rendering a Spearman-rho less-than-significant score of association and thus being denied entry as a theory into the geopolitical model.

Sometimes certain bunches of similar theories come with slightly contrasting descriptions, and the author has been as careful as possible either to combine similar theories into one or instead to leave others separate with their more unique depictions. For instance, in the former case, ocean cycles, the westward movement of civilizations, and the Age of the Pacific all seemed to hold roughly common descriptions. Accordingly, the three assembled into just one compartment although keeping their original labels and configurations. Or for the pentagonal thesis, equatorial paradox, and *camino del sol* concepts, all revealing a diminishing strategic relevance as one distances from the northern countries and regions, these grouped together into one category. But Mackinder's heartland clearly should stand separate from Spykman's rimlands,[2] and shatterbelts from checkerboards.

Other theory-possibilities likely could be added beyond the already assembled sixty, and these should be included and refined after this text is published if a common depository might be located in the future, a facility that will be suggested and encouraged in the concluding chapter. But for the moment, our sixty will readily satisfy the purpose of this book, to select a sufficient number of theories that will fit the definition of the geopolitical model as a way to show the promise and visibility of raising classical geopolitics to becoming a recognized and separate international-relations model.

We are now able below to examine a good assortment of theories that have been selected for the geopolitical model, these numbering among a multitude of the traditional geopolitical themes. Each separately will fit within one of five distinct categories: (1) core-periphery and other dichotomies; (2) pivotal regions and places; (3) borders and frontiers; (4) spaces; and (5) a variety of additional concepts/theories. Some other authors may contrast their categories with these designations. Geoffrey Parker divided his description of geopolitics into bipolar, multipolar, and center-periphery worlds.[3] What will be suggested for this present array appears rational to the author, those parts resembling different sorts of spatial patterns and placements.

Below are the five theory categories for assembly into the geopolitical model. An appendix will define each theory more briefly in alphabetical order:

Core-periphery and other dichotomies: heartlands, rimlands, containment, imperial thesis, normative and alternative processes, dependency thesis, ocean-cycles/westward movement of civilizations/Age of the Pacific, pan-regions, American isolationism, clash of civilizations.

Pivotal geopolitical regions and places: balance of power, checkerboards, shatterbelts, linchpin states, linkage thesis, convergence zones, Monroe Doctrine, offshore balancing, encirclement, geostrategies, spheres of influence, pivotal locations/theory of positional supremacy; *camino del sol*/pentagonal thesis/equatorial paradox, asymmetric states, balancer states/bandwagoning and balancing, key nations, buffer states, Intermarium, bridge-countries/gateway states and regions, lintel states, Great Game, choke points.

Borders and frontiers: frontier thesis, land-locked countries, natural/harmonic/equilibrium borders, organic frontiers, irredentism, borders-cause-wars thesis, contagion or diffusion across borders, falling-dominos/field and linkage theories, integration/globalization.

Spaces: space consciousness/space mastery, earth dependence/emancipation theory, manifest destiny, autarky, action space, distance-weakens thesis, sea power/land power, sea-lanes-of-communication, demography, closed spaces/law of valuable spaces, immigration/diversity.

Additional concepts-theories: county shape and size, hydraulic empire/despotism, fluvial laws, natural and energy resources, environmental determinism/possibilism, catastrophic environmental events, challenge and response, petro-politics, climatic theories, weapons states.

As a good starting point, we will begin with the more familiar binary core-periphery and other dichotomies section—that is, an examination of the locations and positions of countries, regions, resources, choke points, buffers, and so forth that will reside within a central place, as set apart from their opposing and surrounding environments or peripheries. What is the impact between the inner and the outer parts of these locations, and consequently, how have these contrasting spaces come to influence states' policies and actions?

1. Core-Periphery

This separation of locations, of central position versus outer position, may bring certain advantages to one or the other but also certain liabilities as well, and one will want to estimate how these spatial placements influence the affairs of certain states and regions. We should assume that a middle/outside perception of one's spatial position is acted upon conscientiously or unconscientiously by the individual state players for such an impact to be of value to our study.

The central Eurasian Heartland marks the most famous of all the classical concepts-theories, that impenetrable inner continental space seen in Halford Mackinder's keen imagination, an area united within its interior bastion but distant and thus secure from threatening maritime forces on the Eurasian perimeter. This prime example of the core-periphery formula exudes a picture of a core continental region offering some inner pivotal advantage for the possessor to consolidate resources within such a confinement so that its impact will naturally extend outward at places most advantageous to it within and beyond its perimeter margins. Central placement thus brings advantage for further territorial expansion with the benefit of security from periphery invasion.

Mackinder kept shifting the bounds in his Eurasian Heartland map throughout his major writings,[4] but this need not bother. His approach pertaining to Europe/Asia held these essentials: the heartland consisted of interior continental spaces encompassing the Arctic-flowing river watersheds in the north-central Asian regions, rimmed by lofty mountains, vast plains and harsh deserts, and expansive distance from the major oceans. The dominant country occupying this space was Russia, but Mackinder also warned of a worst-case scenario of Russia's being replaced by or joined with Germany as owner of these lands,[5] a much greater threat to England. Germany was uniquely positioned adjacent the passageway into the hinterlands of central Russia, Mackinder noting this leverage by giving strategic importance to Eastern Europe. More recent authors place China as a possible candidate for heartland possessor, too.[6]

Of particular importance was the heartland's isolation from Atlantic and Pacific seacoasts, where the maritime nations could not so easily occupy the central locations. Distance translated to security and the ample resources strengthened and unified the core. The heartland's placement formed a defense against periphery invasion, extent of territory being the core's advantage as Napoleon and Hitler were later to discover in their failed attacks.

Mackinder saw this central position becoming a global pivot once new technologies gave heightened efficiencies to rail transportation at the turn into the twentieth century. This transformation awarded a strategic advantage to landward states, canceling the earlier benefits of sea over land communications. Railroads linked the ample interior spaces and resources together, providing greater ease in carrying arms and men to defending the access points to the interior as well as to probing the more vulnerable places at the less defended coastal areas. And according to Mackinder, expanding the heartland's power onto the exposed maritime bases of the ocean coasts would balance, and could eventually surpass, the power of rival maritime coalitions. A world conquest by the continental forces at that time would "be within sight."

This latter projection of power thrusting outward from center to periphery assumes an inevitable aggressiveness, perhaps in part taken from historic suspicions of Russian expansionism so much dramatized at that time as well as later in Cold War propaganda. There seems little to indicate this likely expansion by the heartland's possessor, although that image appears a potential by Mackinder and by other commentators.[7]

A more recent heartland by C. Dale Walton moved this global center of gravity onto eastern Eurasia,[8] a region extending from Pakistan to Siberia, Japan to India and Australia, but with a Chinese pivot. In a "Post-Columbia Epoch" that began with the Soviet Union's fall, Walton predicted that US global hegemony eventually will wane, a new hegemon relocating to a multipolar Pacific Rim. He advised that North America continue balancing the East Asian powers as its best way to remaining a global power in this evolving geopolitical nexus. In a similar account, Zbigniew Brzezinski recommended North American activism in this region, with the United States assisting in settling regional disputes and in supporting a balance of power encirclement of China in league with its regional rivals.[9]

Students of geopolitics stand mixed in gauging the regional and strategic impacts of pivotal heartlands. Its most prominent example came in Mackinder's version, where classical geopolitics saw its start in the Anglo–North American world. But a number of other writings now add to the original concept, either favoring Mackinder or discrediting him. Frankly, a precise calculation of the relevance of this theory remains quite unlikely. How realistic in theory and in history is a heartland? Does a central continental position really matter, for how can the wastes and isolation of middle Asia exert global impact or indeed bring about a world empire?

Nonetheless, Walton's and Brzezinski's vision of an East Asia pivot holds some relevance with its center in China, particularly if the strategic impacts of Europe and America diminish. That region encloses India, Japan, Russia, and Korea, all with a tendency toward restricting a potentially expansive China. And it seems the United States also has found this region's importance with increased involvement in the area with a new strategic and regional policy of offshore balancing.

Among the several critics of Mackinder's pivot is William Kirk,[10] who questioned both the importance of the Eurasian selection itself and the emphasis on land power. Instead, Kirk noted a "pull" factor coming from the peripheral areas and attracting the envy of peoples of the heartland, this showing the outer regions being more advanced in wealth and culture than the interior lands, and thus more attractive to the hordes beyond to attacking the wealth of the more sophisticated marginal areas. Hence, several "sub-tropical" marginal "Zones of Initiation" have risen to a more important global reach, encircling the continental core and exerting heightened new ideas and greater technology and power. These peripheries seemed to represent better examples of "geographical pivots" in history. Kirk, likewise, questioned Mackinder's emphasis upon land power, arguing instead for some combination both of sea and land strength required for the rise of the larger countries, dependent upon the place and policy of the time. His analyses could as well be extended to the several other pivotal examples including the East Asia region.

Meinig followed this revisionist path by placing focus upon "positional supremacy," extending his description of the outer crescent or rimland areas as maritime or continental in orientation. His extension was based upon consideration of "functional" or cultural-political considerations that would shift over time and from place to place.[11] Like Kirk, Meinig offered more flexibility, adaptability, and updating to the original.

This author deems the heartland thesis should be taken seriously for two reasons. Mackinder's original proposal continues to dominate the study of classical geopolitics, whether its expanse can measure precisely or not. The theory, too, is believed to have strategic relevance by states persons of the past and the present, and this alone makes the heartland a pertinent inclusion within the typology of classical theories. One must only peruse policy statements by George Kennan, Henry Kissinger, Zbigniew Brzezinski, and others in like positions of authority to understand the impact of the heartland perspective upon the larger countries, particularly for US foreign policy.[12] And recently, Russian and Chinese strategists have taken new interest toward the heartland thrust, too.[13]

Cold War geopolitics stands as a good example for the actions and policies stemming from the original thesis. Strategists sought to "contain" Soviet expansionism from the heartland by establishing rimland dykes or military bases in pivotal coastal lands of expected interest to the Russians. An offshore balancing of naval and marine forces within this Mackinderistic design have extended for decades from Western Europe to the Persian Gulf to Korea and Japan, all marginal zones encircling the Eurasian pivot. The Monroe Doctrine fit nicely into this scheme by advocating exclusion of intruding Eurasia forces as US rivals in Middle America, a fear of a shatterbelt forming there to replace the North American influence sphere. The Cuban missile crisis offers good evidence to this vital US interest.

Secondly, the heartland theory does show some pivotal insight despite its best example residing in the cold wastelands and distant isolation of north-central Eurasia. Central locations encourage heightened involvement in regional and international affairs. Core nations frequently expand outward with a security interest for controlling surrounding territories, this internal leverage awarding some advantage in the choice of one's allies and opponents, in probing the stronger and weaker points of their neighbors, and in being able to prioritize which resources should become national security goals. Certain vulnerabilities accompany the core positional advantages. Residing in the middle of a region reveals an encirclement of potential hostility, a threatening condition one would want to avoid, one seen in the imperial thesis outlined below. With the more borders/more wars thesis, central location accrues to heightened conflict.

Take as a contrasting instance the advantages held by the United States derived from its simultaneous pivotal and perimeter locations. It prizes distance and isolation from Eurasia and also near-presence of weaker, nonthreatening neighbors. These traits feature its "island" characteristic, prompting a significant naval power and an ability for selective military intervention upon the distant Eurasian rimlands. All of these diverse attributes bring geopolitical bonuses, where North America's encirclement by Eurasia blends with its own encirclement of Eurasia. North America is pivotal by living astride both northern oceans, a balancer or gateway state with two sea fronts able to stabilize the balance of power at either fringe of Eurasia to its advantage. Consequently, the United States alone holds a unique continental position among the Great Powers for being both core and peripheral to its strategic surroundings.

Why not North America a strategic heartland? Mackinder's description could fit more appropriately the United States than Eurasia: (1) an isolated region protected by distance and weaker neighbors; (2) an internal and unified land enhanced by rivers, lakes, and canals, and with modern communications networks; (3) a resources base of industrial and technological innovation; and (4) an ability to probe beyond America to promote its security by offshoring balancing along the Eurasian flanks. The Mississippi watershed with New Orleans the strategic key further anticipates this northern extent. This may well have been a distant vision of President Jefferson in his famous purchase, being first guided to buying the port and the rest falling under that pivot. Once more, might these American characteristics reveal a strong heartland candidate?

Other outcomes of core versus periphery deserve our attention, including Brazil's encirclement by its Spanish neighbors, Mexico's dependency on the United States, Venezuela's noninvolvement in South America's wars, Germany's two-front dilemma, and China's landward confinement, weak maritime impact, and hostile nations surrounding.

Another continental heartland, much less known, locates in Bolivia in its Charcas heartland of middle South America.[14] With this configuration, the territorial focus rests upon the space between the cities of Sucre, Cochabamba, and Santa Cruz, with the latter town, Santa Cruz, being the supposed key to dominating the interior of South America and ultimately of the entire continent. Two alternatives of the thesis include that of Paraguay as a hinge-state heartland,[15] and that of General Golbery Couto e Silva's welding zone of western Brazil and eastern Bolivia,[16] overlapping to some extent the Charcas triangle. In the last description, the Brazilian military governments of the 1960s through the 1970s built an array of jungle highways that in part led through the welding zone and toward Charcas. Allegedly, these paths aimed toward the two strategic passes onto the Pacific coast, raising some suspicions that these road systems were guided by the heartland-induced recommendations of Travassos and Golbery. They could have intended to fulfill Brazil's manifest destiny quest for lands on the Pacific-American littoral.

Rimlands, the continental perimeter but still strategic periphery, configures the Eurasian marginal regions bordering Mackinder's heartland that would include western and southern Europe, the Middle East, and Southeast and East Asia. The Dutch-American Nicholas Spykman drew this encircling region of strategic leverage, noting its placement between heartland and the outer maritime worlds being of greater importance to global stability and American security than either of the continental or maritime extremes.

In Spykman's words:

> The rimland of the Eurasian land mass must be viewed as an intermediate region, situated . . . between the heartland and the marginal seas. It functions as a vast buffer zone of conflict between sea power and land power. Looking in both directions, it must function amphibiously and defend itself on land and sea.[17]

Gerace's insightful article offers a clear separation in this regard between Mackinder and Spykman:

> Mackinder and Spykman are actually quite different. In Mackinder there is one pattern of conflict in history—that between seapower and heartland. In Spykman, however, there are two—that between seapower and heartland, and that between an independent center of power in the rimland with both seapower and heartland allied against it. These patterns alternate around the shifting distribution of power within important regions of the rimland. It is this dualism in Spykman that is ignored. . . . Yet it was the second pattern that he saw as coinciding with major wars in modern times. The first is real, but is no longer the overriding theme that it is in Mackinder.[18]

Spykman's views anticipated the security danger toward America coming from the Eurasian marginal lands, a threatening balance of powers arising against both heartland and outer perimeter. Departing from the later containment against an aggressive Eurasian interior that reflected Mackinder's concern, he opposed European integration and any sort of rimland unity because this posed the greater challenge to peace and to America.

Figuring within the core-periphery dichotomy resides the imperial thesis, a concept showing a territorial growth outward from an undefended central core, reaching to an eventual expansive empire earning security and wealth by the absorption of more outlying territories. Such spatial growth is followed by an inevitable contraction of the territorial gains reverting back to the original center resulting from the failure of the imperial core to sustain the envelopment of the hostile and rebellious outer margins.[19]

The Principality of Moscovy, centuries ago, began its territorial expansion, in large part to seek security through distance, the core lacking natural frontiers for protection. The additional territory, too, increased the wealth of the central ecumene as well. This outward expansion lasted centuries and came about through conquest, annexation, and purchase.

Nonetheless, like the rise and fall of ancient Rome, the Russian imperial expansion over new territories eventually halted, and for several reasons the periphery contracted and became separated from the core: (1) neighboring countries resisted the absorption of new imperial lands on their frontiers, creating a hostile encirclement of Russia and resisting further enlargement; (2) inhabitants of the imperial acquisitions, differing in culture and race from the core peoples, grew restless and with increasing frequency rebelled to gain their autonomy against Moscow; and (3) costs of central management heightened, requiring the core armies to police both frontiers and the diverse subjects near the borderlands, causing bankruptcy and autocracy of the center. Hence, the periphery, becoming independent once more, enfolded against the center, ending the empire.

Such a scenario could conceivably play to Brazil, Mexico, and other larger states including the United States. In Mexico's case, the peripheral frontier lands traditionally oppose the central authority of Mexico City, with a century ago, Emiliano Zapata from the south and Francisco Villa from the north marching in coordination to conquer the Central Valley in 1914. Brazil's *bandeirantes*, also, sought interior South American lands, causing suspicions and resistance from Spanish neighbors.

For the United States, we can observe a similar scenario, seeing territorial growth steadily westward from the English-American coast with little opposition from Native Americans or Europeans in that expansion. Blocking Ohio Valley shatterbelts encircling the new republic quickly evaporated once Napoleon Bonaparte's aggressions had drawn his rivals in Europe away from America.[20] The potential for imperial disintegration, of late suffered by the Russians, has likely been averted because of North American wealth and geographic unity, a relatively stable and pragmatic political system, isolation from Eurasia, and the absence of major difficulties (with the exception of the North/South civil war) being the primary factors. But has the nation fully integrated all of its western lands still—namely, the plains and mountain states, Texas, the West Coast, and Hawaii, into the eastern core of the union? Time may tell a similar disintegration.

This topic of global empire fits the spatial requirement of geopolitics and also of the core/periphery perspective. Dimitry Sims depicts the United States as a "benign liberal empire," and he criticizes the republic for its "messianic instincts" toward involving itself in wasteful and unnecessary crusades.[21] Whether the North American Empire is destined for decline, as most other historical examples have suffered, continues as a debate among Cold War proponents, and perhaps more examination of this feature is needed within classical geopolitics. In the next chapter will be explored the ancient Roman rise and decline within a geopolitical context.

Somewhat akin to the imperial thesis is Geoffrey Parker's General Geopolitical Process, which merits our attention.[22] Asserting that states' behaviors resolve themselves into either conflict or associative outcomes, the former being the more frequent, he divides his survey into three progressive "stages" showing states' spatial expansion, then hegemonic success after this broadening, and eventual decline and territorial fragmentation. During Parker's first stage a continental power will gain a regional leadership whenever it confronts a maritime opponent. Normally the land power will emerge the stronger by absorbing a greater expanse of wealth and lands than will be possible for the sea power, being limited to coastal lands and vulnerable ports and bases.

The countries of the maritime periphery have been able to prevent complete dominance despite their weaker positions and resources, and in time the greater powers will "fragment," creating "a number of smaller states that [will] seek to establish a balance among themselves until such time as the next bid [by a rising state] for [Great Power] dominance takes place," a final rotation in the cycle and one that Parker labels an "alternative geopolitical process." The European Union would set itself as the prime example of the latter instance of fragmentation, then replaced by regional association. This alternative process is attractive as a possible scenario for a coming world order, depleted of hegemons and Great Power dominance and more concerned with global integration, resolution of environmental challenges, and return of a classical multipolar system, perhaps growing into an effective world governing system.

The dependency thesis, also a periphery-core structure, exhibits wealthier and technologically advanced core areas, basically North America, Europe, Japan, and some metropolitan centers of the emerging markets, amid a periphery of semideveloped regions, these kept weak and vulnerable to the strengths of the core in an almost mercantilist or colonialist fashion. The center emits this advantage because it already possesses abundant natural and energy resources, and these are supplemented further by sophisticated technology, central locations, an educated middle class, and strong consumer markets, whereas the periphery lacks all of these advances. The outlying regions stagnate without facilities for competing against the core in the regional and global arenas because the periphery cannot unite with other like areas, these partisans of the quadrant producing similar primary products and/or being reliant upon the core for sustenance.

Dependency qualifies as a geopolitical structure because its basic features (core/periphery) show a spatial positional description, with other variants attaching also: heightened poverty and weakened governments with a growing number of failed and rogue states; a corresponding lawlessness and mounting difficulties making these areas less attractive to core investment; and a clustering of countries of the global south, lands much removed from the dominant northern sectors and with an absence of strategic relevance. Might these poor and marginal regions devolve soon into complete failures, gated off from the rich north and left to their own suffering without hope of relief, a "spaceship earth scenario" of two very contrasting world societies, the one vigorously protecting its living standards against the depressions and threats of the other?

Some describe a "semiperiphery" composed of countries that hold sufficient wealth and technology to arm themselves with "weapons of mass destruction," threatening the militarily dominant center. One might expect core leaders to respond against these nuclear alarms with sanctions and invasions, as in the cases of Iran and Iraq.

Dependency theory exhibits two different blames for this two-tiered configuration of poverty amid wealth. Some radical theorists claim in dependency an imperialist conspiracy of the rich becoming richer because of their exploitation of the poor. In this theme, Lenin saw in the profits of the capitalist a consequent blocking of the dialectical progression of historical stages advancing the northern capitalist nations toward socialism. Specifically, proletarians or capitalist labor was propped up by wealth gained from exploiting of the southern regions, and consequently, these workers lacked incentives for revolting against their elitist managers. Lenin's solution came as a revolutionary one, of upheaval against international imperialism by way of wars of liberation aimed at northern profits in the southern colonies so that the dialectic could continue on, workers against capitalist, and soon the arrival of socialism, thus ending southern dependency.

A more moderate and liberal bent envisioned the dependency structure as a natural flow of under-regulated capitalism where the international system lacked effective institutions for moderating the excesses of monopoly. Here, a peaceful redistribution of wealth could happen, once such institutions would bring about a "New International Economic Order," reversing some of the wealth in a voluntary and substantial assistance to southern modernization. This latter solution for the problems of dependency possesses fewer ideological trappings, although both patterns resemble the spatial features of distances, resources, and regional separations.

Next, we see an ocean-cycle thesis of centrally located rivers, seas, and oceans that have facilitated the rise of civilizations—for instance, in the ancient Middle East, the Nile and Euphrates-Tigris river ways, and since classical times, the Aegean and Mediterranean seas, the North Atlantic Ocean, and more recently the Pacific Rim. These bodies of water favor maritime nations, placing such waterways pivotal to broadening the sea-oriented countries' impact and prosperity and in utilizing many of the advantages of central position in regions and continents that focus upon the earth's waters.

An expansion of the ocean-cycles thesis shows a progression of these regional centers steadily shifting to the global west,[23] the westward movement of civilizations, facilitated by central waterways. Perhaps Eurocentric and reductionist in favoring that specific direction, one can still visualize from ancient times to the present the advancement of the ancient Greco-Roman empires yielding to the later expansion of Western Europe and subsequently onto North American hegemony.

Chinese civilizations could meld into this thesis as well, when Asia predominated in manufacturing before the onset of European colonialism, a western expansion and plundering into Asia created by the Europeans' availability of coal and by their utility of steam power for military use based upon this energy source.[24] In present times the coming Age of the Pacific forecasts the diminishing of Europe and the growing vigor and prosperity of the Asian.[25] Authors allege a likely movement of the global pivot toward these eastward directions, the Asians enjoying renewed stability and security. Some in the West resist this possibility, suggesting American offshore balancing to contain an expansionist China, an encirclement of the Chinese by its Asian rivals, Japan, Russia, India, and Korea, plus American involvement in leading such a checkmating.

This *ocean-cycle thesis* yields to a further discussion of the Mediterranean's position within ancient Roman geopolitics in the next chapter, but one could include certain other important sea and river systems as well for the bolstering of civilizations. The Mississippi River, when compared with the Amazon, shows a good example of the relative importance of waterways, where the Mississippi is less extensive in water flow than the Amazon but its more pivotal location in the rich and populated heartland of North America has proven vastly more vital to the historical development of the United States. The Saint Lawrence Seaway rates a similar advantage. In contrast, the Amazon contributes marginally to the prosperity of Brazil, and it could pose a security threat to the republic of absorption by other nations because of the region's isolation in respect to the Atlantic coastal centers of the country.[26] This author had resisted including pan-regions within traditional geopolitics because it derived from the German *Geopolitik*, which linked it to their aggressive lebensraum and autarkic themes from the earlier writings of Ratzel and others. Yet, even the American scholar Isaiah Bowman promoted this thesis,[27] within the guise of the Monroe Doctrine, Manifest Destiny, and similar expressions that have since come in similar designs. Henry Kissinger, too, made such references to his favoring of the northern power zones in pentagonal expressions,[28] stating his lack of interest in southern matters. A parallel condominium structure has been alleged to conspiracy of the permanent five members of the UN Security Council, its opponents decrying a hegemonic "freezing" of northern dominance and of the preventing of southern nations from developing themselves, a structure of exploitation fitting the image of both the dependency and the pan-region arrangements.

The pan-region thesis offers a global structure of three or four diverse regional compartments, each divided according to a north-south or longitudinal configuration. In these we see, almost in Orwellian descriptions of the novel 1984, a pan-Europe, a pan-Russia, an East Asian or "co-prosperity sphere," and an Oceania or Pan America.[29] The advantages visualized in this structure derive in autarchy or self-sufficiency in resources for each sector, the different climatic and resource zones of the regions linked within to provide all of the necessary ingredients for a greater strategic autonomy. Also shown is an interdependent specialization among states within the pan-sectors that resemble those of common markets and free-trade zones today. Indeed, particularly among the South American writers, and especially for the Uruguayan scholar Bernardo Quagliotti de Bellis,[30] regional integration is a primary topic in geopolitical discussions within the Southern Cone.

Pan-regions reflect the wealth distributions of oceans and continents on our earth where the sea expanses and limited southern landforms contrast to the more ample and richer land surfaces in the planet's northern half. This reality shows the spatial advantage given the north in having more of its land surfaces within the more productive and healthier temperate zones, the residences of the major civilizations of the past and present. These temperate lands, with their greater national power and wealth, award a significant advantage to the northern lands of the earth.

The Colombian geopolitical writer Julio Londoño Londoño[31] called this north-south maldistribution of wealth *el camino del oro*, where the farther a country's position from an imaginary northern hemisphere line stretching from Tokyo and Beijing to Washington, DC, and through London, Paris, Rome, and Berlin and extending on to Moscow, the less influence that country would exert in global strategic matters. Reflective of his argument, South America itself could be designated a geopolitically independent region, distant from strategic global affairs. Several authors refute the importance of the contrasting core-periphery dichotomies, this impact voided because of new technologies that might now benefit the south. Saul Cohen maintained that "spatial-centrality" theories and "cycles of hegemonic growth and decline" are obsolete.[32] He enlisted, instead, systemic and developmental approaches that depend more upon resources and technology than upon regional and continental pivots. To Cohen, it matters little the position of a country; more vital is its developmental level that will grow into more complex and integrated realms and regions:

> Essentially, the principles hold that systems—both human and biological—evolve in stages, from atomization and undifferentiation, specialization, and specialization-integration. Applying these principles to the geopolitical map is complex, for various parts of the world are at different developmental stages. . The capacity of different parts of the system to evolve relates, in large measure, to their distinctive operational environments.[33]

Similarly, Alexander de Seversky's *air-isolationism* posits that countries' economic resources and advanced technologies facilitate domination of regions regardless of locations, central or otherwise.[34] Both sources rejected the importance of the traditional core-periphery dichotomies.

Nonetheless, Grygiel[35] and Walton[36] call for a return to geography as a common fixture to international relations, declaring that human involvement, that being within Cohen's development and Seversky's technology, among many similar examples, should not replace the spatial impact that we study in classical geopolitics. So, we see two different directions here, the latter descriptions of relative placements of states, resources, and regions perhaps more in tune with our model of geopolitics.

An American isolationism resides next on our list, reflective of separation from balances among Eurasian states and of residence in the wealthy and protected lands of North America, the unique isolation enjoyed by the United States should rank as a separate instance of a concept entering the geopolitical model. These advantages include: (1) distance awards an American security; (2) isolation allows consolidation of continental wealth without opposition; (3) reliance upon naval over land power avoids the danger of local armies overturning civilian governments; (4) role of balancer state offshore the Eurasian flanks attracts US allies to its favor; and finally, (5) distance and isolation make America less feared by Eurasian states in having their territories jeopardized.

All other Great Powers lack this American advantage of strategic isolation and wealth: China in its East Asian encirclement; Japan checkmated by China, Russia, and America; Russia between Germany and China; Germany, France, and England all vulnerable to each other's pressure; Brazil surrounded by Spanish Americans; and India fearing a nuclear, unstable, and hostile Pakistan. Based upon these factors, the odds of the "unipolar moment," or the demise of the United States as global hegemon being reduced by challenger states, appears remote at the moment.

Samuel Huntington's *clash of civilizations* envisioned eight or nine world civilizations, each based upon common cultures, languages, and religions, and each occupying a separate but unified geographic region.[37] The Cold War having ended, the previous ideological and nationalistic challenges among nations and blocs, he predicted, will shift from the political-ideological alignments onto new social and cultural dimensions where different and rival civilization centers will compete and fight instead. Conflicts would arise along cultural march lands or frontiers, and some borders would suffer particular hostility, those including the Muslim, Chinese, and Western. Huntington believed that the cultural centers themselves would remain united and not be susceptive to civil wars. Huntington's thesis provides some relevance to the recent Western intrusions into Iraq, Syria, and Afghanistan and to the several terrorist attacks from those centers toward Western Europe and the United States. But Russia, China, and India, among other nations, suffer such incidents as well. The weaker parts to this thesis would challenge the cultural unity within such regions—for instance, the Sunni divide against the Shia factions does not emit that quality. Likewise, international conflict in the post–Cold War era stems from other sources including competition over resources and frontiers as well as struggles within nations for unity or autarky.

The *clashing-civilizations thesis* fits the core-periphery structure and the bipolar patterns as set in the Eastern threats against Western civilization,[38] historically seen by Europeans in the "Russian colossus" of the Great Game, the "Yellow Peril" threat of the Orient, and the Muslim incursions from the Ottoman Empire.

2. Pivotal Geopolitical Structures

Closely associated to the various core-periphery configurations are an assortment of structures that show systemic patterns of strategic and pivotal relevance. Overlapping with systems theory that carries spatial elements similar to those of classical geopolitics, we observe within the boundaries of structures, or systems, actions and reactions that emit positional patterns of states, regions, and resources common to a spatial nature.

This section about leverages begins with mention of the balance of power because this seems to relate to other themes below. But the author and reader should proceed carefully here, for stated again, balance of power pertains to the realist model as well as to the geopolitical model—only the emphases differ. Realist balances reflect power, one country's or one alliance's physical force-levels framed against those of opposing countries or alliances, a "power politics" configuration. As stated in Chapter One and elsewhere in this book, one goal is to separate this power label from geopolitics where it so wrongly affixes. The only connection to "power" in geopolitics comes indirectly from security instances of pivotal positions, places, and resources, and one should refer to these connections as leveraging or pivotal rather than as raw muscle. We must not equate placement with power because this deflects from the essentials of our classical model.

Within the realm of geopolitics, balance of power pertains to pivotal placements, ones balanced against opposing positions that will contribute to the national interests and security of a country and alliance. Again, we should disregard the measuring of one state against the other, balanced or not balanced. Rather, the focus rests upon the pivot itself between/among the positions—both the structure's configuration and the patterns within that configuration. Pan-regions, checkerboards, shatterbelts, Great Game, heartlands/rimlands, sea-land power, and core/periphery represent unique alignments. Stability/instability, peace/war, friendly/hostile, development/stagnation all serve as instances of patterns within these alignments. The location of energy and natural resources, of choke points, of strategic ports and rivers, of population clusters, and the like, could be added to these impact considerations.

A contemporary example is demonstrated once more in the two-oceans balancing of the United States, where North America, from afar and offshore, can leverage to its favor the larger countries at either Pacific or Atlantic extreme of the Eurasian continent. Its ability to intervene among the several states would tend to stabilize those peripheral regions and add to American safety, but this involvement is positional and pivotal in impact, not power-centric.

The *checkerboard structure* offers another balance of power stance, of contrasting rivalries and alliances arising at various intervals throughout history in world regions, from the Peloponnesian war in ancient times to the Vietnam conflict of several decades back. The diplomatic patterns in South American foreign affairs show another example of this geopolitical structure.[39] Checkerboards resemble the dictum "My neighbor my enemy but the neighbor of my neighbor my friend"—frontiers bring international tensions between neighboring states but this potential balances out by establishing alliances in leapfrog fashion with neighbors of neighbors more distant across regions and continents. One portrayal of this phenomenon is shown in the mandala circles, the center being one's country but the surrounding circles alternate according to opponent or ally.

Checkerboards stabilize current South American diplomacy,[40] a feature of the next chapter. The alignment of Brazil, Chile, and Colombia as opposed to Argentina, Peru, and Venezuela has existed since independence, a formation exerting some impact upon earlier South American wars. The 1982 Falklands/Malvinas war fought between Britain and Argentine revealed a checkerboard with Argentina supported by Peru and Venezuela opposed by Chile and ignored by Brazil.

The particular geographic outcroppings within the checkerboard tend to determine the level of stability within that structure. For South America, several reasons may contribute to a stabilized continent for the moment. Great distances among larger countries and their normally isolated frontiers dampen direct contacts between neighbors that might prompt violence. The costs of an extensive war would be significant because of distances, but there is also the possibility of having to fight two-front conflicts, an expensive encirclement. Most of the republics could not afford extensive continental wars. Buffer states along the South American corridor of conflict further isolate adjacent neighbors. Widespread conflict could encourage Brazilian expansionist ambitions against its Spanish encirclement, and such a threat would curtail open strife. And finally, the United States could also intervene in a continentwide conflict, were it to be prolonged and widely destructive, and this action would encourage the republics not to engage in violence.

A checkerboard of ancient Greece in the Peloponnesian war drew a wider expanse of rigidity and violence, and the pattern discouraged peace settlements. The participants' frontiers were close enough among the several city-states and empires to stimulate rivalry, and a stalemate between Athenian sea power against Spartan land power prolonged the strife. The Athenians' failed attack against Syracuse weakened the city, and the neighboring Persians played off one side against the other until they helped finance a Spartan fleet that turned the contest in favor of Sparta, an assist that defeated the Athenians after a thirty-year struggle.

A contrasting geopolitical structure surfaced in ancient India in Kautilya's *Arthasastra*, a mandala or "circle of states" closely resembling later checkerboards. To describe this feature, Modelski writes:

> We might call [Kautilya's circle of states] a checkerboard model, because the basis of it is the proposition that one's neighbor is one's enemy and that one's neighbor's enemy is therefore one's obvious friend. The regular alternation between friends and enemies produces, for the system, a checkerboard effect.[41]

As in Machiavelli's *Prince*, Kautilya advised his king on strategies for securing the kingdom such as alliances, diplomacy, and warfare. The mandala configuration assisted in the king's choice of allies and alliances similarly to the way in which our checkerboards might contribute to contemporary states persons.

Shatterbelts have taken on a variety of past labels including "crush" or "clash zones," "middle tiers" or "belts of political change," and "devil's triangles" with "zones of contact."[42] Shatterbelts have been commonly placed in Middle Europe and the Middle East and less so in Southeast Asia by the earlier geopolitical writers. In their original designs, the noted characteristics of these structures featured areas in political, ethnic, and economic turmoil but still of attraction to the interventions of larger neighboring countries. Escalation of this strife among both levels of countries, local and strategic, would contribute to the beginnings of both world wars. "Catalytic wars," in which smaller countries enticed the larger outsiders into intervening in their behalf against local rivals, further characterize the dramas of shatterbelts. In sum, shatterbelts spawn conflict and war and they represent dangers to global and regional peace.

But this earlier depiction required a more studied definition and application because the shatterbelt came with factors other than mere violence itself. With this in mind, the author utilized a cluster-analysis computerized routine that measured four variables of dispersion—political, social, economic, and ethnic—these four being those given shatterbelts by the traditional authors. The subsequent research did not find uniformly high amounts of depression within any of these shatterbelt combinations. That is, political unrest might have appeared, but the other features, ethnic, economic, and social, revealed lower decline. Said differently, the three clusters of nations assembled within the statistics saw different assortments among the four variables: one cluster drew high levels of political disorder, yet experienced medium levels of ethnic, social, and economic depression. A cluster low in disorder ranked higher in the other three variables. The final grouping rated low in those variables but in middle position for political stability. To fit the classical definition for shatterbelts, all four factors would have had to have experienced submerged figures in common, although none of them actually did so. Hence, the need was felt for a more workable definition.

A redesigned shatterbelt, one apparently accepted within the field,[43] shows a similar two-tiered pattern, a local conflict set within a strategic rivalry among outside Great Powers. This geopolitical composite became apparent (1) when rival states at both levels, regional and strategic, experienced tensions among themselves; and (2) when these tensions attracted consequent intervention into such regions by outside strategic competitors in alignment with local contestants. Some sort of alliance agreements between local and strategic states completed the new definition—policies to align the levels within a locale in conflict were essential and not simply the rise of regional conflict itself.

Shatterbelts emerge whenever certain countries at both local and strategic levels decide to ally themselves with/against their local and strategic friends/ opponents. Such coalitions are formed by policy choices and not by specific regional characteristics. In sum, we see strategic rivals set against the others within certain regions, these regions also in turmoil and local states agreeing to the interventions of their Great Power sponsors. These alliances often escalate to a higher potential for warfare.

During the 1980s, six such formations could be located by utilizing the suggested definition, most of them rimming the Eurasian World Island. Once the Soviet Union fell, leaving the United States the sole superpower, shatterbelts disappeared, with the contemporary exception of a shatterbelt in the Ukraine civil war, Russia and the West supporting their local clients. Other shatterbelts could form in Central Asia, the original Great Game of a century ago, with China, Russia, and the United States vying for petroleum access. Other likelihoods might emerge in the Pakistan-Afghanistan areas as well as upon the Korean peninsula and over Taiwan.[44] These instances represent rough possibilities, and their appearances are unlikely at the present time because Great Power challengers appear reluctant or unable to compete against the United States in these and other regions of likely instability.

If a shatterbelt were to arise within an area, prompted by strategic alliances agreeable to local factions, the likely settings could erupt into war. These configurations pose serious threats to international peace; they are not solutions to conflict but instead contributors. They come about in areas already suffering strife among neighbors but where the Great Powers decide to intervene with their own interests at stake. Great Powers' lack of interest in or resistance toward entering this competition, and the erection of certain "fire-breaks" against escalation such as prior agreements to arbitrate, sanctions and threats, or pursuit of other avenues toward peacekeeping, would offer ways toward preventing likely escalation.

Paul Hensel and Paul Diehl sought to test further the concept's application, their definition closely fitting the author's:[45] "The term 'shatterbelt' generally refers to a geographic region that is plagued both by local conflicts within or between states in the region, and by the involvement of competing major powers from outside the region." They might have inserted the larger states "choosing to intervene within the areas of conflict" at the end of their definition.

In Cold War terminology, Saul Cohen[46] and Zbigniew Brzezinski[47] coined two additional terms tied to shatterbelts. The first, "linchpin states," held locations of strategic value and of economic and military attraction that would enable the Western alliance to contain the alleged spread of Soviet influence in the Third World, such states including Germany, Poland, Iran, Afghanistan, Pakistan, South Korea, and the Philippines. In addition, Kissinger's linkage thesis asserted a connection between Soviet intrigue and Third World instability and anti-Westernism. To halt the disruptions of this linkage, he advised the United States to provide trade and technology transfers leading to possible accommodation with Russia and China.

Cohen described a preshatterbelt condition in his outline of convergence zones, areas centrally positioned between interests of adjacent Great Powers.[48] These zones could emerge as gateway regions or as shatterbelts. Fitting this image, he criticized the George W. Bush administration's decision to occupy Iraq that upset the previous multilateralist consensus for stabilizing the country.

A concept meant to block the entry of shatterbelts into regions is the Monroe Doctrine of 1823, based on the US interest in excluding Eurasian powers from the Caribbean. Although this sort of exclusion parallels that of regional spheres of influence, the doctrine should remain separate because it closely associates with the Eurasian heartlands and rimlands. One would expect most of the larger states having similar traditions (the Brezhnev Doctrine of the 1970s; China over the Korean peninsula) within their foreign-security policies, those being, to ward off shatterbelts in adjacent regions and to preserve within these lands their own influence spheres. This geopolitical classic for the United States warns Eurasian states to keep military and political interventions away from Middle America, for such an occupation would threaten the security of its southern approaches. Middle America, or the Caribbean and its Central and South American watershed, has shifted historically between eras of shatterbelts and of spheres of influence,[49] and for the Cuban missile crisis of 1962, Soviet warheads in Cuba represented a clear shatterbelt violation to Monroe's declaration.

Nations will protect against the possibility of encirclement by opposing neighbors. This danger appeared in the imperial thesis where territorial expansion outward and distant from an empire's core eventually attracted resistance by suspicious neighbors on the empire's periphery. Most of the Great Powers of Eurasia suffered this encirclement, in particular Russia, China, and Germany. But North America, while surrounded on both sides by the distant Eurasian flanks, is less threatened from that immediate danger by the wide ocean expanses and by weak and friendly neighbors.

Indeed, the United States enjoys more encirclement benefits than encirclement liabilities, since it encircles Eurasia as well as being encircled. The grand-strategy of offshore balancing particularly addresses this advantage in which America can support a favorable Asian multipolar balance intent on containing an expansionist China as well as balancing to its favor the European nations against a possible Russian threat. The Monroe Doctrine warns against such Eurasian engagement toward America.

This *encirclement* factor is noted in the contrasting checkerboards of ancient Greece and present-day South America,[50] where the two structures resemble each other but the pattern within differs widely. The distances and isolation among the major South American states tended to forestall regional conflict despite the historical encircling structures, one republic being surrounded by rival republics on either frontier dampening conflict. Shatterbelts did not appear, nor extracontinental intrusions.

The ancient Greece city-states saw encirclement that prolonged their war and increased the destruction. Here, Athens could encircle its rivals' coastlines by enlisting superior naval reach, whereas Sparta was supreme on land but unable to breach the protective embankments of its opponents. Shatterbelts intensified the encirclements by attracting Sparta's allies, Persia and Syracuse, into involvements that caused the conflict escalations.

Further encirclement examples include Brazil, at times its territorial expansions drawing the suspicions of South American neighbors.[51] The encircling republics helped prevent Portuguese-American ambitions toward a manifest destiny of stretching Brazilian sovereignty onto the Pacific coastal lands. Both Mackinder[52] and Spykman[53] were well aware of this encirclement concept, too, for the former a "girdle" surrounding the heartland, and for the latter the rimlands caught between heartland and oceanic allies.

Several commentators describe a facet of geostrategy.[54] Jakub Grygiel shows this to be a policy emitted by statespersons who will align the geopolitical needs of states to resources and energy wealth as required of national power.[55] Where these policies reflect geostrategic realities, a country will maintain its power and security. Geopolitics to Grygiel included gaining necessary resources, communications that render access to such resources, and stability of states' frontiers. Geostrategy involves statesmen's policies of attaining these types of elements that enhance the power of the larger nations. Such expanded geostrategic portrayals also receive mention in Cohen's "geostrategic realms," or strategically pivotal spaces,[56] which were composed of several smaller "geopolitical regions."

Spheres of influence associate with dependent countries and regions controlled by more powerful outside states, normally such lands carrying strategically important locations and resources. A variety of examples of such regions exist, but in contemporary times an influence sphere of Middle America has seen relevance for a century by the United States, and the same dominance over Southeast Asia by China, Africa by Europe, and the Balkans by Russia. Brazil and Argentina have competed for influence within central South America, with the former usually winning in Bolivia and Paraguay. Such structures could be in the form of buffers or protectorates, although normally the design accords to military, political, and economic subservience. In the case of Middle America, the area in past centuries has shifted between that of a shatterbelt and of a sphere of influence,[57] and such a phenomenon would not be unusual for other spheres as well, for these realms hold strategic importance that attracts the powerful peoples that lie nearby. But inherent to spheres of influence but not to shatterbelts, these dependencies behave as rather passive actors within international politics, being reactive zones of weaker states and economies. Wars do not normally begin here, because the outside controlling hegemon will not allow an escalation out of control, the rival states blocked from exerting impact within these sequestered regions. In contrast, shatterbelts attract the potential for spread of regional and international violence because their areas are open to competition among nations at both levels of strife.

Pivotal locations of regions/states arise in certain land and maritime locations that project distant relevance, their impact reaching well beyond their central cores and onto adjacent areas. A number of geopolitical visions exhibit this concept. For one, the global northern hemispheres dominate the southern, for in the northern temperate areas reside the healthier climates and more productive landforms and thus the powerful states and empires. Their dominance extends over most of the southern regions.

From a southern perspective, the Colombian writer Julio Londoño Londoño, in his *camino del oro,* estimated diminishing influence of countries the more distant from a northern longitudinal line joining the major capitals of America, Europe, and Asia. Several other examples of northern dominance can be added as well: the pentagonal theme of Henry Kissinger, wherein the five centers of global power dominate—just North America, Western Europe, Russia, China, and Japan truly matter within the scope of vital policy goals.

Related versions of pivot include key states and pan-regions that allege this northern wealth and control in which the stronger leader-states divide the world into influence spheres of autarky. One hears complaints lodged against the permanent seats of the UN Security Council charged with conspiring to rule world politics, this threat a condominium. Various strategically placed countries, such as Brazil, Nigeria, and Egypt, perform as surrogates to the global powers in pacifying their respective regions. Finally, pan-regions form into lattitudinally designed compartments meant to certify a mercantilist and autarkic system. Another extension of marginality and not pivotal to strategic importance are independent regions, the best example being South America, distant and isolated from the northern temperate sectors. Themselves pivotal within regional diplomacy, they remain inactive players in world affairs with their geopolitics internal to their zone. Lesser so, sub-Saharan Africa, South and Southeast Asia, the Middle East, and Australia and New Zealand characterize semi-independent areas because their lands hold some chance for being shatterbelts and spheres of influence of the northern power brokers.

Back for a moment to contemporary South America within its independent classification, for the continent is buffered from North America by Middle America,[58] and from Africa and Asia by the wide Pacific and Atlantic oceans. Sometimes claiming world status but checkmated by Spanish American encirclement, with Argentina, Peru, and Venezuela heading checkerboard resistance and with tepid US support, Brazil now leads continental integration. But the giant republic still exerts little impact upon northern affairs despite its ranking among the larger global economies. The geopolitical factors of distance weakening and peripheral isolation re-enforce these tendencies. In the author's studies of Latin America's geopolitics,[59] he seldom ran across published references to Mackinder's heartland, Spykman's rimlands, or Cold War containment. Nor have shatterbelts entered the region since colonial times or US military interventions so notorious to Middle America. One can examine South America as a purely closed system of classical concepts-theories, buffer states, checkerboards, organic frontiers, space mastery, for instance.

Within these pivotal-country examples, the balancer state can attach in which a nation positioned strategically beyond or within a region can drive an impact because of its unique spatial location. For centuries, the English traditionally played this role of leveraging balancer adjacent the Continent. Although aloof but still able to manipulate, its offshore balances enhanced its diplomacy and security with selective interventions beyond its shores and onto neighboring coalitions.

Two pertinent examples pertain to this balancer-state concept, although a variety of historical examples could be added as well. The two-ocean position of the United States helps to maintain its global hegemony by locating its naval forces to advantage at either extreme of Eurasia. North America can play off China against Japan, Russia and India in East Asia, and can likewise balance its NATO allies against Russia.[60]

This American paramountcy extends global stability beyond the "unipolar moment," because the United States continues to open the sea lanes to the commerce of all nations, protects states' access to raw materials and markets, and contains any country that might want to extend its sovereignty at the expense of neighbors. The American advantage, an encirclement of Eurasia, would make it difficult for any of the remaining Great Powers to alter this balancing, so long as the United States possesses the strength and the will to enforce its favorable leverage.

Paraguay presents a second example of a weaker state balancing within a framework of opposing larger countries, its pivotal position a flanking of Brazil and Argentina. The republic's foreign policies have alternated between that of balancer and of bandwagoning, the former of not taking sides and the latter of siding with one, normally Brazil, against the other.[61] Such a central location in all likelihood helped keep Paraguay independent. It gained the country some profit in the construction of the hydroelectric facility at Itaipú, although the nation lost substantial territory in the Triple-Alliance war of the 1860s when its policies failed to achieve its security.

Offshore balancing,[62] mentioned often above, rates as a separate theory because it suggests an evolving "grand strategy" for North America, placing its emphasis upon a maritime strength toward creating favorable Eurasian rimland balances. Layne outlined his suggestions for the United States thus: (1) retrench its global commitments by reducing involvements in core regions that may protect Japan's and Germany's defenses but that do not favor American interests; (2) accept a structural shift from the current unipolarity to a multipolarity by allowing the rise of new global players including China; (3) replace current interdependent trade and investment policies among its allies for more profitable neomercantile approaches that will focus instead upon domestic problems such as public debt, balance-of-payments deficits, and the rest of our growing internal concerns; and (4) rely upon the US Navy to assist toward an offshoring balancing favorable to containing an expansionist China or Russia or some other threat. This strategy, in transition from an earlier preponderance,[63] may prolong US global hegemony because of its maritime advantages.

A *key-nation concept* presents a design by strategic nations to stabilize by proxy regions of their interest, not by themselves intervening into such areas but by enlisting and supporting resident surrogate-states or key-nation allies to do their regional bidding of control. The approach normally would happen according to an alliance strategy where the interests are parallel for both outsider and regional countries toward stabilizing the pertinent area. The key-country examples vary over time, but from the US perspective, Egypt and Turkey in the Middle East, Brazil in South America, and Kenya and Nigeria in East and West Africa, respectively, would account for some of these pivotal-location examples.

The key countries would intervene within their influence spheres to maintain order and subservience to the advantage of both themselves and their

Great Power sponsors. This was a charge made by Carlos Mutto against Brazil as a US surrogate, alleging that:

> Brazil is on the march everywhere: in the Amazon, pushing Venezuela, seeking friendship with Colombia, building roads to Peru, squeezing Bolivia and Paraguay and threatening Uruguay. Yet Brazil's economic growth is contingent on good relations with her smaller neighbors.[64]

Mutto went on to write: "An imperialist Brazil has figured in the international politics of the Americas for some time. . . . Henry Kissinger advocates the formation of regional leader-nations to help Washington control certain strategic areas." An instance of Brazil threatening intervention against revolutionaries in Uruguay and Chile would solidify cooperation between Brasilia and Washington, Brazil the key nation surrogate or *sepoyan* in the service both of itself and of the northern hegemon.

Buffer states perform as smaller and weaker countries positioned near and between larger neighbors, their purpose to cushion and absorb possible strife within their regions. An appropriate example figures as the four buffer countries of South America,[65] Ecuador, Bolivia, Paraguay, and Uruguay, whose territories have been much affected by warfare and dismemberment because of their central locations. Despite suffering losses, these buffer configurations contribute to stabilizing continental politics not only by separating the major checkerboard countries (Brazil, Argentina, Chile, and Peru), thus limiting their escalatory potential, but also by providing battle grounds for fighting wars and for transferring conquered lands to the aggrandizing appetites of the larger competitors.

A *corridor of conflict* has risen from the central positions of the four South American buffers, a zone extending from the continent's northwest to its southeast. With the exception of the recent Falklands/Malvinas war, that was not internal to the continent but happened in the South Atlantic against Great Britain; all five historical wars fought among the South American states came within this corridor, resulting in a Polandization or fragmenting because of territorial losses among the buffers.[66] These transfers of land, again, helped stabilize the geopolitics of South America, lessening the chances of conflict spread from the competing checkerboard alignments.

One may look upon Middle America as a regional buffer separating the South American from the North American sector.[67] Never has the United States openly intervened militarily against indigenous forces in South America. The

North American preoccupation has been to prevent a shatterbelt from arising along its southern border, in the Caribbean, and, as important, in Mexico. The resulting South American isolation has prevented shatterbelts within its domain. The rugged topography and distances between the coastal populations helped create a Spanish encirclement of the Portuguese and likewise encouraged the checkerboard patterns that predominate, buffering Brazil from consolidating its alleged pursuit of hegemony over the continent.

The United States extended its imperial frontiers westward with little resistance, but that thrust immediately before and after independence was halted temporarily by several shatterbelts of European states supporting Native American tribes in Florida and in the Ohio Valley and Great Lakes opposing the English-American advance.[68] These evaporated once Napoleon Bonaparte's aggressions in Europe drew his opponents away from America and their military support of Indian allies. Later, Great Britain attempted buffering against US expansion in Louisiana, Texas, Panama, and the American Northwest.

A thesis running counter to buffer states was composed by Zbigniew Brzezinski, that of bridge-countries. These entities encourage entry into regions and continents by outside nations in the interests of finance, resources, and security. In suggesting friendly relations with Japan and the countries of Western Europe, he urged North American attentiveness in maintaining such allied contacts: "Europe is America's essential geopolitical bridgehead on the Eurasian continent." Further, he asserted:

> North America succeeded in entrenching itself on both the extreme western and extreme eastern shores of the Great Eurasian continent. The defense of these continental bridgeheads (epitomized on the western "front" by the Berlin blockade and on the eastern by the Korean War) was thus the first strategic test of what came to be known as the Cold War.[69]

Saul Cohen offered a variation of bridge-countries in his gateway-states and regions:

> Gateway states play a novel role in linking different parts of the world by facilitating the exchange of peoples, goods, and ideas . . . . The characteristics of Gateway states vary in detail, but not in the overall context of their strategic economic locations or in the adaptability of their inhabitants to economic opportunities. They are distinct politically and culturally and may often have separate languages or religions, as well as relatively high degrees of education and favorable access to external areas by land or sea.[70]

These states, according to Cohen, served as financial centers and were dependent upon trade and importing raw materials that would convert into finished products. Contemporary examples include Hong Kong, Singapore, Finland, and the Bahamas.

Lintel countries bring a further dimension to the buffer states concept, countries not only partitioning larger neighboring states but likewise stabilizing the immediate region in doing so.[71] In its lintel configuration between Brazil and Argentina, Paraguay balances or bandwagons the two neighbors, its traditional strategy as a brace or barrier to protect against its own absorption. This depiction creates a regional stability in which Paraguay's independence is solidified because neither Brazil nor Argentina could absorb the lintel republic without its rival's opposition, giving some amount of balance and permanence within the region and continent.

The *Great Game* concept should be included within this section because its example expands upon several of the terms already mentioned. The Great Game idea first arose in the nineteenth-century rivalry for Afghanistan and to a lesser extent for Tibet and surrounding areas between the interests of imperial Russia and Great Britain. Some skepticism exists regarding the actual seriousness of the English-Russian competition,[72] but nonetheless the spatial image has re-emerged today in reference to international competition for Central Asia and its petroleum.

Zbigniew Brzezinski's *The Grand Chessboard: American Primacy in Its Geostrategic Imperatives* has popularized the "Great Game" term in the contemporary media. Such a rivalry provides good examples of buffer states and of shatterbelts within the geopolitical lexicon. Nick Megoran revisited Mackinder's "pivot," but he shifted its entry space to Uzbekistan, that country replacing Eastern Europe as the strategic approach for control of the heartland, with the lands of Central Asia becoming likely candidates for new shatterbelts.[73] US Admiral Alfred Mahan found a similar area in Central Asia,[74] which he labeled the "Debated and Debatable Middle Strip," visualizing confrontation between land-power Russia and the western imperial sea-power nations. So, we can see geopolitical relevance here, too, with conditions arising for a variety of theory applications.

Choke points refer to territorial and maritime straits, passes, channels, and canals that hold significant pivotal importance, their positions exerting impact over an extended land and sea territory or region. Examples include the Straits of Malacca, the Beagle Channel, and the Suez and Panama canals. Mountain passes, highway intersections and rail systems, river estuaries and watersheds all contain spatial importance as well.

In the case of the United States, its areas of vital interest might encompass the estuary at New Orleans that controls the Mississippi watershed, associated rivers that originate within the heartland of North America, the Great Lakes exhibiting similar northern routes to the continent's center, Middle America with particular focus upon the Caribbean passageways and the Monroe Doctrine, the stability of Mexico and the Panama Isthmus, and the Hawaiian and Alaskan peninsulas. But one could agree with Nicholas Spykman, who argued that none of these places provided complete protection for North America, a fortress America perimeter of defense not able to withstand a hostile Eurasian encirclement. Instead, the United States must intervene well beyond American waters and onto the rimlands of Europe, the Middle East, and East Asia for its defense, and this projection is well understood within the Pentagon's security establishment along the lines of the Mackinder/Spykman format.

The Panama Canal offers another example in this geopolitical sketch, although the isthmus has lost much of its former strategic importance. The United States has not only returned ownership of the canal to the Panamanians, it also has neglected funding for expansion of the waterway to serve larger vessels. Probably a major reason for this lack of interest is North America's maritime dominance over both of its surrounding oceans; hence, little need currently arises to defend against any reappearance of a Middle American shatterbelt or in resuming control of a transisthmus canal.

3. Borders and Frontiers

As another theme of the classical writers, borders combine political and geographic aspects of space, the essence of our topic. A good example of this spatial linkage presents as sovereignty, of national autonomy or independence against interference by outsiders within a state's political boundaries, this concept relating both to political geography and to geopolitics. Still, one could observe a weakening of nations' sovereignty in the wake of expanded trade, travel, new technologies of communication, and growth of international law and organizations. With this decline of sovereignties, a parallel growth of international laws and organizations contrasts with the realists' dread of international anarchy.

Land-locked countries will initiate this section, those continentally interior nations without seacoasts or good access to oceans. Such places suffer isolation, less economic and political development, and weaker international recognition than would be the due of coastal ecumenes. In the case of Paraguay, access to the outside depends upon the La Plata River for trade and upon an overland-transit agreement with Brazil. Bolivia's loss of its sea-front, detached from defeat in war, remains a stress in its relationship with Peru and Chile, and recovery of this territory represents a dominant factor within its foreign policy.[75] Russia's quest for an ocean-outlet portrays a good example of a major country suffering this dependency. Many attribute its historical imperial ambitions tied to a desire to attain a warm-water ocean port, a quest warned against by Mackinder and others throughout the decades of the twentieth century.

A variation of the land-locked theme is the assertion that sea power normally translates to expanded national power and wealth and to greater global impact, as contended by Admiral Mahan.[76] His maritime-power thesis runs counter to Mackinder's heartland theory, one giving land-power states within the center of Eurasia the nod for such strategic pivot. The balance between this sea power versus land power debate seems best resolved by Spykman's rimland, which refines these contrasts to include both sea and land orientations within his middle location as a place for major international happenings. Meinig developed this dichotomy further by his "extrainsular" and "intrainsular" depictions of rimland states with alternating maritime or continental orientations depending upon security conditions and the policy whims of statespersons.[77]

Natural borders are commonly featured as desirable within traditional geopolitics, frontiers following rivers, oceans, mountains, and deserts that denote clear march frontiers, although river watersheds often tend to unify as well as to divide regions. The clarity of natural demarcations attracts fewer territorial disputes among neighbors and brings more regional stability.

In South America, many borders lack clarity, but these tend not to conflict because they happen in remote, largely uninhabited and poorly surveyed areas. These do revert to controversy when valued resources are discovered near them—for example, petroleum in the Marañón Valley. The proposition of *uti possidetis juris*, originating during ancient Roman times, attempts with some success to retaining the colonial bounds as originally laid out. General Londoño Londoño posited his triple-points thesis,[78] where international disputes are more likely to arise when three different frontiers overlap, but his thesis failed after statistical scrutiny.[79]

Another version of natural frontiers rests with *equilibrium borders,* where the eventual frontiers come naturally to rest between the outer domains of neighboring states or empires, the limits on either side extending to the farthest points their natural power can take them amid the resistance of neighbors.[80] Logically, a majority of frontiers fit this example in such situations; yet because these are dependent on relative power among countries and on the rise-and-fall cycles of empires, they can be susceptible to instability, disputes, and conflicts.

Organic borders arose early on within the writings of the German and Scandinavian schools of classical geopolitics, led by Rudolf Kjellén.[81] Their inspiration would become influential as well among the South American writers to the present day. Nations resemble human organisms by following our own familiar life cycles: being born and growing into adolescence and maturity, then succumbing to older age and finally to death. Countries' borders would expand and contract similarly to such life cycles, widening in territory as reflective of national strength and diminishing reflective of weakness. Later on in the fascist revision (and distortion) of this concept, "younger" countries represented the more vibrant states, possessing the ability and the right to extend their frontiers onto the lands of "older" and weaker countries that did not deserve such spaces. Common sketches of "dead" and "alive" frontiers received their inspiration from this format.

As was explored in Chapter 3, this organic cycling of nations bred into the notorious concept of lebensraum promoted by National Socialists, who tainted the reputation of classical geopolitics when they based legitimacy for territorial expansion under this organic label. A similar notation, less pejorative, was "manifest destiny," or the divinely sanctioned spread of ownership of lands across a sparsely populated continent. The expansion of nineteenth-century North America from Atlantic to Pacific offers an example, but this concept can attach as well to Portuguese-Brazilian expansionism toward the South American Pacific coastlands.

The premise that borders cause wars—or the more frontiers, the more international conflict—can be tested with statistical method for certain world regions. Richardson found a significant correlation applicable globally and in the context of South America;[82] the author located this association among the ten South American republics,[83] where a simple Spearman rho score amounted to a significant statistic. Brazil and Peru suffered the most war involvements in possessing relatively more international frontiers, whereas Venezuela and Chile, the more isolated republics with fewer exposed borders, experienced the least amount of strife. Similar to other spatial variables, the more-borders/more-wars thesis rates as rather obvious because it would seem that nearness of states and their exposed frontiers would make conflict more available. Nonetheless, statistics lends to a wider substantiation.

Evidence shows that the more populated frontiers experience more strife and likewise the busier trade across such boundaries,[84] a reflection of the close-ness/distance dichotomy.[85] In a comprehensive literature review by Hensel,[86] with an expansive quantitative assortment of variables taken from the Cor-relates of War (COW), several configurations passed statistical testing for as-sociation: "[F]or more severe forms of conflict, at least 80 percent of fatal dis-putes and wars [began between 1816 and 2001] were fought between states that shared a land or sea border." Finally, as argued by Stephen Kocs: "[His] data indicate that given contiguity [bordering states], war initiation depends heav-ily on the presence or absence of a never-resolved territorial dispute. War was about 40 *times* more likely to break out between contiguous states if they were involved in a never-resolved territorial dispute than if they were not."[87]

Advocating the annexation of territories for uniting peoples of common ethnicity or of past nationality into new states or into adjacent states, the facet of irredentism reveals another geopolitical expression. Since most countries' borders have redrawn over time, some states affirm irredentist claims toward their neighbors. Examples are many in recent history—for one, Germany's *An-schluss* of Austria and absorption of the Sudetenland from Czechoslovakia in 1938. Additionally, Argentina's quest for the Falkland/Malvinas Islands; Bolivia's drive for its lost Pacific ocean front; Mexico's "lost" northern territories; Kurd-ish urges for a homeland; mainland China's determination to annex Taiwan and parts of the South China Sea; India and Pakistan vying for Kashmir; and Ireland's demand for its whole island.

Two current examples of irredentism bring particular interest, the Aztlan and the Zionist claims. Both argue a historical return of their peoples to a for-mer homeland, providing some legitimacy to current resettlement claims and borderlands. The myth of Aztlan encompasses the alleged ancient lands of the Aztec settlers, who once lived in what today would be the state of Arizona. This tribe later would move, or was forced to move, southward to found its great empire in Central Mexico. Once conquered by Cortez and his Indian allies, the Aztec nation later would take up Spanish and Mexican land grants in its northern provinces, soon to be controlled by the United States. The peoples' supposed return to their former homeland has been utilized to bolster Chicano or Mexican-American legitimacy to land claims and civil rights under the Treaty of Guadalupe Hidalgo of 1848. Unfortunately, one could well doubt the historical reliability of that epic, because no evidence exists for an original Arizona homeland (rather, it likely was located in present-day Mexico itself) and because not the Aztecs but the anti-Aztec peoples migrated northward later on. But the Aztlan myth holds the coloration of irredentism, nonetheless.

Contemporary Zionism fits an irredentist label, of a political movement of self-determination that rests upon aspiration for a Jewish national homeland. This objective is expressed in the Israeli Declaration of Independence:

> The Land of Israel was the birthplace of the Jewish people. Here their spiritual, religious and political identity was shaped. Here they first attained to statehood, created cultural values of national and universal significance and gave to the world the eternal Book of Books. After being forcibly exiled from their land, the people kept faith with it throughout their Dispersion and never ceased to pray and hope for their return to it and for the restoration in it of their political freedom. Impelled by this historic and traditional attachment, Jews strove in every successive generation to re-establish themselves in their ancient homeland. In recent decades they returned in their masses.

This Exodus but later return provided legitimacy to the creating of the Israeli state, although the original borders were vague and are still disputed.

The *contagion or diffusion* phenomenon offers a related thesis to conflict and to national borders, of the spread of riots, rebellion, democracy, military dictatorships, and other such features via a geographic "demonstration effect" across international bounds. Govea and West studied the possibility of riot contagion in thirteen countries of Latin America for the years 1949 to 1963 by gathering data on such domestic disturbances from the *Hispanic American Report*.[88] Enlisting the "contagious Poisson" assumption, that an action by one person or country correspondingly changes the actions by another person or country, these authors utilized a simple t-test of frequency distributions. The results found just four countries showing "chronically" high Poisson figures, with two others revealing "mixed" diffusion impact and the remainder, none. Interestingly, the contagion-impacted countries displayed contrasting national attributes from those who did not encounter diffusion, noting that "rioting may spread due to highly specific and situational factors" and not to common backgrounds.[89]

A further example of contagion was found in Central Africa for the years 1960 to 1972, where Huff and Lutz located a country-to-country transmission of political unrest seen in military coups d'état. These authors discovered statistical significance in two spatial factors: proximity to neighbors and centrality within the region:[90]

> The countries that have experienced coups d'état tend to be in closer proximity to one another, and spread effects are visible about those countries having the initial coups d'état.... Another geographic feature of this diffusion process is the high correlation between the number of coups d'état per country and *centrality*.... This evidence suggests that the more centrally located a country, the greater the likelihood that it would have experienced a coup d'état at some point during the thirteenth year period.

One could add the recent Middle Eastern "democratic spring" of rioting and regime transfers to these examples, too.

Next, we might hesitate entering the ideological realm of *the falling dominoes concept,* the politically charged description of country-to-country diffusion that reveals, first, the existence and threat of socialism in one country, then its "contamination" extending into neighboring states reflective of their apparent weaknesses of succumbing or falling to communism. But the final outcome for all of these victim states is a regional collapse, all becoming communist unless the United States enters to reverse the trend. This may have been the thinking of US strategists during the Vietnam involvement, but probably the checkerboard configuration might have posed a more suitable interpretation.

O'Sullivan suggests replacing the dominoes concept with a modified linkage theory, a "network connecting all the world's trouble spots to the Soviet Union and the USA."[91] He proposed erecting a field-theory structure of other "fields of influence, rather than the drastic clink of a [one-dimensional] domino," these being relative distances and the actual existence of physical borders, comparative population levels, national policy objectives of participants, the historical and cultural rivalries of the players, among other describers. Here, O'Sullivan visualizes "nations as nodes of a more fully connected network of economic and political links weighted in terms of the ease of communication and influence between states." For instance, in metropolitan Europe, the vital connector runs astride trade lines more than nationalist divisors. The eastern American coastline extends as a unified urban sprawl, with state boundaries less noticed than traffic communications. What attracts one to these distinctions is O'Sullivan's attempt to refine and later apply traditional geopolitical concepts—likewise the ambition of the present book.

Nonetheless, it still might profit to retain the original falling-dominoes thesis within this book's lexicon for several reasons: (1) similar to Mackinder's heartlands, the recognition here also falls upon accepted policy, particularly during the Reagan presidency. It remains fixed within the American foreign-affairs vocabulary. And (2) the socialist attachment could easily shift to less ideological traits more attune to contagion, such as dictatorship, recessions, and so forth.

An additional border-related concept requires some mention before concluding this part on neighboring states' borders and contagion. We might surely assume, first, the possibility of the actual disappearance of some national frontiers, certainly an occurrence throughout history. While some contemporary states are facing territorial fragmentation, the author could visualize amalgamation of future lands into larger national compartments as well. One might conclude that the diminution of national sovereignty could happen with globalization or with international capitalism composing a market and investment interdependency, accompanied by the amalgamation of peoples, information, and cultures across frontiers. Sovereignty, or the spatial autonomy of governments within their territories, appears to be diminishing because of a blurring of frontiers with expanded trade, investment, and travel across such bounds.

This border-weakening dynamic may be happening more directly with functional economic and political integration, the erasure of national tariffs in order to broaden regional markets by eliminating such trade restraints and by coordinating regional policies that have succeeded for the European Economic Community, and more distantly for some joining together of the American states within a unified free-trade area. Integration as a spatial concept has become a central theme of contemporary South American geopolitics,[92] seen in the Mercado Comun del Sur or MERCOSUR, which has experienced modest success and has been much written about by the leading scholars who author articles in the Uruguayan integrationist journal, GEOSUR.

One common vision of globalization attaches adjacent countries and markets into broader contacts, created by an advancement of communications such that spaces gradually diminish because of the new electronic technologies. Information transfers instantaneously across national frontiers, business and government leaders travel electronically and not physically, and media sources all extend their tentacles into even the remotest of news events. This phenomenon figures to diminish national sovereignties along with dimming the visibility of their frontiers.

4. Spaces

More within the realm of the early German scholarship of Friedrich Ratzel and others of his generation than of the English or North American traditions, space or an expanse of territory held an organic or dynamic feature as derived both from scientific materialism, the domination of mankind by certain natural laws, and from environmental determinism, a strong impact from one's environment affecting one's behavior.[93] These perspectives combined led to a variety of classical concepts, some later distorted and made ideological by National Socialism.

Certain of the earlier organic features still hold relevance as geopolitical labels from which we may yet gain. Such concepts as will be displayed below are commonly touted within South American geopolitics, where isolated frontiers and uninhabited lands continue to be viewed as important. And in US foreign policy, we have seen debate concerning how expansive its global interests should be, whether a "new isolationism" of offshore retrenchment or of a wider global "preponderance," an active presence within Eurasia including intervening within the central Muslim oil-producing states. We appear to continue seeing the space element in foreign-affairs discussions, but we tend to ignore its continuing contemporary importance.

Perhaps the most significant feature of space consciousness, or the relevance of territorial expanse as a gain in national security, was the original ideal of leaders possessing clear spatial or geopolitical instincts for territorial expansion and thus for protection. Organically, the advocates alleged, countries expand or contract in land and in population, a sign of success toward state security within the vision of its leadership. Those holding to an expansive consciousness visualized the need for territory and resources that would augment wealth, security, power, and influence. Because the international environment suffered continual threats, countries failing in this consciousness faced likely extinction. Awareness, on the other hand, meant survival and greatness, and this path was advocated by the early geopolitical writers.

The spatial themes were first conceptualized by Karl Ritter and Friedrich Ratzel during the final decades of the nineteenth century, both of whom saw a world of steadily diminishing resources and lands,[94] a common viewpoint at the time, including that of Mackinder. Hence, national struggles for lands to colonize would become commonplace within the international system, and those states winning new lands would prove their legitimacy as vibrant and "youthful" sovereignties. These natural "laws" became premised on the "fit-test-survive" formula—the stronger expand in size while the weaker will be absorbed by others. Such a survival thesis became "scientifically" legitimized under the label of classical geopolitics.

Interestingly, despite criticisms alleged by North American scholars disfavoring geopolitics and particularly the organic tradition, one can observe this same feature in both US policies and scholarship. The American Manifest Destiny offers a good example of the former. And within certain areas of recent realist literature, this trait also appears. For instance, Christopher Layne and his colleagues came close to such determinism in their descriptions of why a unipolar power-balance will not persist. Please follow this realist premise brought forth by Layne:

> In an anarchic, self-help system, states must always be concerned that others will use increased relative capabilities against them. By enhancing their own relative capabilities or diminishing those of an adversary, states get a double payoff: greater security and a wider range of strategic options. The reverse is true for states that remain indifferent to relative power relationships.[95]

Within this "structurally determined" system of balancing, the words "fated," "inevitability," "virtually driven," and like expressions of the contemporary commentators reveal close similarity to the former classical German organic determination of states' natural and certain growth and decline.

From the German *Geopolitik* came a variety of other spatial "laws" (or, in our reference, "theories"), including the notion of *raum*, or territory, and *lage*, or location, the terms together showing that the policies of a state should pursue a positional nature that would bring ultimate success in growing national wealth and security. Similarly, the space mastery thesis argues that states should populate and develop their peripheral hinterlands so as to prevent absorption of such lands by aggressive neighbors. The law of valuable areas follows, that states naturally gravitate to competition for uninhabited lands that emit wealth and strategic advantage.[96] In this latter case, Peru and Brazil provide prime examples, both aggressively craving such interior South American spaces from buffer-state neighbors.

Once again, our study could salvage certain early German perspectives relative to the organic tendencies of geopolitics. "Organic" shows a dynamic quality, a common criticism of geopolitics, and it seems obvious that the international environment can best be interpreted as exhibiting constant change and rebalancing in frontiers, communication technologies, new energy sources, and the like. Contemporary China rising and the Soviet Union falling both reflect the organic quality. Whether or not the United States will continue as global hegemon within the current strategic power balance, or compete effectively within the new challenges of the still-young twenty-first century, offers another question within the organic of classical geopolitics. Stated once more relative to change, the dynamism in geopolitics comes in the organic nature of foreign-policy events and not in our spatial theories themselves, which tend not to change.

A variation of the space mastery and consciousness propositions would be found in Manifest Destiny, as has been featured in both North and South America and elsewhere. The term is well known to the North American who enlisted it to encourage and justify the expansion westward to occupy North American lands from Atlantic to Pacific coasts. Both a belief and nearly a specific policy, the concept parallels a variety of other advocacies, including the spread of democracy and Western civilization and religion, as well as of the annexing of Texas, California, and Oregon at the expense of our neighbors.

Likewise, Brazil drew upon a similar theme to extending its sovereignty westward, although this ambition lacked success for reason of Spanish encirclement on the Pacific littoral and of the imposing topography of impenetrable Andes heights and Amazon jungles. Yet, development and colonization of sparsely populated hinterlands and frontiers pose a common theme in South American geopolitics—for instance, the law of valuable territories and the organic theories are popular within the Southern Cone's geopolitical literature.

Next, two opposing spatial concepts deserve description, earth dependence and the contrasting emancipation theory.[97] For the former attribute, mankind is essentially limited by the restraints of nature, with few exceptions, and thus he is not able to escape the fetters of his environment, being largely "nature limited." A rather static and conservative approach, this idea shows a determinist stance in that such enslavement is long term—mankind cannot be freed of shackles by his own devices or by modern technology. Escape is simply not possible, and we must accept the dictates of nature and adopt ourselves to them.

The parallel to this captivity, emancipation, provides a more optimistic prediction of the capacity for human freedom to succeed through various means of release from the constraints of this predicament, for reasons of science and human evolution. Mankind becomes "nature directed" such that he is able to remove many of nature's constraining bonds. This conclusion of human optimism answers a criticism voiced against classical geopolitics, not only that our study is trapped in determinism but also that it ignores the advances of modern science and technology.

Two further portrayals of space mastery follow because both alternatives seem to hold some wisdom, for one must follow the dictates of our natural surroundings, natural catastrophes, resources depletion, earthquakes, global warming, plus disruptive mountains and deserts. Nonetheless, some of these difficulties could be resolved by human and social engineering, and we need encouragements and financing devoted to possible solutions to global warming, energy scarcities, and other such crises. So, again in our analyses of this current chapter, we want exposure to these suitable traditional concepts/theories, and then to apply them if we can where they might lend a deeper understanding to our surroundings. That offers the value of theory, and in our case, of the precepts of classical geopolitics.

Autarky, or national self-containment or self-sufficiency in the economic sense, sets also within the classical geopolitical literature. In this regard, Derwent Whittlesey states:

> Thus the state will be in economic balance and independent of the products of foreign parts of the World. . . . Either such nations would have to fight eternally, or they would have to isolate themselves within their frontiers and reduce their living to the measure of their internal productivity.[98]

Nonetheless, Whittlesey stood against a strategy of isolation, predicting possible war outcomes because such isolation would prove not productive and thus nations will renew conflict, but even more forcefully over attaining necessary scarce resources. We also see this concept tucked within pan-regions, where the northern rulers exploit southern colonies for markets and industrial commodities. Since our globe's minerals, waters, and other riches are not evenly distributed, some states enjoy ample natural rewards while others wane in comparison. It is assumed that the basic advantage of trade, of states' comparative advantages, will arrive as countries seek to distribute these ill-allocated resources more equally by exchanging one's abundance for another's scarcity.

Hans Mouritzen authored a similar concept in his action space, or "the ability [of states] to remain unaffected by other [state] actors." By distance, power, or other factors that might relate to autonomy, a country may enjoy the luxury of adapting or rejecting a "past geopolitical" experience in preference for a "present geopolitical" reality. The Cold War competition between Russia and North America, for instance, reduced this action space for dependent nations restrained by strategic competition; yet once the Cold War rivalry ended, the "deterritorialization" reflecting the previous threat reverted back to a "reterritorialization" of traditional or past territorial geopolitics.

For instance:

> Swedish neutrality has been armed and politically active during the Cold War, as it performed a semi-balancing of the Soviet Union . . . . With the melting down of European bipolarity, however, circumstances changed drastically. Neutrality was no longer meaningful, since there was only one remaining European power pole . . . . Sweden could compensate by joining the European Union, the "New Europe," and sharing in its growing influence.[99]

The Baltic countries joining NATO, and Poland more in tune with Britain and the United States than with the EU, offer additional examples.

The premise that distance weakens, or the *loss-of-strength-gradient*, holds that as the extent of spatial contact widens, the impact of a nation's strength diminishes. In a number of instances, one could incorporate this association within Mackinder's heartland thesis, where distance from maritime power renders the Eurasian land core more security. Or in the similar assertion, that North American safety rests not in a fortress America but in its isolation from Eurasia and in its ability to select and maintain alliances and secure bases with the continent's major rimland states, these points also within the Mackinder mold.

Albert Wohlstetter refuted this distance-weakens principle, arguing that new technologies of weapons and communications have negated this belief.[100] He argued that "the capacity for long-distance lift of the major powers far exceeds that for short-distance lift inside the theatre . . . . Adding several thousand miles to the distance at which remote wars are fought increases the total cost of fighting by only a very tiny percentage." Wohlstetter appears correct in his estimate of technologies; yet, the traditional concept holds to some extent as well. The United States could fight a war in Nigeria with the same relative expense as a war in Nicaragua: the costs of the different distances would equate. But that said, the United States possesses stronger police interests in the latter than in the former, such that closeness would count more than a place more distant and on another continent of less concern.

As discussed elsewhere in this volume, the earth's northern regions possess greater natural wealth than the southern regions, the cause being the former's advantage of having a better ratio of temperate lands over ocean waters. This advantage translates to a greater wealth in capital and technology, meaning for the most part the hegemony of the northern zones of North America, Europe, and China. The *camino del oro* and pentagonal concepts show this southern dependency as well as its diminished presence within global affairs. It would be difficult with this difference in global wealth to visualize a southern-world challenge to the continued domination of the north.

A contrast to these locations of advantage and disadvantage, based upon the distance premise, comes in the equatorial paradox, as associated with climatic or environmental determinism. Here, space away from the equator translates to higher levels of economic development, a 70 percent probability predicated upon the distance-from-the-equator factor. In "stimulus-response" terminology, tropical warmth creates apathetic life-styles, whereas middle latitudes enjoy weather variability, and these stimulations will lead, it is argued, to capitalistic work ethic, less disease, and higher food production, among other factors, and thus to higher accumulations of capital, technology, development, and prosperity.

This author related UN General Assembly voting on United Nations peacekeeping to the Latin American states during the 1950s and into the 1960s.[101] Strongest among his independent variables was "distance from the United States," measured according to a stepwise regression in which the distance variable stood well over the other nine variables in statistical relevance, scoring a rho of .76, or accounting for 76 percent of variance. Hence, the further the Latin Americans distanced from the United States, the more favor they gave to UN peacekeeping. In contrast, the closer nations were in opposition to such interventions, a possible showing against aggressions from North America.

Almost universally within the literature, the sea power/land power dichotomy has characterized countries, a comparison assisting in comparing the ancient Peloponnesian war to contemporary South American diplomacy—Athens led its alliance in sea power, Sparta commanded its allies in land power, and the South American republics were devoid of navies almost completely. In each case, the differing checkerboard structures held patterns that were distinguished by the two orientations. More on these comparisons in the coming chapter.

Theorists contend over which orientation holds advantage, whether a country's proper direction should be toward sea or land. Land-power proponents argue that navies require bases, and these can be intercepted from a central place. The middle areas of continents enjoy security via distance, topography, and ability to pivot onto the weaker coastal enclaves. Maritime countries, it is alleged, gain advantage in their mobility along the rimlands and their greater access to mineral, energy, and food wealth in outer marginal and distant territories. Some indication might show that coastal states tend toward democracy.[102]

Mackinder and Spykman differed on this equation, the former trusting the continents, the latter both lands and seas. Perhaps a majority might side with naval realms.[103] As seen in Modelski's "hegemonic cycles," all of his historical hegemons were sea oriented, each gaining ascendancy from superior navigation and ship technologies that led to rewards in lands and trade. The United States, a two-ocean maritime nation, possesses the ability to balance larger states on either extreme of Eurasia, holding a pivot toward maintaining its global paramountcy. Nonetheless, one could conclude that any advantages of sea power over land power would depend upon the time and place at hand and not upon a general rule of superiority of one over the other.

Sea lines of communication relate to sea power, these routes being vital passageways to the nations holding this orientation. Interruption by pirates or nearby strife would hamper trade and security of the maritime nations. The Straits of Malacca, the Panama Canal and the Caribbean straits that approach it from the Atlantic, the Mediterranean outlets of Gibraltar, the Bosporus, and the Suez Canal would all be good choke-point examples. On land, mountain passes and vital transit centers serve these characteristics as well. Grygiel places oceanic communications within his definition of geopolitics: "the location of natural and economic resources and the lines of communication linking them. It is a map of sorts, assigning strategic value to places."[104] One could imagine the billeting of American troops at rimland bases in Western Europe, the Persian Gulf, and Korea-Japan, all near essential sea passageways.

Demographic patterns represent a further spatial characteristic, of distributions and densities of peoples over lands and resources that exert a political impact such as under- or overpopulation upon places on earth. This concept should deserve a place by itself—for example, excessive human congestion causing disruption and possible conflict in crowded regions. Robert Kaplan predicted a likely explosion in the near future within the southern world's megacities where migrations and birthrates are contributing to rapid growth in already poor areas. Kaplan visualized that:

> [a] Eurasia of vast urban areas, overlapping missile ranges and sensational media, will be one of constantly enraged crowds, fed by rumors transported at the speed of light from one Third World megalopolis to another. . . . It is in the cities of Eurasia principally where crowd psychology will have its greatest geopolitical impact.[105]

In particular, he saw Indian, Pakistani, and Bangladesh "shatter zones" that may suffer the greatest unraveling because of overcrowding, the "worst nightmare" conditions causing failed states, massive human dislocations, crime and terrorism, and dangerous violence.

We might imagine a world in which the wealthy north tightly partitions itself off from the poverty-stricken south, made possible by its superiority in military and economic strength. This division would anticipate Kaplan's megacity nightmare, contributing to all sorts of harms noted above including failed states, piracy, pandemics, and environmental destruction. The dependency thesis reflects this growing disparity in resources and capital, and this unfortunate path may not change under the present directions now taken. The "New International Economic Order," a voluntary reversal of wealth from the rich to the poor, has received little support to date. The absence of good solutions to national and global wealth disparities could spell major disruptions to world peace.

Closed spaces bring another spatial impact observed by several classical authors including Halford Mackinder and Frederick Jackson Turner. In the waning decades of the nineteenth century, a concern was raised over the regional and global "effects of the passing of empty lands for settlement," an "overlap between geography, biology, and public debate."[106] Mackinder envisioned coming international rivalries and wars as a result, and much of his intent was to encourage a British imperial unity of focusing its wealth and power such as would secure the English race and culture. Turner described a similar land scarcity in the American West. This idea could be applied in the contemporary scenes of overpopulation, pollution and global warming, the exhaustion of sustainable resources, and other such factors within the environmental context.

Peter Slowe offered a similar slant in his law of valuable areas, mineral-rich spaces but located in isolated lands still holding sparse populations and development.[107] His example rested with the "Amazon triangle" competed for by Brazil against Peru and Ecuador. Such regions, differing from closed spaces, represented still-available areas wealthy enough for further advantage if colonized.

Immigration concludes this fourth section, the movement of peoples over spaces that impact upon local cultures as well as upon foreign policies. William Hay credits a series of migrations affecting later European geopolitics, citing such factors as "political fragmentation" in Europe leading to the eventual division between the east and west sectors, starting with the separation of ancient Greece from Rome to the several political divisions of the present day.[108] This facet prompted Halford Mackinder's heartland thesis of Asiatic hordes threatening European civilization and of the closing of the Columbian era to colonization and empire.

The Jewish and Aztlan homelands reflect immigration patterns as well. Of more recent vintage, illegal immigration throughout the world colors national and international policies and conflict, desperate workers in poorer countries seeking advantage by moving to more prosperous regions. Immigration is geopolitical because it reflects spatial, demographic, and resource aspects, these conditioning international political concerns.

Diversity, or the merging of diverse peoples in national spaces, brings some interesting perspectives, particularly for the United States, a historic "experiment" of a Great Power blending races, cultures, and religions. Contemporary events around the globe demonstrate a fractured politics reflective of this diversity, but could the reverse in North America be visualized as well? Its wealth, geography, and traditions could present a contrasting picture, one of unity and progress. If a success-in-diversity happens, these benefits might accrue: (1) proof that diversity can emerge in unity, democracy, and prosperity; (2) combining different peoples could prompt innovation and progress; and (3) America might provide a leadership in demonstrating how peoples can live together in harmony and fellowship.

5. A Variety of Other Geopolitical Concepts

A country's shape impacts upon its history and stability, affecting security, national unity, and economic viability. The rectangular configuration of the United States, tied within by internal waterways that facilitate communication, shows benefits not enjoyed by Chile, Brazil, Russia, or Canada. Circular and rectangular patterns tend to enhance unity, whereas elongated and irregular configurations disrupt the development of nations.

Fluvial laws of rivers bring advantages to states that correspond to classical geopolitics:[109] (1) Mediterranean or landlocked countries strive for an ocean outlet; (2) centripetally flowing rivers unify nations; (3) states expand to dominate entire river watersheds; (4) major river estuaries embody strategic and sometimes shatterbelt zones where larger countries compete for control; (5) states that occupy estuaries expand along adjacent seacoast lines; and (6) the direction of a river's flow reveals the regional interests of a country's foreign policy. Nonetheless, none of these generalizations could be stated as "laws," or spaces that have been tested systematically, although one could note instances where these areas may resemble historical logic.

A concept related to fluvial laws is that of *hydraulic empire* or *despotism*, conditioned by rulers' control of water systems in climates of draught. Originally drawn by Karl Wittfogel[110] and taken up by Larry Diamond,[111] the premise rests on a region's dependency for flood control and irrigation that would require maintenance over lands and waters owned or controlled by an elite class or caste. Historical examples come from ancient China and Egypt to pre-Columbian Mexico and Peru. In North America, the growing scarcity of waters has exposed interstate and intrastate conflicts. Similar scenes have risen in Africa and the Middle East. One wonders, too, with changes associated to global warming, that such systems of hydraulic competition could easily contribute to rivalries and wars in the near future.

A state's ample possession of natural and energy resources enhances security and prosperity. Adequate wealth facilitates democracy and development, whereas regions lacking riches suffer. In this latter instance, North America as well as Europe and East Asia are fortunate in having more than their share of natural wealth, and this imbalance has impacted upon national histories and power. We see these disparities in the dependency and other theses, and a solution to the growing gaps between wealth and poverty based on availability of resources has yet to be resolved.

An assortment of geopolitical scenarios arises from rivalries among nations competing for valued resources. One factor contributing to US occupation of Iraq could have stemmed from American dependency upon oil and the attractiveness of Iraq's petroleum reserves. The possible emergence of a central Asia shatterbelt may originate from the same competition for oil, with China, Russia, India, and the United States all moving toward this objective.

Other instances of resource scarcity can be seen in the growing visibility of "failed states," countries so lacking in wealth that effective governments no longer exist. From these failures come pandemics, crime and terrorism, smuggling of drugs and guns, forged currencies, and other such factors. Migrations of desperate peoples flow into the wealthier cores, creating social and demographic dislocations. A parallel transition, "rogue states" reflective of poverty, encourage radical leaders bent on threatening others with weapons of mass destruction, North Korea an example. Both instances derive from geography, the placement of countries within spaces devoid of the resources that would support healthy political regimes.

An additional step into the issue of resource deficiencies moves us to considering several worst-case scenarios: (1) of failure in finding energy sources to replace dependency upon petroleum; (2) of megacities' violence created by poverty; and (3) of the north's continued wealth amid the southern absence of hope. Other examples could easily be added. But once more, what if the plight of the south in comparison to the north cannot be resolved? Will a "new world order" evolve into a globally "gated" one, somewhat resembling pan-regions and condominiums showing a divided and dysfunctional world of poverty within pockets of wealth? One should fear this future.

Next, a premise so damaging to the classic stances, environmental determinism, presents the vision that our physical environment, rather than social and economic factors, determines history, politics, and society in general. This theme, now shunned by political geographers for the distorted and racist attachments of past authors, tainted this field of research for decades. Ellsworth Huntington deserves criticism for enlisting what others alleged to be his flawed methodology, claiming that effects of "climatic energy" controlled human actions, a direct and inevitable "stimulus-response" pattern that separated races:[112] favorable temperate climates attracted higher human accomplishments, and within these zones of North America, Western Europe, and Asia came the greatest civilizations. But Huntington attached a negative feature to his environmental equation similar to Darwin's "natural selection," that certain races gained more than others from favorable weather. The damage was done with these assertions, and political geographers to the present day will warn off their colleagues and students from such speculation.

Other anthropologists and cultural geographers of Huntington's time and since, including Ellen Churchill Semple, attempted replacing the tarnished "determinism" with the more neutral "possibilism," and they drew conclusions from more rigorous methodologies than had Huntington done. Among those could be listed Thomas Griffith Taylor and Jared Diamond. Today it is widely claimed that environment may condition humans' and states' behavior, but a variety of other factors should be examined as well. States Erhard Rostlund: "Environmentalism was not disproved, only disapproved."[113] Further, this author suggested that the disapproval derived from faulty assumptions and methodologies and not from connections between man/state and their natural environments that could be researched properly and objectively. So both political geographers and geopolitical enthusiasts may, with some growing confidence, continue their studies of attempting to associate one's environment with one's behavior, albeit, with care and elevated from the individual to the state.

These debates of political geography accrue to our classical geopolitics, where critics see studies of spatial connection attached to claims of determinism and racism. Like political geographers, most geopolitics adherents favor the classical version of environmental possibilism, the likelihood that a nation's placement impacting upon its actions and policies, but not exclusively.

With the above debate between determinism and possibilism recognized, we extend this discussion further by offering a related topic, of certain catastrophic environmental events in nature that could directly impact upon a country's political behavior, this presenting a further tie between human events and our surroundings. Several thoughts can be drawn in these respects:

Earthquakes, tsunamis, and volcanoes: Not only do these disruptions create economic havoc, they expose political liabilities of elites' governance as well. For instance, the Nicaraguan earthquake of 1972 helped end the Somoza Dynasty when government inefficiency and corruption became exposed. Likewise, Mexico's 1985 quake revealed neglect, as did the Japanese tsunami of 2011. One can see this factor, also, in the Haitian disaster of 2010.

Global warming: Evidence shows polar icecaps melting at rapid paces, bringing rising sea levels to flood low-lying but populated Asian coastal areas, forcing migrations inland to already overpopulated megacities. Volatile weather patterns—droughts, tornadoes, floods—tend to accompany this warming, along with possible political disruptions.

Polluted oceans: Pollutions are depleting marine food and oxygen supplies, reducing nutrition and health of peoples inhabiting coast zones. Extensive "dead zones" appear expanding in size, and few international efforts seem effective toward solution. Depleted seas stir conflict and prompt reckless actions among nations. On land, deforested spaces also deplete oxygen and bring soil erosion.

Pandemics: Diseases spreading from animals to humans happen around the globe, the worst of recent note after World War I of swine flu. Despite World Health Organization precautions, the likelihood of serious diseases occurring again rates high, and mass fatalities would unsettle societies and contribute to economic depression and warfare.

Scarcities of oil, water, land, and other resources: Any scarcity of resource could cause competition among peoples, and strife by the stronger against the weaker might well be predicted. Nonetheless, the reader should take care here, for Theisen, Holtermann, and Buhaug,[114] in a very thorough statistical study, found no evidence that draught in Africa related to civil war.

Nature reacts erratically sometimes to create imbalances, whatever the sort. In response, states would need to adjust to such challenges; unfortunately our record in this regard does not sparkle. The future may well be occasioned with conflict and disruptions that will destabilize our foreign policies and domestic governments.

If we attached an environmental qualifier to bring our discussion to a more positive conclusion, the challenge-and-response thesis gives geopolitical insights into successful human reactions toward overcoming difficult terrain and climate, that when a power is threatened, it will respond to that threat by an effort to create offsetting strengthens. In another example, an "epic" or liberal culture exudes optimism, one assuming "successes" in foreign adventures. North American Manifest Destiny, overcoming obstacles in absorbing the Western frontiers, reflects this image. Interventions in Vietnam and Iraq reveal additional features of American "exceptionalism," that the North American is not "ordinary" and can excel at whatever confronts him.

Brazilian general Carlos de Meira Mattos challenged his republic to develop the Amazon watershed and to integrate it with coastal industrial and population centers despite the dangers and hardships of the jungles.[115] One hears these calls to a higher destiny in other Latin American states toward uniting and populating distant and isolated hinterlands.

A negative designation, the "resources curse" of petropolitics, links a nation's public-revenues dependence on exporting of oil and gas, these geopolitical factors, with a decline of civil rights and democracy, causing an inverse association between resource dependency and freedom. Several environmentalists contend that, as oil and natural gas prices rise, human liberties descend.[116] Diamond found that, for the twenty-three states most dependent upon petroleum export earnings, none were defined as democratic. This dependency or imbalance provided a major reason for a "democratic recession" noted by Freedom House in 2007.[117]

Ross suggested at least six causes for this petroleum windfalls curse: (1) a "taxation effect" in which repressive governments buy off social pressures that might bring a broader accountability; (2) a "spending effect" where rulers can afford elaborate patronage expenditures; (3) a "group-formation effect" that will tie groups to a dependence upon the governing elite; (4) a "repression effect" of stronger police, security, and intelligence forces, paid to protect the elite and to imprison dissidents; (5) an "anti-modernization effect" that weakens the occupational and educational strengths of the middle sectors; and finally, (6) a suppression of women by extinguishing their employment and educational opportunities and confining them to home and to enhancing patriarchal cultures.

Two additional examples connect to this petropolitics: (1) Any sort of resource dependency in addition to oil, such as copper in Chile and Peru and sugar in Cuba and Brazil, has brought social imbalances creating political disruptions. The original Zapata revolt that spurred the Mexican Revolution originated in corporate land purchases for sugar that forced local peasants from communal areas. (2) The present wealth disparities allegedly benefiting the globe's north against the south, in addition to similar claims within the United States of a disappearing middle class, may stimulate conflict as well. Successful actions toward equalizing wealth, both globally and within states, remain uncertain; yet, one could surmise a more stable future were solutions to these imbalances discovered.

Charles Krauthammer offered an extension of the geopolitics of dependency within the oil-rich countries,[118] the concept of weapons states in which smaller powers gain security and prestige by having weapons of mass destruction. He described this proliferation thus:

> It was inconceivable that a relatively small Middle Eastern state within an almost entirely imported industrial base could do anything more than threaten its neighbors. The central truth of the coming eras is that this is no longer the case: relatively small, peripheral and backward states will be able to emerge rapidly as threats not only to regional, but to world, security.

Iran and North Korea fit this image, with Pakistan arriving on a similar course, all bent on enhancing power and prestige by such weapons of terror. This scenario negates the factors of central position and of distance from northern continents; still, his contention of linking oil revenues and extreme ideologies onto nuclear weapons merits our attention, and our fear.

This review concludes discussion of the common classical theories that would fit into the geopolitical model according to its spatial definition. Others could readily be discovered as well. We now will proceed onto the next chapter for testing the application to selected events by enlisting these geopolitical features.

6   Applications of the Model

The usefulness of theories rests in their contributing to insights that may assist toward a deeper interpretation of events and policies within the real international environment, both in the historical and contemporary cases and in the regional and strategic realms. Accordingly, in such an endeavor, how can we utilize our geopolitical model with its sixty-odd theories in ways that will present a better view of foreign affairs, in seeing events more clearly and in prescribing possible solutions for improvement? For this proposal: look for spatial patterns that appear connected to relevant events and ponder whether the two, theory and event, interact in ways that might expand one's experience.

To lend the reader more assistance in this theory-to-event application, one might consider these four suggestions:[1]

1. Carefully examine the event you have selected.—Have you assembled all of the parts of the event? Can you trace its evolution as a happening—past, present, and future? Are there parts that do not seem connected or are missing? Can you connect or find these missing parts?

2. Closely study the theory you have selected.—Does the theory seem clear to you? If not, try to clarify it. To which situations might it apply? How relevant is it to your understanding? Are there other theories that might pose better fits? Might there be several theories that can be utilized together for more understanding?

3. Does the theory seem to fit the event?—Do you feel you have gained insights from connecting theory to event? How great are those insights—narrow or more expansive? Do you know more about the event by enlisting the chosen theory? How much more? Are there other theories that could help to broaden your view?

4. Make sure you have selected the correct theory.—If what you have ap-

plied does not give you much depth, it probably is not a good fit. Try several other theories to see if another linkage offers more clarity. Theories that do not pertain often can lead to problems—for instance, US involvement in Vietnam—containment or checkerboard?

The eight choices for theory-application below include several of the author's previous publications. Other selections met his interest toward testing theories that could be drawn from the geopolitical model.

1. The Peloponnesian War of Ancient Greece as Compared with the Contemporary Diplomacy of South America

Look for these theories for Greece: checkerboards, choke points, contagion, distances, frontiers, heartlands, pandemics, sea and land power, shatterbelts, spheres of influence, topography.

Look for these theories for South America: buffers, checkerboards, distance, encirclement, heartlands, independent world region, sea power/land power, spheres of influence, and topography.

Several escalation-to-wider-conflict episodes foretold the coming of war— the first, the 435 B.C.E. Corinthian-Corcyran interventions into the rebellion of Epidamnus, a former colony of Corinth. Despite the city's being outside the spheres of influence of both Athens and Sparta, the intervention attracted the involvement of the rival states, Athens with alliance to Corcyra, Sparta with military assistance to Corinth. This configuration meant a shatterbelt, as described earlier, a local conflict attracting the rivalries of outside strategic players that helped cause an escalation-to-war where Athenian and Corinthian battle fleets engaged, Athens enjoying its first victory of the approaching war at Sybola.

Three other shatterbelts appeared during the initial war years, each setting Sparta against Athens as strategic rivals and both cities fighting the other alongside local allies and enemies: (1) the "Megarian Decree" declared by Athens against Spartan ally Megara, which restricted trade between the alliances, probably as a punishment for Megara's assistance to Corinth in the Epidamnus intervention; (2) the Athenian siege of rebellious Polidaea, another Corinthian colony; and (3) the later Athenian attack on Syracuse where Sparta lent its support against the invaders.[2] Shatterbelts reveal a policy decision by rival strategic actors to intrude in strife-ridden areas where smaller entities also are in conflict, each outside intruder siding with one of the local rivals. Without that decision to intervene by the strategic actors, shatterbelts would not emerge. The local forces, too, would have to accept the intrusions of their strategic allies. At that point of horizontal and vertical alliances, we observe the escalation to war, and such happened in ancient Greece.

Once war commenced, the opponents' strengthens were shown in a land-power, sea-power balance of power, two more traditional concepts that reside in our geopolitical model. Five times Sparta invaded and ravished Attica, the territory surrounding Athens. But its superior armed forces were unable to lure into battle the weaker Athenian land forces, protected within the walls surrounding the city and its port at Piraeus. But the sea-power superiority of Athens, in turn, could not subdue the Spartans, who lacked a sea-power facility. This balance of power constellation stalemated and prolonged the deadly Greek struggle, the one side's predominant landward strength withstanding the onslaughts of the other side's predominant maritime strength. The eventual Spartan victory came only after Persian financing of a competitive Spartan fleet that was finally to end the war after the naval victory against Athens at Aegospotami in 405 B.C.E.

The Athenian protective walls that kept away the Spartans held liabilities as well as security, for during the second year of war a disastrous plague broke out that killed off a third of the population and reduced the military's strength for years. The enclosing fortifications, which had promoted pandemic, reflected the ability of Sparta to force this defensive tactic on Athens—their refusal to chance a land battle and instead relying on a sea-power strength, and particularly on a dependence on importing food and other supplies through its protected port facility. That strategy would spell disaster when Sparta closed this choke point advantage and starved Athens into submission.

A predominant spatial structure of the war appeared in the checkerboard configuration, the leapfrog pattern of neighboring areas in rivalry but of neighbors of neighbors aligning. Here, Sparta with Persia, Boeotia, Corinth, and Syracuse, stood apart from Athens and its allies, the Aegean colonies, Argos, and Corcyra, these alliance sides remaining in place for the war's entire length. Differing from contemporary South America, a region displaying a similar checkerboard but instead showing stability, the Greek version held an inevitable war-prone fixation. And like the land-power/sea-power contrast, these patterns within the checkerboard helped to prolong and intensify the lengthy Greek drama. The four shatterbelts reinforced the features of the checkerboard, making any relaxation among the alliances not likely. Shatterbelt fire-breaks and facilities for negotiation that might have prevented the original escalation and the intense strife of the checkerboard failed to surface.

The rigidity of the Peloponnesian checkerboard may well have intensified and prolonged the war. Some of the fault lies in the absence of conciliatory leadership for both alliances, where temporary truces soon reverted into conflict, and the bloodshed in sieges and battles became intensified. Furthermore, both the sea-power/land-power balance stalemated resolution, and the four shatterbelts prolonged the violence, playing their parts in the conflict's extension. Other geopolitical features may have contributed to the war's impasse as well, the lack of a dominant heartland hegemon that might have pressed reconciliation among the rivals. But this checkerboard balance stayed in equilibrium and in bloodshed until the final years.

Sparse distances or spaces among the frontiers of some of the alliance players may also have influenced the structure's rigidity, for the major checkerboard players were not isolated from one another, and this lack of separation may have fortified a fear that maintained the stress and resisted a permanent truce. The infrequent battles, caused by the refusal of Athens to engage the Spartans on land, were not decisive in bringing the war's end, that coming instead with the naval victory by Sparta. And finally, some instances of harsh topography plus the intervening seas among Persia, Attica, the Peloponnese, and Italy, tended to isolate the opponents and postpone an ending solution.

The failed Athenian invasion of Sicily (415–413 B.C.E.) proved a fatal mistake that contributed to the later Spartan victory. Here, a strong land and sea force from Athens attempted subjugation of Syracuse but soon suffered annihilation because of distance and difficult terrain, poor Athenian leadership, adroit Spartan guidance to its Syracuse allies, and a confused Athenian strategy of expanding the theater of strife that did not correspond to the original prudent war interests. Pericles' earlier moderation was ignored, and Athens took a distant and reckless offensive on land and sea bent toward ridding its checkerboard encirclement. Its defeat seriously depleted wealth and manpower, encouraging its colonies and tribute cities to revolt, and its opponents, importantly Persia, to become more aggressive.

In this Athenian Sicilian debacle the geopolitical patterns would include the several theories of distance weakening, disadvantageous topography, influence spheres (Athens intruding into that of Sparta), and a contagion or spatial spread of conflict that ensued within the Athenian Empire and elsewhere because of the defeat at Syracuse. And once more, we observe the ubiquitous shatterbelt structures, the local strife in peripheral Sicily drawing in the outside strategic competitors, and the confining and dangerous encirclement of Athens, brought on by the predominant checkerboard configuration of city-states.

It seems rather strange that the strategic Hellespont choke-point straits of the northern Aegean, the food lifeline to Athens from the Black Sea and the Ukrainian grain fields, would not have been recognized as being strategically important by Spartan and Persian leaders earlier in the war, and thus defended more vigorously by Athens. Indeed, locating this Athenian vulnerability took the insight of the Spartan admiral Lysander to exploit, and the Persian rulers to finance a Spartan fleet to neutralize the Athenian sea advantage in the Aegean. The Spartan sea victory at Aegospotami destroyed the Athenian fleet, strangling the city and its seaport, and consequently terminating the long struggle. Although most of the earlier events of the war had happened distant from the Hellespont, the struggle ended abruptly once this strategic choke point was lost to Athens.

Theory affords further depth into an event and thus a platform for explanation and comparison. The spatial patterns of war in ancient Greece offer a good first testing place for study within our geopolitical model. Accordingly, several comments may be appropriate to going more deeply into the conflict and then to contrast these points to the peace of contemporary South America.

Shatterbelts: At least five of these configurations arose during the war, in each case where local struggles attracted the strategic involvement of the two antagonists, Athens and Sparta. These geopolitical designs could be labeled in modern times as "catalytic wars," the tail (local allies) wagging the dog (the strategic sponsors), showing that rigid perceptions and alliances can hamper the decision-making abilities of hegemons and local states and draw each into destructive and unwanted confrontations.

Many wars start from the escalations of shatterbelts, and the Greek war draws no exception. But these engagements are not inevitable, for different policies and actions could have been set in place that might have prevented such violence. For example, the leading political participants of both Sparta and Athens might have been more effective at resisting the war passions of their governing bodies and instead have insisted upon moderation, as Pericles and Archidamus had wisely preferred. Or the two city-states could have better contained or ignored their weaker allies' pleas for intervention by erecting "firebreaks" against unintended escalation. Finally, the opposing hegemonic-led leagues might have established means toward mediating conflict, above all in direct negotiations between Athens and Sparta, making it possible to reverse the perception of the war's inevitability and thereby to strengthen the peace factions within both cities.

A balancer city or nation, a strong power that might have intervened to prevent the conflict or to decide the winner, was not present at first. Persia later played this latter role to the advantage of Sparta but not at the war's outbreak. Suspicions by neighbors of territorial expansion by Athens may have stimulated distrust, a fact that did bear some truth when the city's imperial actions took just that course. We could add as well the ubiquitous frontier disputes and the rigidities of the rival alliances and similarly the absence of a dominant heartland in a position to temper the stalemate. But other factors helped to push the distrust beyond these structural considerations—city loyalties, trade rivalries, ideological differences, poor leadership and short-sighted assemblies—all contributed to the inevitability of the war.

Checkerboard: In contemporary South American geopolitics, the prevailing checkerboard structure has helped bring a stable peace, for reasons peculiar to the region's geopolitics, and these will be discussed below. But the opposite happened in Greece, where geographic conditions helped to cause war in the ancient Peloponnese. The five-city/nation checkerboard of Sparta with Persia, Boeotia, Corinth, and Syracuse arraigned against the four-member coalition of Athens with the Aegean colonies, Argos, and Corcyra, proved to be dangerous to peace and susceptible to conflict escalation. The prevailing checkerboard contributed to the war's outbreak and longevity, as did the shatterbelts, and both were to reinforce each other in tandem.

Costly two-front wars did not retard the Greek contest either, especially from the standpoint of Athens suffering the most from encirclement, probably because she could depend upon her defensive walls and her authority upon the sea. The two alliances within the checkerboard, being equal in space and power, appeared stubborn in opposition to each other, each lacking major defector states and all set toward continuing its struggle. Stalemate, frustration, and increasing rigidity and violence persisted for three decades. Distant Persia played a "divide-and-conquer" game, wanting to break Athenian dominance over the Aegean in hopes of regaining its sphere of influence over the area.

Land and sea power: This land versus sea balancing contributes a further war describer, with Athens dependent upon sea power and Sparta as much upon land power. But the overall advantage in the war's end was to favor Sparta because its army was largely invincible in battle, and hence it could stand unchallenged throughout the conflict, at least in confronting the Athenian equivalent. Consequently, Athens would later lose its maritime supremacy when a newly constructed Spartan armada began its war of attrition in the Aegean after the defeat of Athens in Sicily and after Persia's financing of the Spartan fleet. Here, the greater costs of naval warfare, in material and manpower, as contrasted to the less expensive land forces of Sparta, steadily depleted the resources of Athens, made the city more dependent upon tribute from its increasingly restive allies, and, ultimately, Athens could not match or attract the type of outside support rendered to Sparta by the wealthy Persians.

Strategic choke points: This concept of strategic choke points, meaning a particular locale that extends a strong impact over some greater expanse of space, a maritime strait or canal, an isthmus or mountain pass, or connecting routes within plains, indicates a special place for exerting a country's leverage in struggles against rivals. In Greece, we see these features in the Corinthian Isthmus through which the Spartan armies advanced toward Athens and in the Corinthian Gulf, through which the Athenian navies sought to control the central Greek areas. But securing the strategic Hellespont proved in the final accounting the survival or demise of Athens itself, for through these straits poured the needed grain imports to the city drawn from the Black Sea ports of Ukraine. Once this lifeline was closed by Spartan naval forces, Athens suffered strangulation and the war quickly ended.

Several aspects were missing from this geopolitical puzzle that might have prevented the Peloponnese structure of conflict and have shifted the region into a zone of harmony. Five peace-contributors are suggested that, had they been present, ancient Greece might have resembled the stability of present-day South America.

1. A *power symmetry or balance* existed between the Greek alliances, Athens, Sparta, and their allies, an equilibrium that brought stalemate via a structured checkmating between the rival alliances, lengthening the war and heightening the violence. Were there, instead, a dominant state or alliance within the region, the escalating violence might have become contained and the war shortened or prevented. That happened once Persia intervened.

2. No *buffer states* appeared on the Greek scene, neutral cities that would have cordoned off direct confrontation, absorbed the violence exercised by the larger cities, and enhanced the isolation wrought by distance and topography. Without these buffers the checkerboard rivalries tended to intensify border vi-

olence and to encourage shatterbelt escalation. Buffers were missing because neutrality simply was not permitted among the major antagonists, the tragedy of Melos being a prime example.

3. *Frontier* or march *boundaries* were sufficiently wide to buffer local hostilities and to prevent the constant friction occurring among the rival cities. Had a greater degree of spatial separation and isolation been more evident with greater distances among inhabitants, the wider strategic tensions might have abated.

4. The symmetry wrought by the *sea power* of Athens and the *land power* of Sparta both stalemated and prolonged the war. In the initial years, Athens could not defeat Sparta's army nor could Sparta challenge the Athenian marine. Eventually, Sparta's ability to build a navy equal to that of Athens decided the contest. Had a sea-power capability not been available to either side, Sparta would have won early on, its hoplites easily superior to the army of Athens. Or conversely, had a land-power strength been absent to Sparta, an Athenian victory would have been assured. Nonetheless, the geography of ancient Greece lent itself to both sources of military preponderance, sea and land power, and this brought on a balance that contributed to stalemate and war.

5. Further, we see a temptation by participants to spread the conflict beyond Greece during the wars, with Athens early on invading Egypt, then Sicily, and later facing the strength of Persia. Spartan involvement in these external actions occurred, too. Consequently, *lands external* to Greece also intensified the strife. Had the struggle been confined only to the Greek lands, the extraterritorial adventures and alliances might not have been so strategic to the war's final outcome, and Greece, in more *isolation*, might have become more united or its major players might have recognized the coming stalemate and reconciled their aims.

South America's geopolitical structure and patterns in comparison: Contemporary South America exhibits quite different patterns from the five geopolitical themes of ancient Greece just outlined, showing differences that have stabilized its diplomacy. Today the region reveals a contrasting type of power asymmetry, of a dominant Brazil that its neighbors fear and suspect of a desire for extending its domains onto the continent's Pacific coast via the Charcas heartland of Bolivia. This threat has prompted a Spanish-American encirclement that checkmates a potentially aggressive Portuguese republic, despite the existence of a checkerboard configuration that could hold escalation intent.

The four interior buffer countries of Ecuador, Bolivia, Paraguay, and Uruguay exert positions between the checkerboard actors (Brazil, Chile, Peru, Argentina), a northwest to southeast continental corridor of conflict. The several wars of past decades were fought on buffer territories, with buffer lands sacrificed as rewards to the larger victors, transfers referred to as the Polandization of South America. Despite the suffering, the buffer's losses contribute to the existing stability.

Distances between countries and *harsh topography,* stopping modern roadways and railways, have stabilized the continent's diplomacy by lessening contacts among the larger countries. The Andes are steep and the continent's center is largely barren and sparsely populated. Such an environment reinforces the isolation of the buffer corridor and helps to stabilize the checkerboard structure in the direction of peace and not in a turn to conflict.

Moreover, the South American republics do not hold a distinctive sea- and land-power dichotomy, the navies being of lesser strength and the armies central to national power. This feature likewise has kept the countries more isolated from each other, since transporting and supplying troops would be costly and difficult over the ample distances and rugged terrain.

And finally, South America rates as an independent or autonomous region in strategic world politics, its geopolitics kept sequestered within the continent and away from the rivalries of Eurasia. Unlike the rotation of shatterbelts or influence spheres suffered by Middle America, since independence South America has not seen a serious invasion from a northern Great Power. Hence, no shatterbelts hold sway. The southern continent enjoys a strategic isolation, its geopolitics internally limited to frontier disputes, hinterland development, regional integration, and again, encirclement of Brazil, if that nation were to aspire to continental hegemony. Fortunately for the stability of its diplomacy, Brazil, at present, exerts a policy of conciliation and integration.

To conclude, the Greek and American checkerboards paralleled but the patterns within took opposite paths, the former in hostility, the latter in accommodation. The factors of geography interpreted by theories from our geopolitical model may have assisted the reader toward offering some explanation.

2. The Ukraine Shatterbelt: A New Cold War?

Look for: collective security, distance weakens/closeness strengthens, heartland, immigration, irredentism, shatterbelts.

One rarely can discover the term "shatterbelt" mentioned in the extant foreign-affairs literature. But it appears that the concept will give good insight into conflict situations where local strife may escalate into regional and strategic warfare. Prominent examples of this structure include the Cuban missile crisis of 1962, where the escalation was stopped, and likewise for both world wars, where it instead expanded into war. A shatterbelt arises in a region where local conflict becomes intertwined with strategic rivalry, the result being an escalation of threats. Specifically, the definition shows that whenever regional competitors construct alliances with strategic rivals, a shatterbelt arises.

Shatterbelts are dangerous and war prone, often created when conflict escalations to war go unchecked, such as was suffered a century ago at the dawn of World War I. Such dangers can be avoided by moderate leaders and prudent assembles, sanctions and threats, peace conferences and procedures, and certain types of "fire-breaks," including an effective international resistance against groups or states bent on a spread of conflict toward violence. Finally, it is suggested that shatterbelts may persist for some time at lower levels of conflict, such as in contemporary Ukraine, without serious regional violence, the escalation stopping before a drift to wider war.

It might be wise at this initial moment to pause to emphasize other essential aspects of this geopolitical scenario that may prove instructive toward examining the rise of a regional shatterbelt in Ukraine.[3]

The classical concept of irredentism offers some light into our description relative to eastern Ukraine, this depicting a separatist people advocating annexation or combining of territories as a plan for uniting separated peoples of common ethnicity or of past national identity into forming new states or into joining adjacent existing states. With the fluidity of frontiers following the demise of the Soviet Union, such events would not be particularly unexpected. A good example seems to be that of Crimea, probably an accomplished fact for the peninsula returning to the Russian homeland. Will eastern Ukraine and the wishes of Vladimir Putin follow that irredentist example as well?

A further concept within the geopolitical model features the distance weakens/strengthens variable—giving Russia's nearness to Ukraine a favorable leverage against the remote states of Europe and North America. That distance factor in favor of Russia allows Putin the ability to orchestrate the tempo and the duration of any shatterbelt escalation, a feat much to his political skills and power. Despite Russia's economic vulnerability to Western sanctions, the distance-weakens factor limits the immediate impact the Western allies can exert toward Putin. Were Ukraine located away from the Russian frontier, a conflict such as this might not have been so susceptible to Putin's reach. But the closeness factor of Russia gives in this case the enabling of stalemating the dispute into the immediate future. This element, nearness augmenting Putin's otherwise diminished power, represents a key aspect of this ongoing drama.

Allow a shift in attention now to Vladimir Putin, this affair's central actor, so as to expand upon the discussion of the Ukraine shatterbelt. Putin certainly performs within a pivotal position of leverage that presents him with the choice of directing the main theater of action. His rule within Russia could be described a kleptocracy, a regime of corrupt leaders in the top echelons of an autocratic state. As such, one sees Putin balancing a weakening national economy, dependent upon exports of oil and natural gas to Europe for public revenues within a political system owing its stability to his popularity and success as a politician in addition to his ability to repress any outspoken opposition in his chessboard moves. Unlike Hitler or Stalin, he is not driven by an inflexible ideology, nor is he isolated from public opinion. He must maintain some level of economic prosperity and of popular political support. Accordingly, he must balance domestic forces to maintain his power. He lacks significant foreign allies that might lend him international backing, and he has become increasingly isolated and opposed by other nations as a pariah statesman aiming to upset the present global stability. In sum, Putin holds certain advantages and disadvantages within our shatterbelt scenario, but as an adroit performer, he has so far been able to balance these diverse factors such that the Ukrainian crisis will stay within whichever course Putin may want to pursue for the near future.

Relative to Putin's ambitions, too, rests the doctrine of Eurasianism, a vague *Geopolitik* and anti-Western thesis of the Eurasian heartland, bent on a restoration of Soviet superpower greatness mixed with the return of past territories of the czarist empire. Ukraine represents a central and essential feature for this restoration, and to have this nation point westward instead of toward Russia would pose a strong irredentist restriction to this doctrine and to Putin's desires to fulfill an expansion of Russian influence and lands.

The Ukrainian crisis fits nicely within this Russian political environment. Putin can bolster his domestic popularity and support by his aggressive moves in Crimea and eastern Ukraine. Polls in Russia show popular agreement in his threatening and destabilizing actions, these in creating the required conditions for establishing a shatterbelt. Yet Putin cannot extend his assertiveness too far— that is, to forcing a Russian occupation of the secessionist portions of Ukraine, for this would carry heavy weights both domestically and internationally to his balancing within the Russian system. For instance, a military occupation of parts of Ukraine would themselves be costly to the strained national budget of Putin's realm, pushing the nation closer to bankruptcy. Likely as well, European and US sanctions, plus the plummeting of oil prices, will take a substantial toll on the Russian economy, a danger that Putin and his oligarchs have clearly recognized. Accordingly, Putin will likely not directly invade and annex the eastern parts of the Ukrainian domain. Nonetheless, this does not remove the shatterbelt from our attention because the present configuration could continue at the whim and to the advantage of Putin for some time, perhaps for years.

These factors within Russia have caused the shatterbelt's escalation to plateau and to rise or fall from within the current levels. Simply put, Putin cannot pursue a more aggressive bent because he rightly fears economic and political repercussions at home and abroad. Still, continued tensions in eastern Ukraine can easily be moderated by Putin because distance has isolated the Western allies from direct involvement, and his close frontier can hold tensions at a high enough level to maintain the existence of the shatterbelt itself. In sum, a stalemate will likely emerge—the crisis persisting for a lengthier period with neither a further escalation nor de-escalation. Actual war or a solid peace cannot be envisioned; instead, our shatterbelt should hold constant within these extremes.

The Western allies possess advantages and disadvantages within this shatterbelt constellation as well. Located distant from Ukraine, they exert less impact on local concerns and they cannot stop Putin's ability to continue the stresses on the eastern Ukrainian frontiers by his supporting the pro-Russian militias and paramilitary forces opposing the Kiev government. This lack of a Western physical impact has shown in the Russian acquisition of Crimea, where the takeover could not be blocked by the insertion of Western forces. Were Putin to forcefully occupy and annex the eastern section, certainly tensions would rise substantially, but one would seriously doubt whether such an aggression would be met by any firm Western military opposition.

Nonetheless, the United States and its European friends do have retaliatory methods in their arsenals to press against Putin and to halt any further escalation of the shatterbelt, so long as they stay united in the face of any further aggressive moves by the Russians. Here, the author is describing a very different international structure that could stem the threat of a shatterbelt spread into regional warfare, that being some sort of NATO-led collective security system that could assert enough pressure upon Putin to halt any further drift into strife.

A collective-security regime, written into the United Nations and NATO charters, directs all members automatically to resist any aggression without considerations of particular national interests and policies. Such an endeavor for peace lacks good examples of success in recent history, with the possible exception of forces uniting during the first Gulf War ridding Saddam Hussein's occupation of Kuwait in 1991. Yet this method appears appropriate to the NATO response to the Ukraine crisis, with the weapons of threats, military maneuvers, and above all, economic sanctions.

The Russian stock market has fluctuated wildly since the crisis began, showing a significant flight of capital and investments. With the Russian currency falling drastically in value, a coming recession could be predicted, with the national economy plunging into deep recession.

Finally, it appears that President Obama and his European allies, particularly Chancellor Merkel of Germany, have played their collective-security cards well, increasing threats of more sanctions that would further harm Russian financial stability. Putin's efforts to divide the allies have proven ineffective amid the steady communications and announcements uttered within the Western alliance. This record of unity, at least to date, shows some ability for such a collective effort to bring forth a moderating against the shatterbelt's potential to escalate, despite the distance of Ukraine from Western Europe and North America.

3. Shatterbelts Threatening the Early United States

Look for: choke point, distance weakens, manifest destiny, Monroe Doctrine, rimlands, shatterbelts.

Once more, the classical shatterbelt shall occupy our discussion of a region in conflict, and in this case to postindependence North America. Actually, shatterbelts are presently not common to any place in America. For North, South, and Middle America, they originally arose because of colonial rivalries in the New World among the European powers at the time. For instance, in South America, such patterns came at the estuaries of the La Plata and Amazon rivers, the Dutch, Portuguese, Spanish, and English standing as strategic rivals,[4] and the colonists residing in those areas as regional contestants. But these southern examples came as rather weak ones and never saw escalation into serious violence. And neither the north nor the south has experienced shatterbelts once independence came to their domains. Nonetheless, shatterbelts and interest spheres have continued to alternate within Middle America since the first times of European occupation.

But in the earlier case of the North American English colonists and the later young United States, a series of shatterbelts surfaced for several decades on the western edges of the Atlantic coastal settlements, each posing a threat to the English Americans and a block to western expansion. In these theaters, the French and Spanish, and later English, aligned with the several Native American tribes, providing them with sufficient military arms to engage the colonists successfully. Battles occurred between the Indians and the English Americans, and the armed outcomes were balanced between the two until the decade before the century's turn.

The demise of the shatterbelts originates with Napoleon Bonaparte and his rampaging armies in Europe, causing eventual withdrawal of England, France, and Spain from the Ohio Valley and from Florida, thereby gaining the United States its frontier security. The vast distance of America from the European powers, lessening their interest and involvement, likewise, encouraged this withdrawal. The Native Americans never recovered a military advantage, having lost their European benefactors, and the United States soon pushed westward to the Pacific with remarkable ease and speed, a feat of Manifest Destiny to consolidate its eventual empire.

What also is an important lesson here is the incompatibility between shatterbelts and the Monroe Doctrine. The doctrine was established to prevent Middle American shatterbelts from the Caribbean, as the years passed and the North Americans saw the benefits of a cross-ocean canal or choke point. The American strategic doctrine has been to isolate Middle America, its "soft underbelly," from Eurasian involvement, although despite this goal, the Caribbean has shifted between shatterbelt and sphere of influence during its recent evolution, and the Cuban missile crisis offered the worst-case scenario of the threats brought by Middle American shatterbelts. With some looseness in application, one could extend the Monroe Doctrine beyond Middle America and onto the Eurasian rimlands and beyond, the intention of opposing formation of shatterbelts wherever they might threaten US interests.

4. Shatterbelts Now Emerging in Central Eurasia and Elsewhere?

Look for these theories: distance, geographic isolation, Great Game, independent area, Monroe Doctrine, offshore balancing, resources, rimlands, shatterbelts, spheres of influence.

The reader here might charge, with good justification, "too many shatterbelts!" But please allow this one further description of such possible coming structures, because (1) several may be surfacing currently; (2) these tend toward warfare; and (3) they figure within the author's interest and specialty.

When the author composed his article about testing the shatterbelt concept,[5] he located six regions that fit the refined definition: the Middle East, East Asia, Southeast Asia, sub-Saharan Africa, South Asia, and Middle America. These all arose within the Cold War competition between the Soviet Union and the United States, and interestingly, only one, East Asia, was positioned within Spykman's original rimlands locations. Following the demise of Russia as a global power, all of the six quickly disappeared, a result hardly surprising since it takes two strategic powers to create such regions, and only one side, the Americans, still survived. Subsequently, with North America sole strategic hegemon within a unipolar configuration, we have not seen any of these patterns arising to the present day, with the recent exception being the Ukrainian civil conflict, and that would not have appeared had Russia located more distantly.

In line with the depictions above, if the assumption continues that North America will stay global hegemon within an extended "unipolar moment" for a further decade, reasons for this continuance rest on: (1) its military and economic power stays unchallenged; (2) its geopolitical position of relative isolation and distance from Europe and Asia, astride two oceans, still enabling its domination by offshoring balancing the greater nations at both western and eastern extremes of Eurasia; and (3) its will to continue its role as balancer and as guardian of the strategic consensus.

Still, a potential for new shatterbelts emerging in certain pivotal areas in the decades ahead could be predicted. But first as a measure of elimination, such configurations are unlikely in the Americas, for South America should remain isolated as an independent area and Middle America will stay a US interest sphere within the confinement of the Monroe Doctrine. Likewise, Africa will persist as peripheral to global considerations as well as Australia, New Zealand, and the entire Southern Pacific. Finally, Eastern Europe and the Balkans appear immune to outside intervention, a shift from their involvement as "crush zones" that stimulated the beginnings of both world wars. And the current shatterbelt of Ukraine could figure within the Central Eurasian realms for this potential because the same players, Russia and the West, would perform within those dramas as well.

The Middle East will remain unstable for many years ahead and may offer fertile environments for shatterbelts. But even in this turbulent region, good examples may not arise. Syria suffers a tragic civil war at the moment, with Russia favoring the Assad regime, the Western allies some of the rebels. Both sides receive weapons and funding from outside sponsors. Still, the country has not ripened into a shatterbelt because the outside intervention remains hesitant and limited. Such a pattern could happen with Syria and elsewhere within the region, but the outside Great Power linkages would, nonetheless, need to be stronger than what takes place in the region today. And the so-called Islamic State or ISIS clearly lacks any shatterbelt potential; its violence and recklessness would ward off any major power sponsor.

Accordingly, four possible shatterbelts may arise in the near-future,[6] assuming the United States begins to wane in its hegemonic responsibilities and a challenger (or challengers) to North America enter the world arena, perhaps China and/or Russia the most likely. These next selections of potentially emerging shatterbelts appear to fit the description: Korea, Taiwan and the South China Sea, South Asia, and the six Central Eurasian Muslim states of Azerbaijan, Kazakhstan, Kyrgyzstan, Tajikistan, Turkmenistan, and Uzbekistan.

One of earth's most threatened areas would be the rogue state of North Korea and its belligerency toward South Korea and Japan. The instability of the northern section, its poverty, erratic leadership, and nuclear weapons in addition to the closeness of immediate Great Powers (China, Japan, Russia, with US bases nearby) make this region adhere to the definition of shatterbelts. A southward invasion from the peninsula's north would escalate into regional conflict, although Chinese resistance against a pariah North Korea might prevent that possibility. Indeed, it appears that China's national and regional interests want stability more than conflict in Korea, and thus a rational predictor would argue against the Chinese encouraging its neighbor into combat. A Korean shatterbelt seems remote at the moment, unless China becomes more belligerent especially within the adjacent seas. Were we to see some sort of two-Korea's accommodation or unification, the shatterbelt potential there would disappear entirely.

US ally Taiwan, linked to the South China Sea, could be near explosion, the force preventing eruption dependent on a restrained and moderate Peoples' Republic. Were the mainland set on invading the island or sea a shatterbelt would surface, bringing strife between China against Japan and the United States and others within the region. The internal politics within Washington would not allow its long-term alliance with Taiwan to falter, and conflict would be inevitable. A rapprochement between the two Chinese factions would re-solve this problem; the strong and intertwining trade ties among the three na-tions now tend also to dissipate tensions. China's lack of a substantial sea power limits its authority, too, in the China Sea. Accordingly, a likely shatterbelt in this location is not evitable for the moment.

Pakistan, Bangladesh, and even India may be descending into becoming "failed states," and this could prompt competition there between China, Rus-sia, and the United States, creating another possibility. Possession of nuclear weapons, poverty, and radical leadership, in addition to India/China rivalry, do not augur well for the region's stability. Power vacuums in neighboring Iraq and Afghanistan, with Iranian nuclear ambitions added to the mix, intensify tensions. But the distance and geographic isolation of Pakistan from China and Russia could well limit the conflict to strife solely among the three local players, creating a serious regional conflict but not a shatterbelt.

The fourth shatterbelt candidate comes within the six pivotal but isolated and weak Muslim states of Central Asia, the trigger for strife the strategic com-petition for oil and natural gas in Azerbaijan and Kazakhstan that could bring competition among the outside powers for access to these vital and increas-ingly scarce energy commodities. We could observe resumption of the Great Game rivalries from earlier years.

For this fourth possibility of rivalry in Central Asia, it might prove profit-able to study the several state actors more closely who would perform within this theater. The reader should be reminded again, it is not the actual conflict or the depressed economies or racial/ethnic disturbances that prompt a shat-terbelt, because these instabilities may be current in many cases. Instead, what is vital to the creation of these designs is the willingness of outside powers to decide to intrude in such locations, and in turn, the willingness of the recipro-cating regional powers to agree to interlock with the outside powers. Accord-ingly, we must see these two levels in conflict—vertical and horizontal—the regional neighbors in strife among each other and at the same moment, the outside interveners also in strife with each other on the strategic levels. The two levels joining create a shatterbelt.

With this scenario coming into place, the strategic players in the Central Asia stage probably would be China, Russia, the European bloc, and the United States, with the possible inclusion of India as well, all concerned with accessing and exploiting the oil and natural gas resources of the region. China and Rus-sia, the immediate neighbors, hold traditional ties to the central region, while

Europe and America possess interests and investments there as well—all having footholds in a likely escalation of competition.

The six Muslim states differ marginally in size and stability, and all are ill governed, corrupt, and socially and economically backward. A unity among them is missing, and they could rather easily be set against one another, as just Azerbaijan and Kazakhstan contain the major deposits of these energy sources that the others might covet. The instability, poverty, backwardness, corruption, and unevenness in wealth could cause a vacuum attractive to Great Power involvement, an environment poised for shatterbelts.

5. The Three Separate Americas in Geopolitical Terms

Look for these theories: buffer states, checkerboards, contagion, distance/isolation, encirclement, heartland, independent area, integration, Monroe Doctrine, natural resources, offshore balancing, organic frontiers, power-balances, rimlands, shatterbelts, spheres of influence.

Regions differ in their geopolitical characteristics, in part a reflection of their global locations. When one examines the globe, the most productive climatic zones tend to locate in the temperate spaces. And the northern half shows significantly more land-space within these margins than is displayed in the southern half, filled instead by ample ocean waters. No wonder the historical empires and civilizations appeared in these northern temperate portions, as they possessed more healthful spaces for residencies and development.

Within this geopolitical configuration, three very different Americas exist and inter-relate at differing degrees, the northern, middle, and southern portions:

Northern sector: Strategic in its geopolitics with less interest and involvement to its south, its diplomacy and military projection extends exclusively eastward and westward onto the rimlands of Eurasia, specifically to Western Europe, the Persian Gulf, and Japan/Korea. It ignores South America and neglects Middle America, except when the region threatens shatterbelts. This northern part performs as a Eurasian actor, striving to maintain favorable power balances with the "grand continent" for its primary defense. We do not see an American pan-regional posture within the northern interest.

North America is able to play this strategic role because of its significant natural wealth, its control over Middle America, and its position adjacent the western and eastern fringes of Eurasia that presents it with the ability to offshore balance the forces in these areas to its advantage. The United States likely inhabits the richest space on earth, and it is favored as well by distance and isolation from potentially hostile forces of Europe and Asia. It faces no such threat from within the Americas.

Middle sector: Strategic also but in a reactive and negative way, the smaller and weaker states of the middle portion exhibit a power vacuum and thus a vulnerability to North America as seen in shatterbelts formed by Eurasian rivals to the United States. This vulnerability would be addressed by an effective sphere of influence from the north, otherwise known as the Monroe Doctrine. Hence, a passive Middle America emits a strategic but vulnerable placement to the northern Great Power solely when shatterbelts threaten.

Largely ignored during cycles of northern domination, Middle America presents a depressed, ill-governed, backwater image of little importance to global politics and economics. But once a shatterbelt threatens or emerges, the United States intervenes, militarily in most cases, until the Eurasian presence is removed. A good example of this cycle arose in the two presidencies of Daniel Ortega of Nicaragua, a strategic threat to the north during his 1980s term that brought the US-sponsored Contra mercenaries against his government. But when the Cold War ended in the following decades, Ortega's re-election was ignored by Washington after the demise of the earlier Middle American shatterbelt and a return to the US influence sphere.

Southern sector: Having not suffered armed intervention anywhere from the North American military or from the former European colonial powers since the nineteenth century, the southern portions of the hemisphere lack any sort of strategic Eurasian projection or interest. Its peripheral location shows no indication of likely shatterbelts, nor is its relationship to the other two American sectors particularly close or strategic. Were South America positioned, instead, in the North Atlantic or North Pacific, our strategic description would shift to the area emitting much more prominence in world affairs. As this has not happened, of course, the states there play a very minor role in northern power relationships.

South America holds significantly more wealth than does the middle sector, and the continent shows a tendency for peace and unity. Two states stand out in their size and industrial/technological advancement, those being Argentina and particularly Brazil. Yet neither is a global participant of any note. Being rather hermetically sealed as a location, the region resembles a true museum place for the study of classical geopolitics, with checkerboards, buffer states, heartlands, organic frontiers, distance, contagion, and other such concepts in clear display. The geopolitics of South America has been, since independence, distinctly internal to the region,[7] a focus upon border and land ownership disputes, and more recently upon development and integration within the Common Market of the Southern Cone (MERCOSUR).

Returning to Brazil and its geopolitics, this republic continues to fail in its ambitions for attaining Great Nation status,[8] despite its occasional efforts to reach for that level. Brazil was the only South American state to have fought in World War II, and in several national power indexes it ranks sixth or seventh worldwide in wealth and technology. Nonetheless, a number of factors prevent an extension of its influence beyond the South Atlantic: (1) the South American checkerboard checkmates its ascendancy, with Peru and Argentina balancing against it; (2) the encircling suspicious Spanish republics hold back its alleged aspirations for territory; (3) the absence of US sponsorship of Brazil as a strategic ally; and (4) the manifest destiny failure of Brazil to extend its space.

6. US Geopolitics

Look for these theories: buffers, choke points, containment, encirclement, exceptionalism, fortress America, heartland, immigration, isolation-distance, maritime nation, Monroe Doctrine, natural wealth, offshore balancing, rimland interventions, shatterbelts.

Several themes are presented that will give some detail about the geopolitics of North America, these followed by the geopolitics of Paraguay, the comparison showing that the model's theories pertain to all states alike, large and small and no matter the location.

North American advantages within its geographic setting: All factors required for an advanced industrial-technological society come abundantly together in North America—the necessary mineral wealth (especially coal, petroleum, iron ore) in addition to fertile soil and rainfall and supportive climate for growing foodstuffs, these augmented by a topography that holds rivers and lakes for cheap barge transport and that lacked wide deserts and rugged mountain ranges that might have slowed westward colonization. This combination of geographic factors meant that, in a very short time, the young United States would be able to spread its sovereignty almost unimpeded over a vast expanse of natural wealth extending to the Pacific Ocean and beyond. No wonder that a future global power would emerge from this richly endowed setting, perhaps the greatest combination of these factors of wealth on the entire globe.

This wealth was not recognized by the English during their years of North American colonization, the Crown blinded by what was elsewhere then valued as rich territory to settle. No gold and silver appeared in eastern North America, and no indigenous empires whose inhabitants could be enslaved as miners as had existed for the riches of Spanish Peru and Mexico. England aspired to similar colonial riches, soon ignoring the North Americans in its search for resources elsewhere in Africa and Asia. Such isolation and colonial neglect would make the Americans more self-reliant and ready for independence and successful rebellion once their English masters had attempted improving their administration by taxing colonists more highly. By 1776 the soon-to-be United States possessed the political and economic infrastructures necessary for nationhood, the former autonomy and neglect proving beneficial to later development. Banking, transportation, local government, and other facilities were on their way to developing a modern intrastructure set to advance industrialization once the new nation could fill the colonial vacuum with its own talents and innovation.

Napoleon Bonaparte played his part in this spatial environment, for during the period of rebellion and after, the English colonists faced indigenous encirclement bolstered by European alliances that brought on a series of shatterbelts threatening the expansion westward. His invasions throughout Europe ended these shatterbelt alliances and weakened the military strength of the Native Americans, as seen above in this chapter. Now the whole northern continent lay open to the English Americans, devoid of European buffers. A rapid colonization westward to the Pacific made the United States sole master of this wealthy region.

European divisiveness and its inability to reassert mastery over the former colonies were not the only reasons for North America's rapid consolidation of power. The absence of close neighbors who might threaten added to national protection, for Mexico lacked the strength to resist the US territorial greed, and Brazil, farther to the south, could not extend its sovereignty across the Andes to the Pacific to become another continental nation similar to the northern empire and thus a competitor to North American hegemony.

Significant investments from Europe and later from Asia came to North America because of the factors just described—mineral and agricultural resources, natural transportation waterways, isolation from European wars and rivalries and from immediate American enemies, and labor and consumer markets brought through immigration. These advantages stabilized a political system that would resist foreign wars and diplomatic "entanglements" and advance industrialization and international trade unrestricted by such impediments as fortified borders, rebellious domestic armies, invasions from Eurasia, and other destabilizing factors.

In sum, the United States was so benefited by its American placement that it later would easily ascend to becoming a modern leader nation in world politics and economics, and few other world regions, if any, could compare with that location in North America.

A Geopolitical Description of the United States

America warrants an "island" description, quite similar to the geopolitics of England and Japan. Such an expression underlies its maritime traditions and advantages in trade, in military intervention overseas, and in a distance that awards a security-in-isolation. The contributions of topography assist this maritime portrait, too, for North America is superbly enhanced by its rivers, particularly the Ohio and Mississippi, its Great Lakes, and its canals and ports, all opening up the continent's interior to development, industry, and agricultural production.

North America positions adjacent an even larger continent, the wealthy and expansive super continent of Eurasia, holding strengths equal to those of America. Indeed, Eurasia figures as the core factor within most global geopolitical thought. And similar to England, herein lies the primary, although more distant, threat to US defense. Were the states or alliances of Eurasia to become united and hostile to America, North American strategists believe that Western Hemisphere defenses could not withstand an effective armed onslaught despite the isolation and distance of the Americas. This awareness of vulnerability toward Eurasia has long been present within US defense considerations, and these geopolitical fears continue on today.

In this psychology of vulnerability, America's geopolitics resembles the tenets of classical British foreign affairs. Both countries portray themselves as "islands" near a threatening continental mainland that must be kept divided for security's sake. Neither state will want to commit to a permanent relationship with a continental alliance or country, aiming instead to manipulate the current balances to maintain a favorable security configuration for itself. The recent concept of offshore balancing now offers an attractive "grand strategy" debated within the defense establishment. These descriptions follow guidelines authored by the British geographer Halford Mackinder in his original heart-land thesis that has so strongly influenced the strategic policies of the United States.[9] Again as above, this quotation by George Kennan, the primary author of the containment policy of the later Cold War, reflects Mackinder's impact upon North American security thinking:

> It is essential to us, as it was to Britain, that no single Continental land power should come to dominate the entire Eurasian landmass. Our interest has lain rather in the maintenance of some sort of stable balance among the powers of the interior, in order that none of them should effect the subjugation of the others, conquer the seafaring fringes of the landmass, become a great sea power as well as land power, shatter the position of England, and enter—as in these circumstances it certainly would—on an overseas expansion hostile to ourselves and supported by the immense resources of the interior of Europe and Asia.[10]

The remedy is to forsake a fortress America mentality, a conventional defense of America itself and instead to establish bases on several rimland beachheads of Eurasia, specifically at the present moment in Western Europe, the Persian Gulf, and Korea and Japan.

Keeping Eurasia and its rimlands divided and detached from interior forces is felt essential to North American security. Such a premise is reminiscent of England's previous "splendid isolation" strategy in combination with its dividing and balancing of the continent's larger states. The Dutch-American strategist Nicholas Spykman put the above considerations succinctly in the following statement:

> There is no possibility of achieving an adequate integration of states of the New World in the face of German opposition [writing during World War II], and even if there were, the balance potential of the Americas would still be inadequate to balance the Old World. Because of the distribution of land masses and military potentials, a balance of power in the transatlantic and transpacific zones is an absolute prerequisite for the independence of the New World and the preservation of the power position on this side of the oceans. Hemispheric defense is no defense at all. The Second World War will be lost or won in Europe and Asia. The strategic picture demands that we conduct our military operations in the form of a great offensive across the oceans. If our allies in the Old World are defeated, we cannot hold South America; if we defeat the German-Japanese Alliance abroad, our good neighbors will need no protection.[11]

Isolation and *distance* will not secure the Americas from a Eurasian encirclement, although it could likewise be stated that America encircles Eurasia as well. But, in either case, better to balance Eurasia by intervening upon its rim-land areas in order to preserve a division of forces advantageous to American maneuverability.

Certain pivotal locales or choke points have received attention within traditional geopolitics. Historically, the port at New Orleans represented the key to the Mississippi Basin and thus to access to the internal US heartland. Florida needed to belong to the union, as well as the Pacific Northwest and Hawaii, because US possession of these kept American territory away from the appetites of the British, French, Spanish, and Russians. Building and securing the Panama Canal became vital to security, as was control of the several Caribbean straits leading to the isthmus. To a lesser extent, one could add Greenland and Alaska. And in consideration of the Monroe Doctrine, the importance of Canada, Mexico, and the Central American and the Caribbean nations should be noted as well.

Immigration

One would be remiss not to include immigration within the mix of geopolitics. Certainly, the region's natural wealth and opportunities proved to be powerful "pull" magnets for immigrants and frequently for the most talented and innovative types of individuals. Immigration helped to populate, and thus to secure, the Western frontiers; it created a dual-labor pattern of low-wage earners amid a growing middle class that prompted industrial expansion, and it attracted talented entrepreneurs who expanded technologies and markets.

Another factor pertinent to geopolitics was the cultural, even psychological, impacts that immigration brought to America. Reflective of the English colonial lack of interest in its North American colonies, dissident religious groups found havens here, instilling an antipathy toward Europe and a favoring of isolation, with messianic tendencies coming, too. A strong exceptionalism attached to the country's later foreign policies, of America being a "city upon a hill" and unique within its unilateralism, isolation, and innocence.

Another thesis derived from the early immigration was the concept of a "lower aristocracy" residing in Europe, a subclass of aristocrats losing out to the rising bourgeoisie and thus forced to migrate to a new American world of opportunity. This group tended to be conservative and feudal in cultural and political expression, seen in the later Constitution's Separation of Powers and other features. Ironically, this small but influential group brought Old World values to America at the same instant when those values in Europe were disappearing. In all of these cases, the immigrants arriving to the United States exhibited feelings of suspicion, dislike, even inferiority, toward Europe. Such traits are seen today in US foreign policies.

7. The Geopolitics of Paraguay

Watch for these theories: balancing and bandwagoning, buffer states, checkerboards, crush-zone corridor, distance, heartlands, immigration, integration, isolation, landlocked state, lintel state, pivotal position, position/location, resources-hydroelectric, shatterbelts, sphere of influence.

Our geopolitical model should apply alike to all countries' foreign policies and actions, no matter their size and uniqueness, the student being able to attach appropriate theories for an explanation and guide to all spatial environments, including that of Paraguay.

It is not difficult to claim that Paraguay is not a leading state within the international relations of South America. Its landlocked location rests in isolation within the continent's interior; its resources are meager; it has been manipulated and exploited as a buffer nation by its larger neighbors; and it plays a secondary role within the dominant checkerboard of South American. The country lost a third of its territory with defeat in the disastrous Triple Alliance War of the past century. Nor would one consider Paraguay a likely candidate as a player within a shatterbelt design; it simply is not an important foreign-affairs consideration within a strategic sense.

These points stated, the country's central position remains an insightful one within the testing of our model. Perhaps a dominant and traditional geopolitical theme of Paraguay is the country's vulnerability to absorption by its immediate neighbors, Brazil and Argentina. Both counties have long-held expansionist ambitions of extending their domains into the continent's interiors, and Paraguay lies in the path of those ambitions. It is a wonder that the republic has kept its sovereignty, having survived two regional wars and having been defeated and occupied after one and narrowly winning the second, but with meager rewards after that victory.

A part of its survival may come from certain geopolitical factors—its distance from neighbors, hence its isolation within the continent's center; its placement as one of four buffer states that have separated the leading continental powers from each other but that have themselves suffered warfare and territorial transfers that have taken place; its ability to balance Brazil and Argentina, where one would surely checkmate absorption of Paraguay by the other; its fanatical Guaraní nationalism; and its natural river boundaries that define its territorial limits.

Paraguay resides in a unique pivotal position, perhaps more so than do the other buffers, a good location either for balancing or for bandwagoning Brazil and Argentina to its advantage. The country's foreign policies have attempted playing one neighbor against the other (balancing) or favoring one over the other (bandwagoning), normally Brazil over Argentina. Under the Stronato, or tenure of Alfredo Stroessner, Paraguay aligned with Brazil for the construction of the hydroelectric facility at Itaipú along the bordering Paraná River.

Three additional geopolitical factors should be attributed to Paraguay as well. The Itaipú hydroelectric facility, in large part built with Paraguayan labor and Brazilian financing and engineering, stands as one of the world's largest, and it provides electrical power to the industrial south of Brazil. Sometimes described as the strategic heartland of the continent, the plant ties Paraguay within the Brazilian sphere of influence, and its location and importance to Brazil probably make it likely that Brazil would intervene into Paraguayan affairs were Paraguay to weaken and destabilize. The author can attribute this portrait to Brazilian General Carlos de Meira Mattos, who claimed that the facility had been purposely placed at the Paraná frontier as a way to control the affairs of Paraguay.

Illegal immigration of Brazilians across the border presents another theme to this Paraguayan setting.[12] Ciudad Este, long a smuggling center along the triborder frontier, functions as an entry funnel for workers and investments in agribusiness concerns, primarily in soybeans. This movement happens along Uruguayan and Bolivian frontiers as well, and these intrusions may indicate continued movement of Brazil toward expanding westward its borders at the expensive of neighbors.

Finally, various commentators position Paraguay as a pivotal factor within continental geopolitics. The Uruguayan strategist Bernardo Quagliotti de Bellis saw Paraguay as essential to South American integration, hosting hydroelectric power at Itaipú as well as connecting transit routes among the Pacific, Amazonian, and Plata watersheds. His concept of URUPABOL, or the linking of the three buffer states as central to Southern Cone integration, drew some interest among commentators as well.[13]

The Paraguayan author Julia de Velilla saw Paraguay as a "key," "central point," and heartland, it serving as a "factor of union, port of friendship, equilibrium, and solidarity in the la Plata watershed and in South America."[14] The reader could also conceive of Paraguay as a lintel state, one that stabilizes the Brazil-Argentina relationship within the interior region by its central location.

In sum, all of the various concepts relative to Paraguay's geopolitics— buffer states, distances and isolation, rivers and power plants, balancing and bandwagoning powerful and threatening neighbors, spheres of influence, the Guaraní heritage, illegal aliens and smuggling, continental heartlands and equilibriums—all fit within our geopolitical definition and model.

8. The Geopolitics of Ancient Rome

Watch for these theories: buffer states, center/periphery, central pivot, choke points, climate, demographics, distance/isolation, encirclement, frontiers, heartland, immigration, imperial thesis, land-sea powers, ocean-cycles thesis, resources, spheres of influence, topography.

Rome's geopolitics turned defensive in nature once the empire became established after the demise of the republic: (1) to protect Italy against threat of invasion; (2) to dominate the Mediterranean, restricting alien ships from its waters and closing choke points to the entry of such vessels; (3) to exact Romanization and integration of peoples of the new peripheral lands so as to encourage loyalty; (4) to subjugate small nations within such peripheral lands as buffers against the more distant and rebellious tribes beyond; (5) to construct fortifications along the outer frontiers for protection; and (6) to build an effective road system for rapid communications, linking trade and security for its advantage.

Shatterbelts do not fit within Rome's geopolitics. After the fall of Carthage during the Republican era, and including the later Parthian invasions against the later empire, no other Great Power rose to challenge Rome. Security threats derived largely from "barbarians" and marauders within the western sectors and from the more civilized yet divided city-states and tribes within the eastern sectors. Although these smaller opposing factions grew stronger and more hostile toward the final centuries of the empire, Rome's fall came largely from within its inner bounds, financial bankruptcy and failure to stabilize leadership succession among the primary faults. Since it takes two strategic powers to form a shatterbelt, none appeared because of the dominance of Rome throughout the era, which prevented emergence of serious challengers.

Much of the violence came in civil wars, and such disruptions did not resemble shatterbelts, for these reasons: (1) the struggles, not involving established foreign states, instead drew opposing military forces of distinct regional recruitments within sectors of the empire. Likewise, (2) we do not see the vertical patterns, the strategic powers fighting among themselves with local participants. Finally, (3) the rivals themselves engaged in dynastic or partisan struggles, normally among leading generals who sought imperial authority.

For similar reasons, checkerboards were absent within the Roman configurations, for patterns of alternating factions or countries simply were not present in this framework. Nor were sea and land power struggles in evidence, for naval power pointed primarily to stopping pirates in the Mediterranean. A maritime capacity limited the Roman navy to a supply capacity and in river and sea patrols to protecting the outer margins of the empire and the client states.

Yet, two exceptions could be gleaned where *sea power* proved important, although both were internal to Rome itself, a facet of civil wars and not of foreign engagements. One came in the contest over Sicily between the forces of Caesar Augustus and his admiral and general Marcus Agrippa against Sextus Pompeius in 38 B.C.E.,[15] the latter staking his power upon maritime forces. Agrippa's victory in the sea battle of Naulochus settled the matter, paving the way toward Octavio's eventual consolidation of his forces against Mark Anthony in the maritime battle at Actium (31 B.C.E.) that decided the civil war between the two opponents.[16] But we do not see a true international sea/land power pattern arising.

A connected geopolitical concept relates to the *ocean-cycles thesis* in which empires form around certain seas, a good example being the Mediterranean trade and communications facility for the Romans. Still, Rome never identified itself intimately with the sea, except as a source of commerce and supply, the Egyptian grain shipments to Italy of particular importance. Indeed, the waterway posed as much an obstacle as a transit:

> But the Roman empire was not a small fort under siege. It cannot be visualized as a fort at all, however large: for any fort will always have the advantage of shorter inner lines . . . . In fact, the geographic shape of the empire was most unfavorable: its center was the hollow oblong of the Mediterranean, and the Mediterranean could be as much a barrier as a highway.
>
> The primary barriers were the "vagaries of the weather" that hindered sailing in the winter months. That Sea still served as a central imperial focus, this "Roman Lake" experiencing total domination during the centuries of the Empire. Rome, be-

ing primarily a land force, faced no serious sea-power opponents and saw little need for a focus upon a fighting sea-power component.[17]

Certain other theories hold better application. We might begin with the slogan "All roads lead to Rome," where one could visualize the Imperial City being a heartland described by Halford Mackinder—indeed, the city of Rome positioned roughly at the center of the empire's extensive domain, the expanse of territory formed around the Mediterranean Sea and along the northern and eastern stretches of Rome's borders to Europe and Asia. The classical heartland serves as a connecting pivot between the center extending outward to connect with the outlying periphery, the core being intertwined so as to coordinate the several sectors of the empire. The heartland's outer structure served primarily as a protection to the central ecumene as well as a source for revenue and manpower.

This heartland image appears appropriate to the ancient city. Although the imperial expanse was separated into various distant fronts, each tending to be isolated from the other parts because of poor transit and communication, a rough coordination did occur, with legions and resources being shifted where needed by networks of roads and maritime routes to replenish the empire. Transportation by the Mediterranean was seasonal and not always dependable; still, an internal and systematic pattern of trade, revenue collections, and military security was utilized within this heartland structure.

The heartland depiction can be more extensively drawn according to the three distinct eras of the imperial security framework.[18] With the Republican and later Julio-Claudian realms, an outer ring of client states and tribes brought internal security. No Roman troops stayed in these peripheral regions, and the stability of the system depended upon the fear of imperial power, augmented when necessary by diplomacy, bribes, and subsidies. The costs for defense were minimal, and Roman armies were primarily positioned for further territorial expansion in quest of plunder and resources. One could perceive in this pattern both the concepts of buffer states (perhaps most clearly in the case of Armenia) and of spheres of influence in the subject client states.

After 69 c.e. to the mid–third century crises, the efficiency of clients had diminished and Roman forces were deployed to stabilize the frontiers against rebellion, to fend off the entry of marauders, and to ensure collection of revenue. This new fixture of actively defending territory with Roman legions came at a higher cost, since the clients themselves proved unable to secure the frontiers. A policy of Romanization, intended to pacify the natives of the periphery by awarding Roman citizenship, decreased in effectiveness over time, as the empire became stretched in wealth and manpower and security for the clients could not be assured.

The third and final phase saw reliance upon "elastic defenses" or "defense-in-depth," these being stationary fortifications that sought to contain low-intensity guerrilla-type invaders that the regular armies could not so easily contain. The former images of Roman power and coercion faded, and fortifications gradually lost their effectiveness in defending the subject peoples. As this frontier encirclement contracted against the Italian core, Rome lost both tax revenues and a manpower base from which to recruit the necessary legions. The end arrived when the shrinking perimeter folded into the heartland pivot, the city itself being overrun and its rule ending in 476 C.E.

This Roman center-core or heartland structure corresponds to the *imperial thesis,* a rise-and-fall configuration that posits a *territorial expansion* from a central ecumene for protection and for acquiring wealth, similar to our earlier Russian example. Such territorial extension happens gradually, and the territories annexed, as they extend outward, begin to differ from the more unified core territories in having contrasting ethnicities and other such disrupting factors as topography, demographics, and climate.

Liabilities accrue from this territorial expansion, some serious enough to challenge the survival of the empire: (1) a hostile encirclement by the exposed neighboring peoples, resisting further absorption; (2) a difficulty of pacifying and assimilating the new clients brought into the center's authority by conquest and annexation; and (3) the costs of building and maintaining the center's authority over the expanse of empire, a danger of succumbing eventually to bankruptcy by overstretch of revenues. All of these elements appeared to cause the Roman fall.

This depiction of ancient Rome closes a main part of this book, its purpose again poised toward raising the visibility of classical geopolitics as a usable and recognized international-relations model. With a common definition that constructs the model, the author has placed within it sixty-odd theories adhering to that definition. The insights gained by applying certain of these theories to the eight case studies of this chapter, it is hoped, are suitable to convincing the reader that classical geopolitics indeed should join the pantheon of acceptable IR models.

7   Setting the Course for
a Rejuvenated Geopolitics

As said in the first chapter, the purpose for this book is to construct an improved and more visible classical model of geopolitics. Accordingly, a "call-to-action" is pronounced below for helping to bring about this goal.

1. *Legitimize the study of geopolitics:* Classical geopolitics suffers a distorted image and is wrongly blamed for undeserved ills not of its own making. The negativity comes from the original concept being captured by ideological groups bent on furthering their own perspectives, as was displayed in Chapter 3. Lacking a standard definition has further tarnished its reputation, in addition to the absence of a fully drawn model filled with relevant theories. These detours all diminish the utility of geopolitics and sidetrack it from making the contribution it is capable of making. This book attempts to erase that negativity by (1) drawing a common classical definition; (2) gathering sixty-odd theories that will adhere to that definition; and (3) applying certain of these theories to eight case studies, all three meant to raising the visibility of geopolitics as a separate but valued contributor to the IR-theory field.

2. *Emphasize the classical over the critical, postmodern geopolitics:* Much in critical geopolitics merits close consideration. For instance, postmodern normative theory should receive notice for its critical and prescriptive attentions, something lacking in the classical. We live in a flawed world, and the postmodernists striving to uncover its faults by deconstructing alleged exploitation is laudatory. By its nature, the classical version must put aside focus on the world's problems, its sole function being application of gathered theory to actual events and policy concerning foreign affairs.

But, to meld the normative onto the classical, even if possible, would distract from its neutral contribution—lending theory to interpreting states' actions within a geographic setting. Leaders' decision-making we ignore in preference to assuming that nations themselves represent the primary international actors. We bypass decision-makers on the assumption that rational leaders, consciously or unconsciously, perform within the constraints of their country's environments. One must enlist either one level or the other in his/her study, the decision-making or the state-as-actor, and the normative or the theoretical, but not both, for the two perspectives simply do not mix or combine at all.

This separation between the traditional and the critical can be distinguished even more bluntly. The basic neutral format of the classical model is distant from the partisan in every way, and when it has been forced by ideologues to depart from its nonpartisan place as an impartial tool for policy and for study, it has lost its original credibility and utility. Simply put, and as repeated throughout this book, traditional geopolitics is the study of how geography, or the placement of states, regions, and resources, may condition a country's foreign and security policies and actions. This is the historical and unique contribution of geopolitics. It should not show bias, or it suffers loss of respectability.

Above all, the emphasis of the modernist or classicist is the gathering and applying of theory—the probability that repeated actions and reactions may assist with understanding more clearly certain events, and that these attempts may be useful to conducting policy and to complementing study. The author's impression of the postmodernists takes an entirely different direction, that of deconstructing and critiquing the leadership of states in an interest toward exposing corruption, which they assume naturally to be present. Their stance has nothing to do with theory, whereas geopolitics has everything to do with theory. Again, the two approaches simply do not connect, and they often oppose. Thus, the classical must take its own separate path with little further gain from linking itself to the critical.

3. *Separate geopolitics from the model of realism:* In a different way but still a type of capture that limits the contribution and legitimacy of the classical version, the traditional geopolitics has been damaged by its occasional submersion within the realism model, and in particular within the power politics alleged to realism.

The power description rests appropriately with the realist. There, security defers to power, a protection necessary for peoples and nations in a dangerous anarchic world. Increasing one's power is believed to bring this protection, despite the "security dilemma" wherein neighbors may respond to power increases with their own power expansions in response. Arms races derive from individual attempts to augment security. As described in the earlier chapters, the Kissinger realist design recommends a moderate "framework for peace" or a collective consensus among the larger states as a surer way to stability and peace than would individual states on their own gaining such protection. A stable balance of power will return a similar collective security.

This reliance upon power is foreign to geopolitics, and where placement equates with security, this comes inherently within the spatial placement of nations—their positions, resources, and the like yielding to safety. The task is to recognize that particular location and consequently to deal with its advantages and limitations. Obviously, a country cannot locate itself distant from a threat; it must embed its security within its natural setting by balancing with allies or against threatening neighbors. Building up power alone may not protect at all, and it may endanger.

Another direction in this power discussion might come in the balance of power most noted in the neorealistic stance of Kenneth Waltz, which emphasizes that security derives from the measured powers within coalitions. Others found that wars arose more frequently when balances of either side were equal in power. Imbalances tended to negate warfare. Collective security would resemble this security-in-power intent as well. But the emphasis rests on measuring states' power and not in their spatial positioning, as would be the concern of geopolitics.

In sum, a reinvigorated geopolitics requires separation from the realist model and its power description for it to breathe a new life. This is not to refute the legitimacy of realism or of power but instead to assert that the two models are different in nature and must make their own separate contributions.

4. *Clarify and agree upon an appropriate geopolitics definition:* Without an accepted definition, constructing a geopolitical, or any such model, simply could not take place. A definition, as noted in Chapter 2, functions as "gatekeeper" by which assumptions, concepts, and theories legitimately can enter a model. The parts must correspond to the overall label, and without this facility we would suffer confusion and failure. Specifically, we would face difficulty in separating what is, and what is not, geopolitical. A common classical definition would protect our geopolitics from the ideological "captures" of the past and present that have so weakened the traditional stance.

It is essential for geopolitics to have some academic consensus for maintaining a set definition, and such a consensus should stipulate, at a minimum, the words "geographic" and "foreign policy." Again, as from Chapter 2, the author's definition is this: "Geopolitics is the study of the impact or influence of certain geographic features—positions and locations of regions, states, and resources, in addition to topography, climate, distance, demography, states' shape and size—as these may condition states' foreign policies and actions as an aid to statecraft. Accordingly, this study lends itself both to theory and to policy." It seems that most descriptions show a similarity to this suggestion. But whatever the case, an agreed-upon definition is vital to our mission to resurrect the traditional concept.

5. *Agree on the essential parts to a model of geopolitics, these being assumptions, concepts, and theories that correspond to a definition of geopolitics:* The approach to international-relations modeling taken in this book may be unique to the field, that being, the three parts of a model, assumptions, concepts, and theories, woven within a consistent definition of the area of interest. Once assembled and expanded with the entry of new elements, the only step remaining would be the application of the model's parts to actual events or to potential scenarios, as was submitted in Chapter 6. This rather simple approach seems the best method for assembling all the relevant parts into a whole for study and for policy.

What should follow would be a search, tabulation, and refinement of the relevant parts, these being all of the extant assumptions, concepts, and theories that would correspond to our established definition. This effort would resemble an ambitious project over an expanse of future time and involvement of reviewing the geopolitical, the foreign affairs, and the political-geography literature for features that correspondent to an agreed-upon definition of what is the classical, and then collecting and sorting these into our traditional geopolitical "container" or model.

Such a project may be quite lengthy—the sifting through all types of publications and documents, and even originating new concepts and theories over time. And eventually our task would require some central depository to publish our listings such that all of us would have access to the ongoing collections.

6. *Collect and refine classical geopolitical assumptions:* Once more, the model's assumptions must come as simple statements of belief, not being provable but still necessary to underlying what would be the essence of geopolitics. We could not proceed further without these traits. For instance, we assume at the beginning that a country's relative position will condition its international behavior. Further, we assume that statespersons will normally act in behalf of their countries within an environmental parameter, consciously or unconsciously. How would we know this? We just do—a trust with no further

doubts. Fortunately, once accepted, the other elements of the model become possible.

7. *Collect and refine classical geopolitical concepts and theories:* Concepts resemble symbols, traits, and other descriptions that form the basic and necessary vocabulary of geopolitics. Concepts arrive as abstractions and as passive describers, unlike assumptions that we must believe as true and theories that contribute as statements of probability.

Frequently, concepts and theories blend together, the symbol lending itself eventually to the premise. This would be reason for combining the two elements into a single Chapter 5. For instance, heartlands occupy central continental locations. Yet their central locations, being pivotal, give certain advantages—isolation, protection, mobility, and maneuverability, as well as certain disadvantages—isolation, distance, encirclement, and unstable boundaries. Consequently, we see together both a concept and a theory. Indeed, all concepts can be formulated as theories, the description leading to the generalization.

This dichotomy noted, the suggestion is first, to describe the concept as briefly as is necessary, and second, to expand beyond the concept into the theory. This technique appears natural, and it holds the clarity of keeping concept and theory connected but still distinct.

8. *Collect and refine applications within the geopolitical model:* In this eighth goal, we arrive at the testing-through-application phase, once progress toward the model's assembly starts to happen. We bring to our consideration historical and contemporary examples in foreign affairs, such as with the Peloponnesian war. The checkerboard pattern of the various Greek war participants seemed instructive, revealing the general structure of the conflict and why certain actions took place. The several shatterbelts showed where and how the war began. Other concepts and theories taken from the geopolitical model that offered assistance included the sea-power/land-power dichotomy, the distance-weakens thesis, the lack of buffer areas but the presence of spheres of influence and the rigidity of alliance systems, strategic choke points, rugged terrain and access to resources, the contagion of conflict across borders, the impact of powerful Persia, and other relevant features of the spatial environment. Most international happenings would affix to similar applications.

A further thought would include the assembling of geopolitical linkages or bundles of concepts and theories that may associate together, such as checkerboard with buffer states or shatterbelts with heartlands and influence spheres. Such attempts could assist in the further broadening of the geopolitical model itself, not only with successful applications but also with an increase in our typology of assumptions, concepts, and theories.

9. *Organize a support group of classical geopolitical enthusiasts to forward the above aspirations:* The idea here would pertain to an institution's assistance as a headquarters, most likely a major university with the addition of a professional journal focused upon research and information relative to the classical version of geopolitics. We could well include an official membership of classical enthusiasts, a repository or listing for all of the assumptions, concepts, and theories, and a newsletter bulletin that might feature the various successful applications and insights that might be located, utilizing our geopolitical model. Perhaps initially the Mackinder Forum could satisfy as a beginning. Some connection with foreign ministries could lend support as well. All of these suggestions, of course, must await circulation of this book to a wider audience and, it is to be hoped, winning readers' support for its aspirations.

Appendix: Classical Geopolitical Concepts / Theories

Action Spaces: The ability of some states via distance, isolation, topography, or certain regional balances to remain unaffected by and independent from other states' actions. American countries tend to enjoy this security from Eurasian threats, as do the southern and peripheral world regions, such as sub-Saharan Africa, South Asia, and the Southern Pacific. The Cold War rivalry between the United States and the Soviet Union reduced action spaces because of their ubiquitous competition. But the US, as later unipolar hegemon, created a tendency for expansion of such autonomous spaces caused by the ending of the earlier strategic rivalry with Russia. Countries positioned more centrally, for instance, such as Germany and Poland, suffered more than average interventions from neighbors, thus experiencing diminished action spaces. Switzerland, Venezuela, and Australia/New Zealand experienced the opposite.

American Isolationism: Unique within a strategic platform, the United States can better exert pivotal influence by its offshore balancing, an ability to place its naval strength at either extreme of Eurasia and then siding for or against certain regional rivals and allies to its advantage. The isolation and distance of America enhances its aligning with nations for overseas' regional balances without their fear of territorial absorption by the United States. North American isolation allows it protection from Eurasian dangers and involvements, and from threatening American neighbors, thus awarding a focus upon its sea-power capacities without the need for more expensive and politically vulnerable land-power facilities. Within this isolation as well, the American could capture the wealth of his continent during past centuries without serious opposition and to dominate Middle America according to the Monroe Doctrine.

Asymmetric States: In Saul Cohen's terminology, these countries are "second-order powers" that challenge a status quo by disrupting "the regional [leading states] to rethink long-held positions and, in effect, to open their systems more widely." Castro's Cuba ranks as a prominent example; perhaps Iran and North Korea do as well. "While these regionally destabilizing states may well exhaust their own energies, the perturbations [instabilities] caused by them play a useful role in forgoing more cohesive regional structures."[1] Consequently, the outcome of these states opposing the regional leaders assists toward rebalancing an unstable regional system, and to Cohen, ultimately these states will come to play a positive role.

Autarky: A state's ambition for attaining enough resources, protection, and autonomy to enable self-sufficiency. This is illustrated in pan-regional designs, longitudinal lines separating the earth into three or four distinct autonomous geographic zones, sometimes depicted as Oceania, Eurasia, and East Asia. One could surmise this scenario within a more negative *Geopolitik* of a northern dominance of southern regions, Africa, Latin America, and the Middle East, fulfilling Great Powers' needs for industrial and energy resources. Likewise, the more extreme maps of this design could expose a war-prone checkerboard pattern of conflict across the adjacent zones for each other's wealth.

It is generally established by most economists that autarky should not be recommended as a modern nation's policy. Since the earth has distributed its resources unevenly, international trade replaces the alleged merits of self-sufficiency as a more effective path to gaining trading markets and necessary resources for national development and prosperity. Enhanced security might arrive in the collective as well.

Balance of Power: A configuration of regional states composed of varying numbers, from one to five normally, positioned for equilibrium or disequilibrium among them depending upon state policies and upon the wider political environment. The outcomes are thus: unipolar, bipolar, or multipolar, and their arrangements accommodative (more stable) or hostile (more unstable). Most scholars visualize the classical balance as multipolar and accommodative and as more stable. Yet the present unipolar pattern of the United States as hegemon has proven peaceful, since it appears to be accommodative to the major Great Powers. In classical geopolitical terms, security derives more from position than from power, the alignments of checkerboards a prominent instance.

Balancer States; Bandwagoning and Balancing: Balancers locate either as peripheral-within-regions or outside-of-region states, not intertwined within major power alliances and thus able to bandwagon or align with a dominant side of a regional balance or balance against a dominant side, evening the power distributions within the region. Traditionally, England played this role within European balances, and presently the United States follows with its offshore balancing strategy. Despite its relative weakness, the central positioning of Paraguay between its larger neighbors, Brazil and Argentina, has seen these sorts of balances in its recent history.

Borders-Cause-Wars Thesis: Here, a statistically proven association arises between number of international frontiers of states and their number of war involvements—or, the more borders, the more wars. The association was shown for South

America and the same globally.[4] This rather common sense connection rises statistically with countries having more populated borders,[5] and with states possessing never-resolved territorial disputes.[6]

Bridge Countries; Gateway States and Regions: Areas and states that attract outside entry into and through them into more expansive regions and continents in the interests of security, investments, and energy-industrial resources. Brzezinski saw Western Europe as "America's essential geopolitical bridgehead on the Eurasian continent,"[2] and Cohen visualized these areas as financial and trade centers.[3]

Buffer States: Smaller and weaker countries positioned between/among larger neighbors such that direct contact, and thus possible warfare among the larger adjacent states, are likely avoided. In most cases, as in South America, these buffers stabilize regions by cushioning conflict among the larger powers and by absorbing territorial losses to the benefit of the more powerful. Middle America tends to isolate the Southern from the Northern Hemisphere similarly.

Camino del Sol: A geopolitical reference to the *isolation* of South America from the northern Great Powers,[7] and hence to an alleged world dominance of the Northern Hemisphere. The farther a country from a latitudinal line connecting the major northern capital cities—Washington, DC, London, Paris, Moscow, Beijing, and Tokyo—the less global impact that state possesses. A similar picture arises in the equatorial paradox, which posits a 70 percent likelihood that the level of development of a nation will correspond to its distance from either north or south of the equator. Explanations for this tendency extend from tropical diseases hampering human energies to the tropics providing easy foodstuffs without need for innovation and hard work that would be required of the challenges of colder and harsher northern climes.

These references parallel Henry Kissinger's pentagonal thesis, which numbers a global power monopoly of only the five major power centers of the north that "count." Also within this mix, a condominium concept resembles these five Great Powers of the north controlling major international events of importance. Some evidence exists that the world's more productive temperate landforms, the areas historically spawning the leading civilizations, happen more plentifully in the north than in the south, where in the latter case, such zones extend mostly over ocean waters and the smaller fertile landforms that are scattered and isolated.

Cataclysmic Events: This thesis resides at the one extreme between environmental determinism and possibilism, the former of these being events within nature that directly and immediately impact upon a country's political and governmental behavior—earthquakes, tsunamis, volcanoes, global warming, polluted water and air spaces, pandemics, and scarcities of oil, water, land, and other energy and human/industrial resources. Some political scandals and popular uprisings have followed earthquakes and tsunamis in Nicaragua, 1972, and in Japan,

2011. Cataclysmic events occur so devastatingly that they determine political outcomes.

Challenge and Response: Humans facing and overcoming difficult terrain, climate, and other harsh conditions—these representing, for instance, dangerous jungle environments and rugged mountain ranges when confronted by migrating peoples. American exceptionalism might pose a further example, its success in transforming a wilderness into a rich continent, or manifest destiny, its alleged inherent right and duty to do so despite the daunting challenge.

Checkerboards: A leapfrog configuration of states within a region whereby neighboring states appear as enemies but neighbors of neighbors farther out figure as allies. This mandala patterning can be found in contemporary South America, instilling a stable structure to the continent. For the ancient Greek Peloponnesian war, its checkerboard was rigid and war-prone,[8] creating a setting for thirty years of destruction. Thus, geopolitical patterns can differ within these structures, the outcomes being either stable or not. Checkerboards occur elsewhere in the Middle East, Middle America, and Southeast Asia.

Choke Points: Pivotal land and sea corridors show as choke points, these being straits, passages, canals, channels, and river estuaries whose positions exert impact over an extended distance beyond their immediate locations. Good examples would include the Straits of Malacca and of Gibraltar, the Panama and Suez canals, New Orleans and the Mississippi River estuary. Countries compete for control over such points.

Clash of Civilizations: Huntington and others have asserted that previous ideological and nationalistic competitions among nations and blocs of the Cold War have shifted onto different social and cultural dimensions of conflict.[9] Now, rival "civilizations" struggle in armed strife. Wars will be fought in march lands or frontiers that separate the various civilizations, particularly in borders showing contemporary hostility—the Muslim, Chinese, and Western lands. Huntington believed that the cultural centers themselves would remain united and not engage in civil warfare.

Climatology Theory: A link is fixed between climatic conditions and human and political behavior, perhaps the most prominent example the alleged vigor and health of temperate climates in contrast to the lethargy and stagnation alleged of tropical and polar zones. Another example comes in the connection between lower rainfall prompting migration, depression, chaos, and stagnation. Some evidence derives from the climatic disruptions of global warming in which inconsistent weather may contribute to conflict. Finally, it is possible that favorable climates assisted the industrial rise of Europe and North America after the "little Ice Age," giving rise to domination over Asia and Africa.

Closed Spaces: At the nineteenth century's end, a concern was raised by several writers, Halford Mackinder and Frederick Jackson Turner among these, of the disappearance of lands for colonization and development, thus creating a scarcity causing national rivalries and wars. Such a scenario extends today to overpopulation, diminished lands for food production, exhaustion of sustainable resources, and other such factors within the environmental context. The law of valuable areas represents a variation of the closed spaces in which available resources and agricultural lands lie open to potential colonization but primarily those located in isolated and difficult-to-exploit spaces. A similar prediction of Great Power warfare accompanies this law, a likely example being for petroleum resting in Central Asia.

Contagion: A diffusion phenomenon exhibiting the spread of riots, rebellion, democracy, military dictatorships, and other instances across international frontiers. This "demonstration effect" tends toward a higher likelihood in centrally positioned countries within regions. The "falling dominoes" example, sans its ideological taint, represents another instance of contagion.

Containment Policy: The source for this strategy originated in George Kennan's warning of likely Soviet expansion over Eurasia and onto its rimlands, this threat adhering to Mackinder's heartland thesis. The general assumption held that the Soviet Union, either for nationalistic or ideological reasons, sought to extend its territories to the whole of Eurasia and beyond, perhaps bent upon world domination. Hence, to turn back this threat of a united and hostile Russia, Eurasia, the United States, and its allies must erect "rimland dykes" along the continent's periphery to contain the Russian expansion in the hope that once the allied success in halting the advance occurs, Russia's recognition of its being contained would either mellow into seeking a status quo or instead the empire would collapse as a result of the costs and stresses of its failed seeking of new lands. Violence could develop in this latter case with global war following a Soviet collapse.

Convergence Theory: A possible pre-shatterbelt condition visualized by Cohen in areas centrally positioned between the interests of outside but often adjacent Great Powers.[10] These zones could show either as gateway or shatterbelt patterns. Perhaps pre–World War II Poland might qualify, and contemporary Iraq before the US occupation.

Demography: A spatial characteristic of distributions and densities of peoples over lands and resources that exert a political, economic, or other impact, such as under- or overpopulation upon places on the earth. Excessive human congestion in southern megacities could foster failed states, and from these would spread beyond themselves to adjacent areas such problems as crime, migrations, poverty, disease, political violence, and other such disruptions.

Dependency: A core-periphery regional and global structure featuring the technologically advanced and thus wealthy and powerful core countries and regions dominant over an outer rim of weak, poor, and dependent countries. A maldistribution of natural resources accompanies this pattern, the rich areas more amply endowed in resources than the poor areas. A further claim arrives in that those in poverty are kept in plight within a colonial or neocapitalist pattern, the powerful becoming wealthier at the expense of the poor.

Distance-Weakens Argument: The claim that closer lines of communication will lend certain advantages of nearness—lower costs of transport and travel, cooperative security interests, assembling of influence spheres and key nations, and accomplishment of regional integration. Disadvantages accrue with distance, although some argue against these claims, asserting that modern technologies of communications negate the disadvantages of distance. Despite such technologies, many affirm that this traditional thesis of distance weakening still pertains in the majority of cases.

Earth Dependence/Emancipation: In the instance of earth dependence, man essentially is limited in his capacities by nature, with few exceptions. Not able to escape the fetters of his environment, he is "nature limited." Nonetheless, in the more liberal instance of emancipation, humans hold greater capacity for freedom, given this by science and human ingenuity, which will remove many of nature's constraints. Such a dichotomy can be visualized in states as well as in humans, states being either at the mercy of difficult regional and spatial limitations or able to achieve gains from their own skills and flexibility that would lend them more freedom.

Encirclement: Of course, all countries encircle and are encircled, a premise central to classical geopolitics. What one studies within the phenomenon of encirclement are the supposed advantages and disadvantages of this positioning. Locating on the periphery might award some protection yet deprive the resident of impact within the region. Other factors on either side of this discussion have been outlined elsewhere in this volume. This term can exude a balancing phenomenon and even hostile intent, in which certain nations might seek protection and power with alliance to an outside power. Or they could align with others against a more dominant regional nation. Brazil being encircled by the Spanish republics offers an example, Brazil's neighbors having been successful in denying it access to the Pacific and to a permanent seat on the UN Security Council. The United States, in its capacity as an offshore balancer, exhibits another instance of its involvement in the regional balances on either Eurasian fringe, encircling China or Russia in preventing any sort of aggressive intentions. North America can limit its encirclement by Eurasia by itself encircling the continent's rimland expanses.

Environmental Determinism/Possibilism: We might want to avoid the charge of geopolitics being "deterministic," a claim that holds some justification. Yet the query must be considered: How dominating to ourselves and county is our physical environment—excessively or selectively? Here, we see an evolution of thought and controversy in this theory's divide, evolving from an inevitable causality of earlier writers to the contemporary acceptance of a "possible" or "conditioning" effect toward humans and states toward their spatial surroundings. Accordingly, we presently hold a common acceptance for countries' settings impacting upon their international actions and policies in certain instances. We can do no more to clarify this attachment. Nonetheless, let us refrain from asserting a strict "determinism" and instead stay with the environment as possible "conditioner."

Falling-Dominoes Thesis: The more popular and notorious depiction of this thesis attaches to the spread of communism, one state succumbing to socialism and this "disease" or "flood" then advancing onto neighboring states being tainted similarly, such countries "falling [like] dominoes." Hence, this unproven ideological premise takes this dominoes assumption out of the realm of classical geopolitics. Still, examples of a contagion effect happening among contiguous countries occur within nonideological descriptions of this phenomenon, such as political instability, economic depression, democracy, riots, and the like.[11] Accordingly, when the concept of falling dominoes or sequential happenings may occur among neighboring countries, in these instances we can accept the theory of dominoes falling as tied to contagion, and thus, it will be given a place within the geopolitical model.

Two additional theories could stick to falling dominoes, both being expansive to the dominoes question above. A field-theory structure broadens the original thesis by adding types of borders, comparative population levels, historical and cultural rivalries among the adjacent players, and so forth. Here, the additional variables add more depth beyond the mere one-dimensional frontiers. Additionally, a modified-linkage model serves much the same purpose, replacing national borders with connected functional nodes that erase political lines, these being multinational metropolitan and trade networks, traffic routes, and like regional extensions.

Fluvial Laws: Spatial patterns of rivers and seas would pertain to an assortment of theses: interior land-locked countries inherently striving for an ocean outlet; centripetally flowing rivers unifying countries; states dominating single river watersheds; countries competing for river estuaries; states controlling estuaries tending to dominate the immediate coastlines; and directions of countries' rivers determining the regional directions of their foreign policies.

Frontier Thesis: The argument advanced by historian Frederick Jackson Turner that the unique North American wilderness and its frontier, with colonists moving westward, helped form America democracy and such other traits as equalitarianism, individualism, distrust for authority, violence, and less interest toward artistic and scientific achievements. The earlier settlers encountered environmental challenges in overcoming the wilderness and developing its uncultivated lands. His thesis prompted a variety of offshoots, such as manifest destiny, Monroe Doctrine, exceptionalism, isolationism, and resistance to immigrant and racial diversity.

Geostrategies: Policies designed and implemented by successful statespersons that gained their countries' vital resources and trade routes, protected frontiers, national unity, and other pertinent geopolitical needs of their states.

Great Game: This idea originated in the nineteenth-century rivalry between Imperial Russia and Great Britain for Afghanistan and to a lesser extent for Tibet and surrounding areas. Several later authors revived the Great Game, including Brzezinski and Megoran,[12] with Admiral Mahan predicting a land-power/sea-power confrontation over a "Middle Strip" within Central Asia also resembling this rivalry.

Heartland Thesis: Mackinder's 1904 address outlining his heartland thesis began the Anglo–North American version of traditional geopolitics, the emphasis upon the internal lands of central Eurasia and its strategic inward pivot. Central position afforded several advantages: (1) protection from invasion resulting from isolation, longer distances, harsh weather and topography, and great expanse of territory; (2) maneuverability within and beyond a central pivot; (3) access to continental resources; and (4) ability to probe vulnerabilities of the outer ring of countries and of the maritime bases of the rimland. Mackinder's Eurasian heartland thesis stands as the leading geopolitical concept, one that alleges world domination would reward the heartland's possessor. The Charcas Heartland of Bolivia in South America is recognized within the literature, too.

Hydraulic Despotism: Related to fluvial laws, several ancient empires of despotism formed because of rulers' control of irrigation systems in climates of drought. This premise rests on elite castes' dominance over flood control and water that brought them ownership of adjacent lands and peoples. Yet in contemporary times, we may be returning to this image of political rivalry for scarce water, lands, and resources by elites and their corporations.

Immigration: The movement of peoples over spaces that eventually impact upon local cultures and governments as well as upon foreign policies. Examples would cover later political and economic fragmentation within lands hosting new immigrants, as with contemporary Europe and with illegal migration across borders where workers seek better employment opportunities but create other dislocations associated with their movement. European colonization of North America probably lent to foreign policy the ideals of exceptionalism, manifest destiny, images of racism, and attitudes of unilateralism.

Imperial Thesis: All empires expand, almost by definition, and such expansion carries advantages and disadvantages. Expansion brings security and wealth—security in distance frontiers and in isolation from enemy countries; wealth in the resources the imperial state can access in the newly gained territories. Yet empires must face problems of encirclement by suspicious neighboring countries alarmed at the expansion. Absorbing alien peoples in newly gained territories could stimulate rebellion against the center. In addition, imperial states must bear the costs of expansion and encirclement, all of these liabilities forcing an eventual contraction of space away from the periphery to the original core and toward imperial disintegration.[13]

Integration/Globalization: Integration erases national commercial boundaries and political sovereignties as ways to broaden regional markets by eliminating tariffs and by coordinating policies, the best example being the European Union. Globalization reflects the advancement of communications such that distant peoples and countries come closer via the new electronic technologies.

Intermarium: Similar to a buffering configuration, "the [European] countries from the Baltic to the Black seas have a common interest in limiting Russian power and the geopolitical position to do so if they act as a group."[14] But, for energy sources, Turkey is reluctant to alienate Russia by joining this buffer configuration. No decision has been made to date.

Irredentism: Advocating annexation or combining of territories as a plan for uniting long-separated peoples of common ethnicity or of past national identity into forming new states or into joining adjacent existing states. The Kurds in Iraq, Iran, Syria, and Turkey, desiring a unified homeland, are one example, others being the Zionist claims for Israel and the Aztlan of Chicanos for the American Southwest. The contemporary Ukrainian shatterbelt offers an example as well.

Key Nation Thesis: An alleged tactic of the Nixon foreign policy whereby certain strategically positioned states in outlying regions would receive US assistance meant for them to stabilize such areas that would also forward US interests. Examples include Brazil, Iran, and Nigeria. "Using subordinate regional powers as surrogates, exchanging their willingness to incur risks from a major power opposed to the US for substantial benefits. These [benefits] range from strategic guarantees and support against smaller neighbors to trade advantages and technology transfers. The recovery of West Germany and Japan during the Cold War are classic examples of this."[15]

Land-Locked Countries: Those being continentally interior nations without extensive seacoasts, such states normally suffer isolation, less economic and political development, and weaker international involvement and recognition than coastal ecumenes would enjoy. For some, gaining a sea outlet would appear prominently in their foreign-policy goals. Paraguay maintains some ocean contact from the Paraguay River and from overland-transit agreements with Brazil. Traditionally, Russia and Bolivia have sought an ocean outlet as well.

Linchpin States: A concept tied both to shatterbelts, containment, and the Eurasian rimlands, these states possess locations of strategic value between the margins of potential Soviet expansion and of Western resistance to that expansion. Examples include Poland, Germany, Iran, Afghanistan, Pakistan, South Korea, and the Philippines.

Linkage Thesis: Kissinger's assertion that Third World instabilities and anti-Westernism were connected to Soviet intrigue. To break this linkage, the West would offer rewards to the Russians to reverse such actions, the West affording relaxation of tensions, exchanges of trade and technology, and cooperation within international organizations.

Lintel States: Like buffer states, a single state positioned between two larger countries that stabilizes the surrounding area, like a doorway or window lintel placed above the arch. The two larger countries are poised against each other, as neither can dominate or absorb the lintel state. As in the case of Paraguay juxtaposed astride Brazil and Argentina, it may play a balancing or bandwagoning foreign policy toward its two larger neighbors that may stabilize the entire region.

Manifest Destiny: A space concept within geopolitics when shorn of its nationalistic and religious connotations, the term refers to the inevitability of a country occupying outlying territorial spaces. Such an expansion often manifests as a right or obligation to civilize and develop the new lands. This factor is seen in both Brazilian and US manifestos to spread westward, only the United States being successful. The nineteenth-century attempts to exploit the rubber lands of the Congo and of Brazil by European nations parallel this description.

Monroe Doctrine: President James Monroe's original address that sought to prevent European bases and strategic influence in Middle America, a goal that would work against the formation of shatterbelts in the region. Also a part of the containment policy of the Cold War, violated in 1962 during the Cuban missile crisis when the Soviet Union placed nuclear-armed missiles in Cuba. The doctrine could later be extended to the Eurasian rimlands, the American objective being offshore balancing against a possible hostile Eurasia.

Natural Borders: Frontiers formed by rivers, oceans, mountains, and deserts that denote march borderlands, although river watersheds tend to unify as well as to divide state boundaries. This clarity of natural demarcations attracts fewer territorial disputes among neighbors and therefore brings more regional stability. *Harmonic* and *equilibrium* frontiers show similar tendencies, with the latter being the outer limits of expanding empires or the farthest points their natural power can take them.

Natural Resources: Abundant resources possessed by countries bolster their national prosperity and international impact. Fortunately for some and not so for others, the earth's riches are not evenly distributed, North America perhaps being the most provisioned with such wealth. The dependency thesis would reflect this scenario as well, the core areas wealthy because of their abundant inheritance of natural riches. The petro-politics dilemma poses a different and negative view of such wealth. Future wars could well be fought over resource competition when energy and other wealth become depleted.

Normative and Alternative Geopolitical Processes: Two alternating geopoliti-cal processes, the "normative" in which the successful expansion of a universal or hegemonic state would come to extend domination beyond its immediate regions such as to place adjacent areas under some level of subservience. Such Great Powers control their cores and peripheries to the extent that lesser states accept their stan-dard of domination. After these empires falter, the smaller countries will attempt to resume their autonomy by constructing regional associations that will protect their newly gained independence. The Cold War resembled the first process; the contemporary European Union the second.[16] The imperial thesis and action spaces resemble this depiction as well.

Ocean Cycles; Age of the Pacific; Westward Movement of Civilizations: Cer-tain centrally located rivers, seas, and oceans have ed the rise of civilizations in the ancient Middle East, the Nile, Euphrates-Tigris river ways, and elsewhere in the Aegean and Mediterranean seas, the North Atlantic, and more recently, the Pacific Ocean Rim. These bodies of water appear to favor maritime nations, placing such waterways as pivotal to success in broadening countries' impact and prosperity and toward their utilizing many of the advantages of central position in regions and continents. Some find in the contemporary Age of the Pacific a prediction of this basin as the coming world focus of importance, power, and conflict. Finally, the thesis forms that major world civilizations have moved westward, from Greece through Rome and Britain, onto North America, and perhaps to the Pacific Era and China. Somewhat Europe-centric and mentioned by Mackinder,[17] these civiliza-tions drew strength from sea and oceanic features nearby, the Mediterranean, the North Atlantic, and later, the Pacific.

Offshore Balancing: An alternative Grand Strategy of the United States, a shift away from Cold War preponderance, suggesting these changes: the United States should (1) retrench from commitments to Japan and Germany and allow these countries' rise to Great Power status. Resist intervening in peripheral areas meant to enhance Japanese and German stability. No longer oppose the rise of such sta-tus for China. Accept an eventual shift from a unipolar to a multipolar world; (2) forsake the current interdependent trade policies, replacing these with a neomer-cantilism that will place primary emphasis on protecting US national wealth and on meeting its current domestic needs; and (3) rely upon the US Navy to assist in offshore balancing adjacent the Eurasian rimlands favorable to American national interests, particularly in positioning against an expansionist China by aligning with its encircling Asian rivals.

Organic Borders and States: An earlier German concept whereby states tend either to expand in territory or to contract spatially, based upon their national "ages": youth, maturity, or elderly. Survival would rest with expansion, defeat with contraction. Borders would broaden or shrink in relation to this dynamic nature, the outer skins of the state. Manifest destiny approximates this phenomenon, as well as containment, the imperial and dependency theses, and, more distantly, Mackinder's heartland.

Pan-Regions: The thesis of three or four global longitudinal sectors enclosing regions and continents—Pan-America, Pan-Europe, Pan-Eurasia, and the Asian Co-Prosperity Sphere. Common examples are shown in George Orwell's novel 1984, and in Fascist world maps. Such a structure sought to achieve self-sufficiency and autonomy for the sequestered sectors, dominated by the northern Great Nations. Checkerboard conflicts might arise within this configuration. Similar patterns of northern power would include condominiums and the key nation aspects.

Petro-Politics: A "resources curse" shown in a nation's dependence upon exporting oil and gas while yet reaping great wealth. Nonetheless, this will see a decline in civil rights and democracy, causing an inverse statistical association between resource dependence and individuals' freedom.

Pivotal Locations and Positional Supremacy: Pivotal locations represent an essential element of traditional geopolitics, a unique placement giving impact further out from the central leverage. A variety of other concepts reflect this pivot: choke points, heartlands and rimlands, dependency, ocean cycles, and buffers, among similar terminology. Positional supremacy offers a similar description, that being a "key area requisite for world domination."[18] Such a core area could be a heartland or rimland or both, outlined by cultural or "functional" factors during historical periods advantaging a particular state or alliance.

Rimlands: Periphery lands of the Eurasian margin astride Mackinder's heartland that would include Western and Southern Europe, the Middle East, and Southeast and East Asia. Mackinder's and Spykman's visions differed on their descriptions of this encircling region, the former seeing it as passive, the latter more active and as essential to global stability as the heartland. Many tend to side with Spykman,[19] who recognized that both world wars were found in divided rimlands with either extreme, heartland and outer oceanic margins united against opponents of the rimland.

Sea Lanes of Communication: Transport paths vital to countries dependent upon international trade and upon resources they require but must import. A good example would be Japan. Strategic maritime straits or choke points factor into this concept, as well as offshore balancing and sea power vs. land power, two perspectives vital to North American interests.

Sea Power–Land Power: Countries exhibiting either a maritime or a continental emphasis in their geopolitical projections. A maritime nation would reflect a coastal position with good harbors and an oceanic projection. Landward nations normally lack a sea orientation, being placed internally within continental cores. A common debate stirs over the favored orientation for national power, with naval proponents arguing for the benefits of trade and continental proponents for the weakness of sea powers for vulnerable land bases.

Shape and Size of Countries: A state's configuration affects its national unity, territorial security, and economic vitality. The rectangular shape of the United States, tied together within by internal waterways and passable terrains, facilitates communications, whereas the irregular shapes of Chile, Brazil, and Canada hinder unity. In general, circular and rectangular shapes might strengthen unity, whereas elongated and irregular configurations could be disruptive. A nation's greater territory will factor into strength and prosperity, the larger powers tending to be more active in international relations.

Shatterbelt: A region showing two levels of conflict: (1) a strategic rivalry between outside Great Nations; and (2) a local conflict among countries of that region. A shatterbelt arises when strategic competitors and the regional competitors form opposing alliances within the area.[20] A threat of conflict escalation is common to these configurations.

Space Consciousness and Space Mastery: Drawn from German and South American spokesmen (Friedrich Ratzel and Julio Londoño Londoño), the idea of space consciousness claims that larger states have appetites for additional space, particularly if these nations visualize as profitable open and vacant spaces nearby. Such awareness of additional lands marks success in a survival-of-the-fittest international environment. Space mastery posits that states should populate and develop their peripheral hinterlands so as to prevent absorption of such lands by aggressive neighbors.

Spheres of Influence: Regions under domination by an outside adjacent or nearby Great Power, examples being Middle America by the United States and Eastern Europe by Russia during the Cold War. A shatterbelt structure would replace these influence spheres in that a rival outside competitor would intrude into the area.

Weapons States: These smaller powers aim to gain in security and prestige by the acquiring or producing of "weapons of mass destruction," nuclear, chemical, and biological.

Notes

Preface

1. Glassner, Martin Ira, and Harm de Blij, *Systematic Political Geography,* 4th ed. (New York: John Wiley and Sons, 1989), 223–28.

2. Kissinger, Henry, *The White House Years* (Boston: Little Brown, 1979).

3. Starr, Harvey, *On Geopolitics: Space, Place, and International Relations* (Boulder, CO: Paradigm, 2013).

4. Kelly, Phil, "A Critique of Critical Geopolitics," *Geopolitics* 11 (2006), 24–53.

5. Mastanduno, Michael, "Preserving the Unipolar Moment: Realist Theories and U.S. Grand Strategy after the Cold War," *International Security* 21/4 (1997), 50.

6. Cohen, Saul, *Geopolitics: The Geography of International Relations,* 2nd ed. (Lanham, MD: Rowman and Littlefield, 2009).

7. Grygiel, Jakub, *Great Powers and Geopolitical Change* (Baltimore, MD: Johns Hopkins University Press, 2006).

Chapter 1

1. Owens, Mackubin Thomas, "In Defense of Classical Geopolitics," *Naval War College Review* 52/4 (1999), 59–76.

2. Kelly, Phil, "Geopolitics—Part 1," in John Agnew and James S. Duncan, eds., *A Companion to Human Geography* (Chichester, West Sussex: Wiley-Blackwell, 2011), 512–22.

3. Art, Robert, "Geopolitics Updated: The Strategies of Selected Engagement," *International Security* 23/3 (1998–99), 79–113.

4. Gerace, Michael, "Between Mackinder and Spykman: Geopolitics, Containment, and After," *Comparative Strategy* 10/4 (1991), 353.

5. Kelly, Phil, and Thomas Boardman, "Intervention in the Caribbean: Latin American Responses to United Nations Peacekeeping," *Revista/Review Inter-Americana* 6 (1976), 403–11.

6. Kelly, Phil, "Geopolitical Themes in the Writings of General Carlos de Meira Mattos of Brazil," *Journal of Latin American Studies* 16 (1984), 439–61.

7.   Kelly, Phil, "Escalation of Regional Conflict: Testing the Shatterbelt Concept," *Political Geography Quarterly* 5 (1986), 161–80.

8.   Kelly, Phil, and Jack Child, *Geopolitics of the Southern Cone and Antarctica* (Boulder, CO: Lynne Rienner, 1988).

9.   Kelly, Phil, *Checkerboards and Shatterbelts: The Geopolitics of South America* (Austin: University of Texas Press, 1997).

10.   Kelly, "Geopolitics—Part 1."

11.   Kelly, Phil, "Methodological Challenges toward Constructing a Geopolitical Model," *Dialogue and UniversalismE* 5/3 (2014), 1–13; "A Geopolitical Interpretation of Security Concerns within United States-Latin American Relations," *Security and Defense Studies Review* 14 (2013), 53–68.

12.   Kelly, Phil, "A Critique of Critical Geopolitics," *Geopolitics* 11 (2006), 24–53.

13.   Gray, Colin, "In Defense of the Heartland: Sir Halford Mackinder and His Critics a Hundred Years On," *Comparative Strategy* 23 (2004), 9–25; Clover, Charles, "Dreams of the Eurasian Heartland," *Foreign Affairs* 78 (1999), 9–13; Ó Tuathail, Gearóid, *Critical Geopolitics: The Politics of Writing Global Space* (Minneapolis: University of Minnesota Press, 1996).

14.   Clokie, H. McD., "Geopolitics—New Super-Science or Old Art?" *Canadian Journal of Economics and Political Science* 10/4 (1944), 502.

15.   Sloan, Geoffrey, *Geopolitics in United States Strategic Policy, 1890–1987* (New York: St. Martin's Press, 1988), xiii.

16.   Layne, Christopher, "The Unipolar Illusion: Why New Great Powers Will Rise," *International Security* 17/4 (1993), 16.

17.   Kelly, "Geopolitics—Part 1."

18.   Hay, William, "Geopolitics of Europe," *Orbis* 47/2 (2003), 298.

19.   Gerace.

20.   Kelly, Phil, and Luisa Pérez, "El Paraguay como Estado 'Dintel' y Zona de Contacto en Sudamérica," *GEOSUR* 223/224 (1998), 43–49.

21.   Kelly, Phil, "Il Sudamerica come—zone di pace," *Eurasia: Rivista di Studi Geopolitici* 3 (2007), 49–59.

22.   Burr, Robert, "The Balance of Power in Nineteenth-Century South America: An Explanatory Essay," *Hispanic American Historical Review* 35 (1955), 37–60.

23.   Cohn, Jonathan, "Revenge of the Nerds: Irrational Exuberance: When Did Political Science Forget about Politics?" *New Republic* 1 (1999), 10.

24.   Kelly, "A Critique of Critical Geopolitics."

25.   Parker, Geoffrey, *Geopolitics: Past, Present and Future* (London: Pinter, 1998), 169.

26.   Ó Tuathail, Gearóid, and John Agnew, "Geopolitics and Discourse: Practical Geopolitical Reasoning in American Foreign Policy," *Political Geography Quarterly* 11 (1992), 155–75; Blouet, Brian, "Sir Halford Mackinder 1861–1947: Some New Per-

spectives," Research Paper 13, School of Geography, University of Oxford, England (1975); Hall, Arthur, "Mackinder and the Course of Events," *Annals of the Association of American Geographers* 45/2 (1955), 109–26.

27. Ó Tuathail, Gearóid, "Putting Mackinder in His Place: Material Transformations and Myth," *Political Geography* 11 (1992), 100–118.

28. Spykman, Nicholas, "Geography and Foreign Policy I," *American Political Science Review* 32/1 (1938), 29–30.

29. Hennig, Richard, and Leo Korholz, *Introducción a la Geopolítica* (Buenos Aires: Editorial Pleamar 1977) as republished from *Einfuhrung in die Geopolitik* (Leipzig: B. G. Teubner, 1938).

30. Cohen, *Geopolitics: The Geography of International Relations*, 2nd ed. (Lanham, MD: Rowman and Littlefield, 1990).

31. Kelly, Phil, "Fronteiras e Geopolítica: Uma Discussão das Teorias do Gen. Meira Mattos," *A Defesa Nacional* 757 (1992), 41–49.

32. For a good history of geopolitics, see Dougherty, James, and Robert Plaltzgraff, *Contending Theories of International Relations: A Comprehensive Survey* (New York: Harper and Row, 1981), 54–83; Parker.

33. Sempa, Francis, "Spykman's World," *American Diplomacy* (2006), 7.

34. Gerace.

35. Kelly, Phil, Rubén de Hoyos, and Luisa Pérez, "Zonas Contextuales y en Disputa: Observaciones Generales y el Modelo de la Cuenca del Rio de la Plata," *Argentina Global* 10 (2002), 1–10.

Chapter 2

1. Dougherty, James, and Robert Pfaltzgraff, *Contending Theories of International Relations: A Comprehensive Survey* (New York: Harper and Row, 1981), 20.

2. Van Evera, Stephen, *Guide to Methods for Students of Political Science* (New York: Cornell University Press, 1997), 7–8.

3. Jorgensen, Knud Erik, *International Relations Theory: A New Introduction* (New York: Palgrave-Macmillan, 2010), 1–3.

4. Griffiths, Martin, *Rethinking International Relations Theory* (New York: Palgrave-Macmillan, 2011), 18.

5. Waltz, Kenneth, *Theory of International Politics* (New York: Random House, 1979), 6.

6. Gray, Colin, "In Defense of the Heartland: Sir Halford Mackinder and His Critics a Hundred Years On," in Brian Blouet, ed., *Global Geostrategy: Mackinder and the Defense of the West* (London: Frank Cass, 2005), 25.

7. Snyder, Jack, "One World, Rival Theories," *Foreign Policy* 154 (2006), 54.

8. Starr, Harvey, *On Geopolitics: Space, Place, and International Relations* (Boulder, CO: Paradigm, 2013); Starr, Harvey, and Benjamin Most, "Contagion and

Border Effects on Contemporary African Conflict," *Comparative Political Studies* 16/1 (1983), 92–117; and Govea, Rodger, and Gerald West, "Riot Contagion in Latin America, 1949–1963," *Journal of Conflict Resolution* 25/2 (1981), 349–68.

9. Kelly, Phil, "Fronteiras e Geopolítica: Uma Discussão das Teorias do Gen. Meira Mattos," *A Defesa Nacional* 757 (1992), 41–49; Richardson, Lewis, *Statistics of Deadly Quarrels* (Pittsburgh, PA: Boxwood Press, 1960).

10. Kelly, Phil, "Escalation of Regional Conflict: Testing the Shatterbelt Concept," *Political Geography Quarterly* 5 (1986), 161–80.

11. Kelly, Phil, and Thomas Boardman, "Intervention in the Caribbean: Latin American Responses to United Nations Peacekeeping," *Revista/Review Inter-Americana* 6 (1976), 403–11.

12. Gray, Colin, "The Continued Primacy of Geography," *Orbis* 40/2 (1996), 247–59.

13. Gorman, Stephen, "Geopolitics and Peruvian Foreign Policy," *Inter-American Economic Affairs* 36/2 (1982), 74.

14. Berger, Joseph, David Wagner, and Morris Zelditch, Jr., "Introduction: Expectation States Theory: Review and Assessment," in Joseph Berger and Morris Zelditch, Jr., eds., *Status, Rewards, and Influence: How Expectations Organize Behavior* (San Francisco: Jossey-Bass, 1985), 1–5, 30, 57–58.

15. Kelly, Phil, "Methodological Challenges toward Constructing a Geopolitical Model," *Dialogue and UniversalismE* 5/3 (2014), 1–13; Kelly, Phil, and Luisa Pérez, "¿Por Qué se Necesita una Teoria de Geopolítica?" *Geopolítica* 4 (2004), 5–7.

16. Atencio, Jorge, *¿Qué es la Geopolítica?* (Buenos Aires: Editorial Pleamar, 1986), 41; translation is the author's.

17. Cohen, Saul, *Geopolitics: The Geography of International Relations*, 2nd ed. (Lanham, MD: Rowman and Littlefield, 2009), 11–12.

18. Kelly, Phil, "Geopolitics—Part 1," in John Agnew and James S. Duncan, *A Companion to Human Geography* (Chichester, West Sussex: Wiley-Blackwell, 2011), 512–22.

19. Easton, David, *A Framework for Political Analysis* (Chicago: University of Chicago Press, 1979).

20. Parsons, Talcott, and Edward Shils, *Toward a General Theory of Action* (New York: Harper and Row, 1962), 50–51.

21. Rivarola Puntigliano, Andres, *The Geopolitics of Development: Imagining South America*, 2010 (book proposal).

22. Spykman, Nicholas, "Geographic Objectives in Foreign Policy," *American Political Science Review* 32 (1939), 591–614; also "Geography and Foreign Policy," *American Political Science Review* 32 (1938), 28–50, 213–36. See also Sempa, Francis, "Spykman's World," *American Diplomacy* (2006), 1–18.

23. Spykman, Nicholas, *America's Strategy in World Politics: The United States and the Balance of Power* (New York: Harcourt, Brace, and Company, 1942).

24. Gerace, Michael, "Between Mackinder and Spykman: Geopolitics, Containment, and After," *Comparative Strategy* 10/4 (1991), 347–64.

25. Morgenthau, Hans, *Politics among Nations: The Struggle for Power and Peace* (New York: Knopf, 1948).

26. Kissinger, Henry, *A World Restored: Metternich, Castlereagh, and the Problems of Peace* (New York: Houghton Mifflin, 1957).

27. Waltz.

28. Garnham, David, "Dyadic International War: 1816–1965: The Role of Power Parity and Geographic Proximity," *Western Political Quarterly* 29/2 (1976), 231–42.

29. Levy, Jack, and William Thompson, "Balancing on Land and at Sea: Do States Ally against the Leading Global Power?" *International Security* 35/1 (2010), 7–43.

30. Marks, Robert, *Origins of the Modern World* (Lanham, MD: Rowman and Littlefield, 2002), 5–11.

31. Freeland, Chrystia, *Plutocrats: The Rise of the New Global Super-Rich and the Fall of Everyone Else* (New York: Penguin Press, 2012).

32. Kaplan, Robert, "The Revenge of Geography," *Foreign Policy* 72 (2009), 96–105.

33. Modelski, George, "Long Cycles and the Strategy of U.S. International Economic Policy," in William Avery and David Rapkins, eds., *America in a Changing World Political Economy* (New York: Longman, 1982); Modelski, George, "The Long Cycle of Global Politics and the Nation-State," *Comparative Studies in Society and History* 20 (1978), 214–35.

34. O'Sullivan, Patrick, "Antidomino," *Political Geography Quarterly* 1/1 (1982), 57–64.

35. Cohen, *Geopolitics: The Geography of International Relations*, 33–59.

36. Cohen, Saul, "The World Geopolitical System in Retrospect and Prospect," *Journal of Geography* 89 (1990), 8.

37. Cohen, Saul, "Global Geopolitical Change in the Post-Cold War Era," *Annals of the Association of American Geographers* 81/4 (1991), 557.

38. Cohen, Saul, "Asymmetrical States and Global Geopolitical Equilibrium," *SAIS Review* 4/2 (1984), 193.

39. Cohen, *Geopolitics: The Geography of International Relations*, 6; also "The World Geopolitical System in Retrospect and Prospect," 2, 12.

40. Cohen, Saul, "The Emergence of a New Second Order of Powers in the International System," in Onkar Marwak and Ann Schultz, eds., *Nuclear Proliferation and the Near Nuclear Powers* (Cambridge: Bolinger, 1976), 23.

41. Cohen, Saul, "A New Map of Global Geopolitical Equilibrium: A Developmental Approach," *Political Geography Quarterly* 1/3 (1982), 231, 224.

42. Cohen, "Asymmetrical States and Global Geopolitical Equilibrium," 193–94.

43. Cohen, "The World Geopolitical System in Retrospect and Prospect," 2–3.

44. Cohen, Saul, "The Eurasian Convergence Zone: Gateway or Shatterbelt," *Eurasian Geography and Economics* 46/1 (2005), 1–3.

45. Cohen, "The World Geopolitical System in Retrospect and Prospect," 3–9.

46. Ibid., 10.

47. Cohen, *Geopolitics: The Geography of International Relations*, 5–7.

48. Ibid.

49. Cohen, "The World Geopolitical System in Retrospect and Prospect," 9–11.

50. Grygiel, Jakub, *Great Powers and Geopolitical Change* (Baltimore, MD: Johns Hopkins University Press, 2006).

51. Ibid., 24, 26.

Chapter 3

1. Kelly, Phil, "A Critique of Critical Geopolitics," *Geopolitics* 11 (2006), 24–53.

2. Clover, Charles, "Dreams of the Eurasian Heartland," *Foreign Affairs* 78 (1999), 9.

3. Yahoo, "Market Update" (July 13, 2006).

4. Ó Tuathail, Gearóid, "The Postmodern Geopolitical Condition: States, Statecraft, and Security at the Millennium," *Annals of the Association of American Geographers* (on-line version, 2000), 1.

5. Fifield, Russell, and G. Etzel Pearcy, *Geopolitics in Principle and Practice* (Boston: Ginn and Company, 1944), 15–19.

6. Parker, Geoffrey, *Geopolitics: Past, Present and Future* (London: Pinter, 1998), 12–19.

7. Bassin, Mark, "Race contra Space: The Conflict between German *Geopolitik* and National Socialism," *Political Geography Quarterly* 6 (1987), 117.

8. Fifield and Pearcy, 16–19.

9. Herwig, Holgar, "Geopolitik: Haushofer, Hitler and Lebensraum," *Journal of Strategic Studies* 2/3 (1999), 218–41.

10. Fifield and Pearcy, 16.

11. Bassin, 130.

12. Cohen, Saul, *Geopolitics: The Geography of International Relations*, 2nd ed. (Lanham, MD: Rowman and Littlefield, 2009), 25.

13. Kennan, George, "Sources of Soviet Conduct," *Foreign Affairs* 25 (1947), 566–82.

14. Cohen, *Geopolitics: The Geography of International Relations*, 24–26.

15. Kennan, George, *American Diplomacy* 1900–1950 (New York: New American Library, 1951), 10.

16. Gerace, Michael, "Between Mackinder and Spykman: Geopolitics, Containment, and After," *Comparative Strategy* 10/5 (1991), 347–64.

17. Art, Robert, "Geopolitics Updated: The Strategies of Selective Engagement," *International Security* 23/3 (1998–99), 79–113.

18. Sloan, Geoffrey, *Geopolitics in United States Strategic Policy, 1890–1987* (New York: St. Martin's Press, 1988), 166–207.

19. Jones, Richard, *Critical Theory and World Politics* (Boulder, CO: Lynne Rienner, 2001), 5–10.

20. Kelly, "A Critique of Critical Geopolitics," 24–53.

21. Ó Tuathail, Gearóid, "The Bush Administration and the 'End' of the Cold War: A Critical Geopolitics of US Foreign Policy in 1989," *Geoform* 23 (1992), 439.

22. Smith, Stephen, quoted in Robert Jackson and George Sorensen, *Introduction to International Relations* (Oxford: Oxford University Press, 2003), 251.

23. Dalby, Simon, "Gender and Critical Geopolitics: Reading Security Discourse in the New World Dis-Order," *Environment and Planning D: Society and Space* 2 (1994), 595.

24. Hepple, Leslie, "Metaphor, Geopolitical Discourse and the Military in South America," in T. Barnes and J. Duncan, eds., *Writing Worlds: Text, Language and Discourse in Geography* (London: Routledge, 1992), 139.

25. Ó Tuathail, Gearóid, "Understanding Critical Geopolitics: Geopolitics and Risk Society," *Journal of Strategic Studies* 22/2,3 (1999), 108.

26. Ibid.

27. Ó Tuathail, Gearóid, "A Strategic Sign: The Geopolitical Significance of Bosnia in US Foreign Policy," *Environment and Planning D: Society and Space* 7 (1997), 42.

28. Ó Tuathail, Gearóid, *Critical Geopolitics: The Politics of Writing Global Space* (Minneapolis: University of Minnesota Press, 1996), 15, 60.

29. Dodds, Klaus, *Geopolitics in a Changing World* (Cambridge: Prentice Hall, 2000), 33.

30. Ó Tuathail, Gearóid, and Simon Dalby, "Introduction: Rethinking Geopolitics: Towards a Critical Geopolitics," in Gearóid Ó Thathail and Simon Dalby, eds., *Rethinking Geopolitics* (London: Routledge, 1998), 1.

31. Routledge, Paul, "Anti-Geopolitics," in John Agnew, Katharyne Mitchell, and Gearóid Ó Tuathail, eds., *A Companion to Political Geography* (Malden, MA: Blackwell, 2003), 236–37.

32. Kelly, "A Critique of Critical Geopolitics," 47.

33. Spykman, Nicholas, "Geography and Foreign Policy I," *American Political Science Review* 32 (1938), 29–30.

34. Kelly, Phil, and Thomas Whigham, "La Geopolítica del Paraguay: Vulnerabilidades Regionales y Respuestas Nacionales," *Perspectivas Internacionales Paraguayas* 3 (1990), 41–78.

35. Cohen, Saul, "A New Map of Global Geopolitical Equilibrium: A Developmental Approach," *Political Geography Quarterly* 1/3 (1982), 223.

36. Kelly, "A Critique of Critical Geopolitics," 36.

37. Teggart, Frederick, "Geography as an Aid to Statecraft: An Appreciation of Mackinder's *Democratic Ideals and Reality*," *Geographical Review* 8 (1919), 235–40.

38. Ó Tuathail and Dalby, "Introduction: Rethinking Geopolitics," 2.

39. Brzezinski, Zbigniew, *The Grand Chessboard: American Primacy and Its Geostrategic Imperatives* (New York: Basic Books, 1997), xiii–xiv.

40. Ó Tuathail, "Understanding Critical Geopolitics," 107.

41. Mouritzen, Hans, "Past Verses Present Geopolitics: Cautiously Opening the Realist Door to the Past," in Annette Freyberg-Inan, Ewan Harrison, and Patrick James, eds., *Rethinking Realism in International Relations: Between Tradition and Innovation* (Baltimore, MD: Johns Hopkins University Press, 2009), 164.

42. Kelly and Whigham.

43. Velilla de Arréllaga, Julia, *Paraguay: Un Destino Geopolítica* (Asunción: Instituto Paraguayo de Estudios Geopolíticos y Relaciones Internacionales: 1982), 255. See also Velilla de Arréllaga, "An Energy and Iron Community in the La Plata Basin," in Phil Kelly and Jack Child, *Geopolitics of the Southern Cone and Antarctica* (Boulder, CO: Lynne Rienner, 1988), 147–58.

44. Mackinder, Halford, *Britain and the British Seas* (Oxford: Clarendon Press, 1902), 1–2.

45. Londoño Londoño, Julio, *Geografía Política de América* (Bogotá: Universidad Nacional, Dirección de Divulgación, Colcción Textos, no. 5, 1969), 1.

46. Hersh, Seymour, *The Price of Power: Kissinger in the Nixon White House* (New York: Summit Books, 1983), 263.

47. Spykman, Nicholas, "Geography and Foreign Policy 1," 41–45.

48. Ibid., 29–30.

49. Kelly, Phil, "Geopolitics—Part 1," in John Agnew and James S. Duncan, eds., *A Companion to Human Geography* (Chichester, West Sussex: Wiley-Blackwell, 2011), 512–22.

50. Kelly, Phil, and Luisa Pérez, "Los Shatterbelts de las Américas," *GEOSUR* 273/274 (2003), 7–21.

Chapter 4

1. Sprout, Harold, and Margaret Sprout, "Geography and International Politics in an Era of Revolutionary Change," *Journal of Conflict Resolution* 4/1 (1960), 151–52.

2. Sprout and Sprout, "Geography and International Politics in an Era of Revolutionary Change," 147–48; see also Sprout, Harold, and Margaret Sprout, "Environmental Factors in the Study of International Politics," in James A. Rosenau, ed., *International Politics and Foreign Policy: A Reader in Research and Theory* (New York: Free Press, 1969), 41–56.

3. Sprout and Sprout, "Environmental Factors in the Study of International Politics," 48–49.

4. Ibid., 44–46.

5. Kelly, Phil, "Fronteiras e Geopolítica: Uma Discussão das Teorias do Gen. Meira Mattos," *A Defesa Nacional* 757 (1992), 41–49; James Wesley, "Frequency of Wars and Geographical Opportunity," *Journal of Conflict Resolution* 6/4 (1962), 387–89.

6. Mouritzen, Hans, "Past verses Present Geopolitics: Cautiously Opening the Realist Door to the Past," in Annette Freybert-Inana, Ewan Harrison, and Patrick James, eds., *Rethinking Realism in International Relations: Between Tradition and Innovation* (Baltimore, MD: Johns Hopkins University Press, 2009), 164–88.

7. Spykman, Nicholas, "Geography and Foreign Policy I," *American Political Science Review* 32 (1938), 41–42.

8. Cohen, Saul, "Reexamining Our Geopolitical Views of the World," *US Army Command and Staff College Reference Book*, 20–4, *Readings in Military Geography* 4/1 (1959), 22.

9. Kelly, Phil, "La Geopolítica de la Confederación: Los Escritos del Gral. Colombiano Julio Londoño Londoño," *Geopolítica* 46 (1992), 40–50.

10. Kelly, Phil, "La 'Tierra Corazón' de Mackinder: El Concepto Aplicado a Sudamérica," *GEOSUR* 135/136 (1991), 33–47.

11. Kelly, Phil, *Checkerboards and Shatterbelts: The Geopolitics of South America* (Austin: University of Texas Press, 1997), 161–75.

12. Tambs, Lewis, "Geopolitical Factors in Latin America," in Norman Bailey, ed., *Latin America: Politics, Economics and Hemispheric Security* (New York: Praeger, 1965), 31–49.

13. Child, Jack, *Antarctica and South American Geopolitics: Frozen Lebensraum* (New York: Praeger, 1988); Seckinger, Ron, "South American Power Realities during the 1820s," *Hispanic American Historical Review* 56 (1976), 241–67; Burr, Robert, "The Balance of Power in Nineteenth-Century South America: An Explanatory Essay," *Hispanic American Historical Review* 35 (1955), 37–60.

14. Kelly, Phil, "Geopolitics—Part 1," in John Agnew and James S. Duncan, eds., *A Companion to Human Geography* (Chichester, West Sussex, Wiley-Blackwell, 2011), 512–22; Kelly, Phil, Rubén de Hoyos, and Luisa Pérez, "Zonas Contextuales y en Disputas: Observaciones Generales y el Modelo de la Cuenca del Rio de la Plata," *Argentina Global* 10 (2002), 1–10.

15. Kelly, Phil, and Luisa Pérez, "El Paraguay como Estado 'Dintel' y Zona de Contacto en Sudamérica," *GEOSUR* 223/224 (1998), 43–49.

16. Gray, Colin, "In Defense of the Heartland: Sir Halford Mackinder and His Critics a Hundred Years On," in Brian Blouet, ed., *Global Geostrategy: Mackinder and the Defense of the West* (London: Frank Cass, 2005), 26–27.

17. Easton, David, *A Framework for Political Analysis* (Chicago: University of Chicago Press, 1979).

18. Kelly, de Hoyos, and Pérez.

19. Kelly, Phil, and Luisa Pérez, "Impacto de la Democratización de la Geopolítica en América del Sur," *GEOSUR* 267/268 (2002), 32–42.

Chapter 5

1. Kelly, Phil, *Checkerboards and Shatterbelts: The Geopolitics of South America* (Austin: University of Texas Press, 1997), 128–30.

2. Gerace, Michael, "Between Mackinder and Spykman: Geopolitics, Containment, and After," *Comparative Strategy* 10/4 (1991), 347–64.

3. Parker, Geoffrey, *Geopolitics: Past, Present and Future* (London: Pinter, 1998), 94.

4. Mackinder, Halford, "The Round World and the Winning of the Peace," *Foreign Affairs* 21/4 (1943), 595–605; *Democratic Ideals and Reality: A Study in the Politics of Re-Construction* (New York: Henry Holt, 1919); "The Geographic Pivot of History," *Geographical Journal* 23 (1904), 421–44. Also Sloan, Geoffrey, *Geopolitics in United States Strategic Policy, 1890–1987* (New York: St. Martin's Press, 1988), 6–15.

5. Verner, Pascal, "The Geographical Pivot of History and Early Twentieth Century Geopolitical Culture," *Geographical Journal* 170/4 (2004), 330–36.

6. Robbins, Gerald, "The Post-Soviet Heartland: Reconsidering Mackinder," *Global Affairs* 8 (1993), 95–108.

7. Berman, Ilan, "Slouching toward Eurasia?" *Perspective* 12/1 (2001), 1–9; Ingram, Alan, "Alexander Dugin: Geopolitics and Neo-Fascism in Post-Soviet Russia," *Political Geography* 20 (2001), 1029–51.

8. Walton, C. Dale, *Geopolitics and the Great Powers of the Twenty-First Century: Multipolarity and the Revolution in Strategic Perspectives* (London: Routledge, 2007).

9. Brzezinski, Zbigniew, *Strategic Vision: America and the Crisis of Global Power* (New York: Basic Books, 2012); also Walt, Stephen, "The Myth of American Exceptionalism," *Foreign Policy* 189 (2011), 1–72.

10. Kirk, William, "Geographical Pivots of History," inaugural lecture at Leicester University, Leicester University Press, 1965.

11. Meinig, Donald, "Heartland and Rimland in Eurasian History," *Western Political Quarterly* 9 (1966), 553–69.

12. Sloan, *Geopolitics in United States Strategic Policy,* 18901890–1987, 127–65.

13. Sempa, Francis, "Is China Bidding for the Heartland?" *The Diplomat* (January 21, 2015), 1–2; Ingram, "Alexander Dugin: Geopolitics and Neo-Fascism in Post-Soviet Russia"; Clover, Charles, "Dreams of the Eurasian Heartland," *Foreign Affairs* 78 (1999), 9–13.

14. Hepple, Leslie, "South American Heartland: The Charcas, Latin American Geopolitics and Global Strategies," *Geographical Journal* 170/4 (2004), 359–67; Kelly, *Checkerboards and Shatterbelts,* 27–28, 70; Tambs, Lewis, "Geopolitical Factors in Latin America," in Norman Bailey, ed., *Latin America: Politics, Economics and Hemispheric Security* (New York, Praeger, 1965), 31–39; Travassos, Mario, *Projeção Continental do Brasil* (São Paulo: Companhia Nacional, 1947).

15. Velilla de Arréllaga, Julia, "An Energy and Iron Community in the La Plata Basin," in Phil Kelly and Jack Child, eds., *Geopolitics of the Southern Cone and Antarctica* (Boulder, CO: Lynne Rienner, 1988), 147–58; Kelly, Phil, and Luisa Pérez, "El Paraguay como Estado 'Dintel' y Zona de Contacto en Sudamérica," *GEOSUR* 223/224 (1998), 43–49.

16. Golbery do Couto e Silva, *Geopolítica do Brasil* (Rio de Janeiro: Livraria José Olympio Editora, 1981).

17. Spykman, Nicholas, *The Geography of Peace* (New York: Harcourt, Brace, and World, 1944), 41.

18. Gerace, 347.

19. Gray, Colin, "The Most Dangerous Decade," *Orbis* 25/1, 13–15.

20. Kelly, Phil, and Luisa Pérez, "Los Shatterbelts de las Américas," *GEOSUR* 273/274 (2003), 7–21.

21. Sims, Dimitri, "America's Imperial Dilemma," *Foreign Affairs* 28/6 (2003), 91–102.

22. Parker, 160–66.

23. Spykman, Nicholas, "Geography and Foreign Policy I," *American Political Science Review* 32 (1938), 45.

24. Marks, Robert, *Origins of the Modern World* (Lanham, MD: Rowman and Littlefield, 2002).

25. Walton; Brzezinski, *Strategic Vision;* and Walt.

26. Meira Mattos, Carlos de, *Geopolítica e Trópicos* (Rio de Janeiro: Biblioteca do Exército, 1984).

27. Natter, Wolfgang, "On the Geo-Economic Pivot of History: Neil Smith's 'American Empire,'" *Political Geography* 24 (2005), 245–50.

28. Hersh, Seymour, *The Price of Power: Kissinger in the Nixon White House* (New York: Summit Books, 1983), 263.

29. Marini, José Felipe, *El Conocimiento Geopolítico,* 2nd ed. (San Miguel de Tucumán: Universidad de Tucumán, 1982), 350, 416; Kelly, *Checkerboards and Shatterbelts,* 25–26.

30. Quaglioti de Bellis, Bernardo, *Constantes Geopolíticos en Iberoamérica* (Montevideo: GEOSUR, 1979); see also Kelly, *Checkerboards and Shatterbelts*, 104–8.

31. Londoño Londoño, Julio, *Geografía Política de América* (Bogotá: Universidad Nacional, Dirección de Divulgación Cultural, Colección Textos, no. 5), 1; also Kelly, Phil, "La Geopolítica de la Conferación: Los Escritos del Gral. Colombiano Julio Londoño," *Geopolítica* 46 (1992), 40–50.

32. Cohen, Saul, "The World Geopolitical System in Retrospect and Prospect," *Journal of Geography* 89 (1990), 2–7.

33. Cohen, Saul, *Geopolitics: The Geography of International Relations*, 2nd ed. (Lanham, MD: Rowman and Littlefield, 2009), 5–6.

34. Seversky, Alexander de, *Air Power: Key to Survival* (New York: Simon and Schuster, 1950).

35. Grygiel, Jakub, *Great Powers and Geopolitical Change* (Baltimore, MD: Johns Hopkins University Press, 2006).

36. Walton.

37. Huntington, Samuel, "The Clash of Civilizations," *Foreign Affairs* 72 (1993), 22–49.

38. Parker, 96–118.

39. Burr, Robert, "The Balance of Power in Nineteenth-Century South America: An Explanatory Essay," *Hispanic American Historical Review* 35 (1955), 37–60.

40. Kelly, Phil, "Geopolitics—Part 1," in John Agnew and James S. Duncan, eds., *Companion to Human Geography* (Chichester, West Sussex: Wiley-Blackwell, 2011), 512–22.

41. Modelski, George, "Kautilya: Foreign Policy and International System in the Ancient Hindu World," *American Political Science Review* 57/3 (1964), 554–55.

42. Kelly, Phil, "Escalation of Regional Conflict: Testing the Shatterbelt Concept," *Political Geography Quarterly* 5 (1986), 161–80.

43. Cohen, Saul, *The Geography of International Relations* (Lanham, MD: Rowman and Littlefield, 2015), 48.

44. Kelly, Phil, "Stanno Nascendo delle Shatterbelts nel Cuore dell'Eurasia?" *Geopolitica—Rivista dell'Istituto di Alti Studi in Geopolitica e Scienza Ausiliarie* 1/1 (2012).

45. Hensel, Paul, and Paul Diehl, "Testing Empirical Propositions about Shatterbelts, 1945–76," *Political Geography* 13/1 (1994), 33, 39.

46. Cohen, *Geopolitics: The Geography of International Relations*, 24–26.

47. Brzezinski, *Strategic Vision*.

48. Cohen, Saul, "The Eurasian Convergence Zone: Gateway or Shatterbelt?" *Eurasian Geography and Economics* 46/1 (2005), 1–22.

49. Kelly, *Checkerboards and Shatterbelts*, 164.

50. Kelly, "Geopolitics—Part 1."

51. Burr; Mutto, Carlos, "Brazil's Manifest Destiny," *Atlas* 20 (1971), 21–24.

52. Mackinder, "The Round World and the Winning of the Peace."

53. Spykman, *The Geography of Peace*, 34; *America's Strategy in World Politics: The United States and the Balance of Power* (New York: Harcourt, Brace and Company, 1942), 457.

54. Brzezinski, Zbigniew, *The Grand Chessboard: American Primacy and Its Geostrategic Imperatives* (New York: Basic Books, 1997); Cohen, *Geopolitics: The Geography of International Relations.*

55. Grygiel.

56. Cohen, *Geopolitics: The Geography of International Relations.*

57. Kelly, *Checkerboards and Shatterbelts*, 163–64.

58. Kelly, Phil, "Buffer States of Middle America," in John Chay and Thomas Ross, eds., *Buffer Systems in World Politics* (Boulder, CO: Westview, 1986), 67–84.

59. Kelly, *Checkerboards and Shatterbelts*, 84–135.

60. Kelly, Phil, "A Geopolitical Interpretation of Security Concerns within United States–Latin American Relations," *Security and Defense Studies Review* 14 (2013), 3–54; Walton.

61. Kelly, Phil, and Thomas Whigham, "La Geopolítica del Paraguay: Vulnerabilidades Regionales y Respuestes Nacionales," *Perspectivas Internacionales Paraguayas* 3 (1990), 41–78.

62. Layne, Christopher, "From Preponderance to Off-Shore Balancing: America's Future Grand Strategy," *International Security* 22/1 (2007), 86–124.

63. Levy, Jack, and William Thompson, "Balancing on Land and at Sea: Do States Ally against the Leading Global Power?" *International Security* 35/1 (2010), 7–43.

64. Mutto, 21–24.

65. Kelly, *Checkerboards and Shatterbelts*, 39, 137.

66. Ibid., 43.

67. Kelly, "Buffer States of Middle America."

68. Kelly and Pérez, "Los Shatterbelts de las Américas."

69. Brzezinski, *The Grand Chessboard*, 57, 6.

70. Cohen, Saul, *Geopolitics in the World System* (Lanham, MD: Rowman and Littlefield, 2003), 49–53.

71. Kelly and Pérez, "El Paraguay como Estado 'Dintel' y Zona de Contacto en Sudamérica," 43–49.

72. Morgan, Gerald, "Myth and Reality in the Great Game," *Asian Affairs* 60 (1973), 64.

73. Megoran, Nick, "Revisiting the 'Pivot': The Influence of Halford Mackinder on Analysis of Uzbekistan's International Relations," *Geographical Journal* 170/4 (2004), 347–58.

74. Mahan, Alfred Thayer, *The Problem of Asia* (Boston: Little, Brown, 1900).

75. Glassner, Martin Ira, *Bibliography on Land-Locked States* (New York: Kluwer Law International, 1995); "Wither Bolivia? Toward the Atlantic or the Pacific?" in Phil Kelly and Jack Child, eds., *Geopolitics of the Southern Cone and Antarctica* (Boulder, CO: Lynne Rienner, 1988), 159–74.

76. Mahan, Alfred Thayer, *The Interest of America in Sea Power Past and Present* (Boston: Little, Brown, 1897).

77. Meinig, "Heartland and Rimland in Eurasian History," 556.

78. Londoño Londoño, Julio, *Suramérica; o la Geografía como Destino* (Bogotá: Impr. del Ministeria de Guerra, 1948), 19.

79. Kelly, Phil, "La Geopolítica de la Confederación: Los Escritos del Gral. Colombiano Julio Londoño," *Geopolítica* 46 (1992), 40–50.

80. O'Sullivan, Patrick, "Antidomino," *Political Geography Quarterly* 1/1 (1982), 61.

81. Kjellén, Rudolf, *Staten som Lifsform* (Leipzig: Hirzel, 1916).

82. Richardson, Lewis, *Statistics of Deadly Quarrels* (Pittsburgh, PA: Boxwood Press, 1960).

83. Kelly, Phil, "Fronteiras e Geopolítica: Uma Discussão das Teorías do Gen. Meira Mattos," *A Defesa Nacional* 757 (1992), 41–49.

84. Wesley, James, "Frequency of Wars and Geographical Opportunity," *Journal of Conflict Resolution* 46/2 (1962) , 387–89.

85. Starr, Harvey, *On Geopolitics: Space, Place, and International Relations* (Boulder, CO: Paradigm, 2013), 113–52.

86. Hensel, Paul, "Territory: Geography, Contentious Issues, and World Politics," in John A. Vasquez, ed., *What Do We Know about War?* 2nd ed. (Lanham, MD: Rowman and Littlefield, 2012), 6–10.

87. Kocs, Stephen, "Territorial Disputes and International Law 1945–1987," *Journal of Politics* 57/1 (1995), 172.

88. Govea, Rodger, and Gerald West, "Riot Contagion in Latin America, 1949–1963," *Journal of Conflict Resolution* 25/2 (1981), 349–68.

89. Ibid., 365.

90. Huff, David, and James Lutz, "The Contagion of Political Unrest in Independent Black Africa," *Economic Geography* 50/4 (1974), 364–66.

91. O'Sullivan, 57, 62–63.

92. Kelly, *Checkerboards and Shatterbelts*, 45–47, 156–60.

93. Bassin, Mark, "Race contra Space: The Conflict between German *Geopolitik* and National Socialism," *Political Geography Quarterly* 6 (1987), 117–19.

94. Gyorgy, Andrew, *Geopolitics: The New German Science* (Berkeley: University of California Press, 1944), 150–51.

95. Layne, Christopher, "The Unipolar Illusion: Why New Great Powers Will Rise," *International Security* 17/3 (1993), 12.

96. Pittman, Howard, "Geopolitics of the ABC Powers: A Comparison," Ph.D. dissertation, American University, Washington, DC, 1981.

97. Kristof, Ladis, "The Origins and Evolution of Geopolitics," *Journal of Conflict Resolution* 4/1 (1960), 15–17.

98. Whittlesey, Derwent, "Haushofer: The Geopoliticians," in Edward Mead Earle, ed., *The Makers of Modern Strategy: Military Thought from Machiavelli to Hitler* (Princeton: Princeton University Press, 1943), 398–99.

99. Mouritzen, Hans, "Past verses Present Geopolitics: Cautiously Opening the Realist Door to the Past," in Annette Freyberg-Inan, Ewan Harrison, and Patrick James, eds., *Rethinking Realism in International Relations: Between Tradition and Innovation* (Baltimore, MD: Johns Hopkins University Press, 2009), 177–78, 184.

100. Wohlstetter, Albert, "Illusions of Distance," *Foreign Affairs* 46/2 (1968), 244–45.

101. Kelly, Phil, and Thomas Boardman, "Intervention in the Caribbean: Latin American Responses to United Nations Peacekeeping," *Revista/Review Inter-Americana* 6 (1976), 403–11.

102. Kelly, Phil, and Luisa Pérez, "Las Teorias Continentales en la Geopolítica," *Argentina Global* 18 (2006), 1–10.

103. Parry, Christopher, *Super Highway: Sea Power in the 21st Century* (London: Elliot and Thompson, 2014).

104. Grygiel, x.

105. Kaplan, Robert, "The Revenge of Geography," *Foreign Policy* 72 (2009), 101–5.

106. Kearns, Gerry, "Closed Space and Political Practice: Frederick Jackson Turner and Halford Mackinder," *Environment and Planning D* 1 (1984), 23, 33.

107. Slowe, Peter, *Geography and Political Power* (London: Routledge, 1990), 31–33.

108. Hay, William, "Geopolitics of Europe," *Orbis* 47/2 (2003), 295–310.

109. Kelly, *Checkerboards and Shatterbelts*, 44.

110. Wittfogel, Karl, *Oriental Despotism: A Comparative Study of Total Power* (New Haven: Yale University Press, 1957).

111. Diamond, Larry, *The Spirit of Democracy: The Struggle to Build Free Societies throughout the World* (New York: St. Martin's Press, 2009).

112. Huntington, Ellsworth, "Changes in Climate and History," *American Historical Review* 18/2 (1913), 213–32.

113. Rostlund, Erhard, "Twentieth-Century Magic," in Philip Wagner and Marvin Mikesell, eds., *Readings in Cultural Geography* (Chicago: University of Chicago Press, 1962), 49.

114. Theisen, Ole Magnus, Helge Holtermann, and Halvard Buhaug, "Climate Wars? Assessing the Claim That Drought Breeds Conflict," *International Security* 36/3 (2011/12), 79–106.

115. Meira Mattos, *Geopolítica e Trópicos.*

116. Friedman, Thomas, *Hot, Flat, and Crowded: Why We Need a Green Revolution—and How It Can Renew America* (New York: Farrar, Straus and Giroux, 2008), 93–110; Ross, Michael, "Oil, Islam, and Women," *American Political Science Review* 102/1 (2008), 107–23; Ross, Michael, "Does Oil Hinder Democracy?" *World Politics* 53/3 (2001), 325–61; Diamond, *The Spirit of Democracy.*

117. Friedman, *Hot, Flat, and Crowded,* 105.

118. Krauthammer, Charles, "The Unipolar Moment," *Foreign Affairs* 70/1 (1990/91), 30–33.

119. Ibid., 30.

Chapter 6

Note: Portions of this chapter appeared previously in Kelly, Phil, "Geopolitics—Part 1," in John A. Agnew and James S. Duncan, eds., *The Wiley Companion to Human Geography* (2011), 512–22. Copyright 2011 Blackwell Publishing Ltd. Used with permission.

1. Kelly, Phil, *Reader in Classical Geopolitics* (Ronkonkoma, NY: Linus Learning, 2014), 15.

2. Kagan, Donald, *The Outbreak of the Peloponnesian War* (New York: Cornell University Press, 1969), 205–311.

3. Jalilov, Murad, and Phil Kelly, "The Ukrainian Shatterbelt: A New Cold War?" *Report dell'IsAG* #30—Istituto de Alti Studi in Geopolitica e Scienze—Rome, Italy (2014), 1–13.

4. Kelly, Phil, *Checkerboards and Shatterbelts: The Geopolitics of South America* (Austin: University of Texas Press, 1997), 92–93.

5. Kelly, Phil, "Escalation of Regional Conflict: Testing the Shatterbelt Concept," *Political Geography Quarterly* 5 (1986), 161–80.

6. Kelly, Phil, "Stanno Nascendo delle Shatterbelts nel cuore dell'Eurasia?" ["Shatterbelts Now Emerging in Central Eurasia and Elsewhere?"] *Geopolitica—Rivista dell'Istituto di Alti Studi in Geopolitica e Scienza Ausliarie* 1/1 (2012), 129–34.

7. Kelly, *Checkerboards and Shatterbelts.*

8. Meira Mattos, Carlos de, *A Geopolítica e as Projeçãos do Poder* (Rio de Janeiro: José Olympio, 1977); *Brasil: Geopolítica e Destino* (Rio de Janeiro: José Olympio, 1975).

9. Mackinder, Halford, *Democratic Ideals and Reality: A Study of the Politics of Re-Construction* (New York: Henry Holt, 1919); and "The Geographic Pivot of History," *Geographic Journal* 23 (1904), 421–44.

10. Kennan, George, *American Diplomacy* 1900–1950 (New York: New American Library, 1951), 10.

11. Spykman, Nicholas, *America's Strategy in World Politics: The United States and the Balance of Power* (New York: Harcourt, Brace, and Company, 1042), 457.

12. Nickson, R. Andrew, "Brazilian Colonization on the Eastern Border Region of Paraguay," *Journal of Latin American Studies* 13/1 (1981), 111–31.

13. Quagliotti de Bellis, Bernardo, "Uruguay en la Cuenca del Plata," in L. Dallanegra Pedraza, ed., *Países del Atlántico Sur: Geopolítica en la Cuenca del Plata* (Buenos Aires: Editorial Pleamar, 1983), 161–96.

14. Velilla de Arréllaga, Julia, *Paraguay: Un Destino Geopolítica* (Asunción: Instituto Paraguayo de Estudios y Relaciones Internacionales, 1982), 21, 256–57.

15. Everitt, Anthony, *Augustus: The Life of Rome's First Emperor* (New York: Random House, 2006), 139–40.

16. Ibid., 175–85.

17. Luttwak, Edward, *The Grand Strategy of the Roman Empire: From the First Century A.D. to the Third* (Baltimore, MD: Johns Hopkins University Press, 1976), 81.

18. Ibid., 191–94.

Appendix

1. Cohen, Saul, *Geopolitics: The Geography of International Relations,* 2nd ed. (Lanham, MD: Rowman and Littlefield, 2009), 9.

2. Brzezinski, Zbigniew, *The Grand Chessboard: American Primacy and Its Geostrategic Imperatives* (New York: Basic Books, 1997), 6, 57.

3. Cohen, Saul, *Geopolitics in the World System* (Lanham, MD: Rowman and Littlefield, 2003), 49–53.

4. Kelly, Phil, "Fronteiras e Geopolítica: Uma Discussão das Teorias do Gen. Meira Mattos," *A Defesa Nacional* 757 (1992), 41–49; and Richardson, Lewis, *Statistics of Deadly Quarrels* (Pittsburgh, PA: Boxwood Press, 1960).

5. Wesley, James, "Frequency of Wars and Geographical Opportunity," *Journal of Conflict Resolution* 6/4 (1962), 387–89.

6. Kocs, Stephen, "Territory Disputes and International Law," *Journal of Politics* 57/1 (1995), 172.

7. Londoño Londoño, Julio, *Geografía Política de América* (Bogotá: Universidad Nacional, Dirección de Divulgación Cultural, Colección Textos, no. 2, 1948), 1.

8. Kelly, Phil, "Geopolitics—Part 1," in John Agnew and James S. Duncan, eds., *A Companion to Human Geography* (Chichester, West Sussex: Wiley-Blackwell, 2011), 512–22.

9. Huntington, Samuel, "The Clash of Civilizations?" *Foreign Affairs* 71 (1993), 22–49.

10. Cohen, Saul, "The Eurasian Convergence Zone: Gateway or Shatterbelt?" *Eurasian Geography and Economics* 46/1 (2005), 1–22.

11. Govea, Rodger, and Gerald West, "Riot Contagion in Latin America, 1949–1963," *Journal of Conflict Resolution* 25/2 (1981), 349–68.

12. Brzezinski, *The Grand Chessboard: American Primacy and Its Geostrategic Imperatives*; and Megoran, Nick, "Revisiting the 'Pivot': The Influence of Halford Mackinder on Analysis of Uzbekistan's International Relations," *Geographical Journal* 170/4 (2004), 347–58.

13. Gray, Colin, "The Most Dangerous Decade," *Orbis* 25/1 (1981), 13–28.

14. Friedman, George, "An Analysis of Turkish Geopolitics," *TR Defence: Turkish Military & Geopolitics Portal* (November 23, 2010), 10.

15. Friedman, George, "The Next 100 Years," *New Statesman* 138 (2009), 19.

16. Parker, Geoffrey, *Geopolitics: Past, Present and Future* (London: Pintor, 1998), 162–66.

17. Mackinder, Halford, "The Geographic Pivot of History," *Geographical Journal* 23 (1904), 421–44.

18. Meinig, Donald, "Heartland and Rimland in Eurasian History," *Western Political Quarterly* 9 (1966), 554.

19. Gerace, Michael, "Between Mackinder and Spykman: Geopolitics, Containment, and After," *Comparative Strategy* 10/4 (1991), 347–64.

20. Kelly, Phil, "Escalation of Regional Conflict: Testing the Shatterbelt Concept," *Political Geography Quarterly* 5 (1986), 161–80.

Index